GOLD IN THE CRUCIBLE

Teresa of Avila and the
Western Mystical Tradition

Deirdre Green has a first class honours degree in Religious Studies from King's College London and a PhD in Comparative Mysticism. She is now a lecturer in Religious Studies at St David's University College (University of Wales) and is a specialist in mysticism.

To her scholarly training she also brings her personal experience of involvement in mystical disciplines and mystical groups, thus uniting sound scholarship with experiential understanding.

Velázquez's portrait 'Santa Teresa de Jesús' (Marquesa Casa Riera, Madrid) depicts Teresa writing in an entranced or absorbed condition, the dove symbolising her receptivity to the inspirational powers of the Spirit.

GOLD IN THE CRUCIBLE

*Teresa of Avila and the
Western Mystical Tradition*

Deirdre Green

ELEMENT BOOKS

First published in 1989 by
Element Books Limited
Longmead, Shaftesbury, Dorset

Printed and bound in Great Britain by Billings,
Hylton Road, Worcester

Text design by Clarke Williams
Cover design by Max Fairbrother
Cover photo: © Keith W. Ray

British Library Cataloguing in Publication Data

Green, Deirdre
    Gold in the crucible.
    1. Carmelites. Teresa of Avila, Saint
    I. Title
    271'.971'024

ISBN 1-85230-070-1

The soul was purified by this pain; it was burnished or refined, like gold in the crucible, the better to take the enamel of His gifts. . . . . .

Teresa of Avila, *Life*

He hath promised: 'I shall make them pass through the fire, and I shall purify them even as silver is purified. And I shall try them even as gold is tried in the fire.'

Zohar

List of Illustrations

The front cover shows the statue of St. Teresa outside one of the city gates of Avila.

The frontispiece is the portrait of St Teresa by Velázquez (Marquesa Casa Riera).

Contents

Preface

On the majority of occasions throughout this study I refer to the remarkable woman who is its subject simply as 'Teresa'. This is by no means intended to belittle her stature as a saint of the Catholic Church. It is rather intended to emphasise her humanity. More than is the case with any other saint, we feel we can talk to Teresa as if to a friend. She is ruthlessly honest in her self-exposure and never stands on ceremony; always she is delightfully homely and none the less down-to-earth for her exalted flights of mystical rapture and ecstasy. Those who are following the spiritual path – even if it is by a way or tradition that at first sight may seem very different from Teresa's – will find much in her person and her writings with which to identify, in spite of the centuries that separate her from us. For scholars of mysticism and religion, too, a study of Teresa of Avila yields unique insights into the nature of visionary experience, the influence of Kabbalah on Christian mysticism, the status of women mystics in sixteenth-century Spain, and much more.

This study, then, focuses on Teresa as a mystic, as a human being and as a woman, and attempts to see her in the contexts of the Western mystical tradition and of the issue of 'women's spirituality'. It is different from previous studies of Teresa in that it raises more challenging questions than have hitherto been asked with regard to these issues and with regard to the influence of Jewish mysticism on

Teresa's writings and experiences, exploring the bearings that these questions have on the history of esoteric thought. Relatively little detailed attention is given to the history of Teresa's foundations of the Discalced Carmelite Reform, or to questions of theological doctrine, though naturally the relevant background information on these points is sketched in where necessary.

I am aware that the orthodox may shrink from accepting some of my conclusions. I can only say that if they make Teresa more heterodox, they also make her, for me, more vibrant, more creative, more deeply spiritual.

My thanks are due to the Spalding Trusts for a small grant which covered some incidental research expenses, and to the Pantyfedwen Fund for supporting my research visit to Avila. The nuns of the Convent of the Incarnation in Avila were kind enough to grant me an interview.

I am grateful to Dr A. I. K. MacKay and Dr A. P. Hayman, both of the University of Edinburgh, for their suggestions some years ago regarding earlier drafts of some of the material that has eventually found its way into Chapter 3 of this work. Likewise to Mr Glyn Richards of the University of Stirling for his comments on a much earlier version of Chapter 2, which originally formed part of my doctoral thesis.

My greatest debt of gratitude goes to my husband Keith Ray for taking the photographs of Avila reproduced herein, and for his continuous encouragement and interest.

Deirdre Green

Lampeter, 1988

The beautifully preserved medieval walls of Avila are reminiscent of Teresa's symbol of the castle of the soul.

© Keith W. Ray

CHAPTER 1

Teresa's Life and Work

I have ventured to put together this story of my unruly life, though I have wasted no more time or trouble on it than has been necessary for the writing of it. I have merely set down what has happened to me in all possible simplicity and truth.[1]

Teresa of Avila (or Teresa of Jesus, to use the name she took as a nun) still plays a deep and vital role in the cultural and spiritual life of her home town. Her influence can be felt at all levels, from the peace and tranquillity of the monasteries associated with her Reform, to expressions of popular devotion represented by the images of her venerated in local churches and on sale in souvenir shops. Today, the sixteenth-century nun who so loved simplicity has a thriving cult of her own; an image at the Convento de Santa Teresa has her decked in gaudy finery of which she certainly would not have approved, and no more, I suspect, would she have given sanction to the plentiful collections of Teresian relics on show in the museums or the St Teresa ashtrays and keyrings proffered to tourists. Nevertheless, for the reseacher, these different manifestations of piety, and of more diffuse appreciation of Teresa's legacy, all go to make up a rich and varied patchwork in which each element can tell us something about this astonishing woman.

It is the purpose of this chapter to give a brief introduction to Teresa's life and work in so far as they relate to the central theme of this study. (For more detailed biographical studies, the reader is referred to Marcelle Auclair's highly enjoyable biography *Saint Teresa of Avila*, and Victoria Lincoln's challenging *Teresa: A Woman*.) 'Avila of the Knights', as it was known in her day, standing high on the Castilian plateau and encompassed by its beautifully preserved medieval walls, is a city that evokes the romance and chivalry of old Castile at every turn. It was into this sixteenth-century Castilian 'high society' that Teresa de Cepeda y Ahumada was born, on 28 March 1515,[2] to a family then regarded as noble, although coming only recently from merchant Jewish stock before their rapid social climbing. The handsome family home was situated on the Plazuela de Santo Domingo, and there is now a chapel dedicated to St Teresa on the site of the room in which she was born, forming part of the Convento de Santa Teresa (which is in fact not a convent but a church).

Teresa was one of nine brothers and sisters; her father, Don Alonso Sánchez y Cepeda, had remarried after the death of his first wife, so that the two eldest (or, according to some accounts, the three eldest) children were Teresa's half-brothers and half-sisters. Teresa's own mother, Doña Beatriz de Ahumada, who cuts a rather unhappy figure, was to die, worn out with ill-health caused by continually difficult pregnancies, at the age of 33. Teresa was 13, a critical age for such a tragedy to befall a young girl; her account in her *Life* of how she went, weeping bitterly in her distress, to an image of the Virgin Mary (Our Lady of Charity, still to be seen in Avila Cathedral) and begged her to be her mother is touching in the extreme. Teresa's perception of a woman's allotted role in the Spain of her time, and her subsequent decision to become a nun, were clearly very much influenced by her observation of her mother's unhappy life, as we shall discuss later in this work. Women in Teresa's time and culture had only two options open to them: marriage, which meant constant pregnancy and childbirth, and submission to one's husband in everything; or the religious life. It is not surprising that some women who chose the latter did so, not so much from a wholehearted sense of religious devotion, as because it was the only way they could gain a measure of autonomy and freedom. This is not to deny the reality of genuine spiritual vocation for many women who became nuns: the celibate life of withdrawal and renunciation of the world was, indeed, a way in which many women could realise their spiritual aspirations. But it was also a means of transcending some of the limitations placed on women in sixteenth-century Spain. Having renounced their worldly sexuality, women could take their place alongside men in the ranks of the monastic life; although, as we shall see later, even here they were subjugated.

Teresa was apparently fond of reading the lives of the saints from her earliest years, but she was by no means precocious; she also avidly devoured the romances of chivalry (which her mother, too, loved) and even tried to write one herself. She found great inspiration as a child in the Grail legends and particularly in the conclusion of the Quest of the Holy Grail, when Galahad the Grail knight is taken up to heaven. She used to play at nuns and at building convents; and when she was only 7 or 8 she had discussed with her brother Rodrigo (to whom she was particularly close; he was four years her senior) how they might become martyrs, and they had 'agreed to go together to the land of the Moors, begging our way for the love of God, so that we might be beheaded there'.[3] They did in fact get outside the city walls, but were discovered and sent back home by an uncle; Teresa drily remarks that to her and her brother, the greatest hindrance to martyrdom seemed to be the fact that they had parents! The story smacks as much of romanticism as of piety, and shows us that Teresa was an imaginative child with initiative, courage, a degree of stubbornness, and a longing for romantic adventures, rather than that she was destined to be a saint from birth. Indeed, Teresa herself admits that with regard to this adventure she was motivated not by love of God, but by her childish desire to attain quickly and easily the rewards and blessings which, she had read, were laid up in Heaven for martyrs. For a mystic following the interior life of communion of the soul with the Divine, such motivations are soon seen to be no more than a transposition of worldly self-centredness onto another plane.

As she began to grow up, Teresa tells us, she took very great care of her personal appearance, eager to attract and charm, wearing fine clothes and jewellery, 'taking great trouble with my hands and hair, using perfumes and all the vanities I could get'.[4] She was charming, beautiful and accomplished. She became friendly with some cousins of about her own age and 'heard their accounts of their affections and follies, which were anything but edifying';[5] she also enjoyed the company of a disreputable older relative whom her mother had attempted in vain to keep out of the house. Through these relatives, Teresa was introduced to all manner of frivolous and probably indiscreet worldly pastimes, vanities and amusements, which she later came to regard as reprehensible. She tells us in her *Life* that she should never have wished anyone to sin against God because of her and says that in herself she was inclined to be virtuous; but she was impressionable and easily led, and admits that 'When I thought that nobody would ever know, I was rash enough to do many things v:hich were an offence both to my honour and to God.'[6] She became considerably afraid for her reputation and good name: the pressure to maintain one's reputation or honour (*fama, honra*) was a pivot of social behaviour in sixteenth-century Castile. It is difficult to tell just how trivial or serious Teresa's 'sins' (as she calls them) were. Apparently, one of her cousins was in love with her and another cousin (a girl like herself) and the servants (happy to keep a secret in exchange for a bribe) were parties to the matter. We can imagine secret meetings, letters, all the emotional agitation of a first love affair. Teresa herself uses strong words of this episode in her life, speaking of her mortal sin and of being blinded by passion. Sackville-West believes that however scrupulous Teresa's conscience, she would not have used such words to refer to an innocent flirtation: 'Whatever her apologists may say, for three months something very dark was taking place in Teresa's life; something so dark according to her views that she never brought herself to be explicit on paper.'[7] She was playing with fire: 'the occasion of falling was there, the danger within a hand's grasp, and I was exposing my father and brothers to it.' It was accepted custom that a father or brothers might kill a girl's seducer (a tradition reflected in some European folksongs): it is to such real-life melodramas that Teresa obliquely refers here.[8] Even too open a familiarity might be seen as an insult to 'honour' which the males of the family would feel obliged to revenge. Whether Teresa ever actually had an affair is something of which we cannot be sure. Victoria Lincoln, one of her more broad-minded biographers, believes that she did, but the evidence does not seem to me to be conclusive. To us today, the exact details of what happened may not seem to be the most important aspect of Teresa's person; but in her time, almost everything hung on one single facet of life which composed a woman's 'honour', that is, her virginity before marriage and her fidelity thereafter.

After her elder sister had married, Teresa's father, it seems, grew concerned about her, and so she was sent as a boarder, at the age of 16, to a school attached to the Augustinian convent of Our Lady of Grace in Avila, the equivalent of a 'finishing school' for the daughters of wealthy families (see pl. 2). 'The reason for this move was . . . so disguised that it was known only to one or two of my relatives and myself . . . although something had leaked out nothing could be said with certainty; as I was so afraid for my reputation, I had taken every care to be secret.'[9] At first she was restless, but after settling down, was impressed by the purity, modesty and virtue of the nuns, though at this stage she was 'bitterly averse to taking the habit' herself.[10] After a year and a half at this convent school, she was cultivating more virtuous habits, and now and again thoughts of entering the religious life came to her, but she could not make up her mind to act on them. But illness compelled Teresa to return home for a time, and she happened also at this time to visit an uncle of hers, Don Pedro Sánchez y Cepeda, who made her read religious books to him. 'Though I did not much like them I pretended to,' she admits bluntly. Nevertheless, her short visit to her uncle made a deep impression on her: 'I began to understand the truth which I had heard as a child, that all is nothing, and that the world is vanity which quickly passes away.' She began to fear hell, which she considered she certainly deserved; she weighed up the trials which she thought the religious life would hold in store, against the torments of hell; '. . . and though, even then, I could not incline my will to being a nun, I saw that this was the best and safest state, and so, little by little, I determined to force myself to embrace it. . . . This decision, then, to enter the religious life seems to have been inspired by servile fear more than by love.'[11] To this we must add that the alternative path of marriage did not appeal to Teresa at all, for reasons to which we shall return in Chapter 5. At this early stage in her religious life, then, although Teresa aspired to piety and virtue, she was little more than lukewarm in her religion, and not motivated by the most selfless of interests, seeing her vows largely as an 'insurance' against the loss of her soul in hell. It was not until later in life that Teresa was to experience what is often seen as her true 'conversion', the sudden religious experience which marked her entry on the path of the mystic.

Teresa took the habit, then, at the Carmelite Convent of the Incarnation, which lies just outside the walls of Avila, in 1536 (according to the most commonly accepted reckoning), when she was 21, and professed a year later. (Interestingly, the Convent of the Incarnation was founded on the site of a former Jewish cemetery and the chapel had once been a synagogue. It is now generally accepted that Teresa came from a Jewish family background, and the influence of Jewish mysticism can be traced in her work, as will be shown in a later chapter.) The nuns at the Incarnation followed the 'Mitigated Rule' which allowed a considerable degree of laxity. They were not enclosed and could receive relatives and friends in the parlour, go away on visits and accept gifts of jewellery and so on which they wore with their habits. They used perfumes and kept lap-dogs. As has previously been noted, the convent was the only option open to a young woman who for one reason or another did not marry, and many found themselves there without any genuine sense of religious vocation. The Incarnation, moreover, was a 'fashionable' place to be seen, and its parlours were meeting-places for ladies and gentlemen of entirely worldly persuasions, who would gossip with the nuns over the latest news, or flirt with them under a thinly disguised pretension of spirituality, as the case might be:

> It would not have occurred to any man of good family, young, handsome, elegant, that a nun of equivalent social standing could dream of refusing to chat with him in the parlour. He was known as her 'devotee', she was considered to be helping him to save his soul, and if the good-looking nuns were more sought after than the plain ones, this occasioned no surprise.[12]

It is, moreover, known that some nuns met their devotees (*devotos*) in dark chapels or confessionals and carried on affairs with them.

Later in life, Teresa was to leave the Incarnation and found a Carmelite Reform which returned to the original simplicity of the early constitutions. The nuns at the Convent of the Incarnation at Avila today have in fact been followers of Teresa's Reform – Discalced Carmelites – since 1940; until this time they were Calced Carmelites, as in Teresa's day. Today, the Incarnation is to my mind one of the most spiritual and peaceful places in Avila. Teresa lives on here, and perhaps this is not surprising, since she spent, in all, twenty-seven years of her life here, returning as Prioress after undertaking her Reform. Today the nuns read and meditate on Teresa's works regularly, and hold weekly discussion

Our Lady of Grace, the convent whose school Teresa attended as a teenager before taking her vows at the Convent of the Incarnation.
© Keith W. Ray

groups on set passages from her books; her original Rule is still kept. A museum can be seen at the Incarnation containing relics, letters in Teresa's hand, musical instruments and other objects used by her, paintings and so on. One can see the parlour where Teresa used to talk to St John of the Cross on spiritual matters; on one such occasion they were both lifted up into religious ecstasy and, according to some accounts, they were actually seen to levitate. (John of the Cross, as we shall see, had a close spiritual relationship with Teresa and was a co-worker with her in bringing about the Reform; he was Confessor at the Incarnation from 1572 to 1577.) There is a reconstruction of the kitchen Teresa used (she used to say that God could be found among the pots and pans, among everyday chores as much as in contemplative prayer) and of her cell.

But when Teresa entered the Incarnation, there was considerable leniency with regard to adherence even to the Mitigated Rule. Nevertheless, this did not prevent her from feeling a new joy which she could not understand and a delight in all the details of the religious life. She was beginning to awaken spiritually; but she was still to spend nearly twenty years on the 'stormy sea, falling and evermore rising again'[13] – twenty years of oscillation between her desire for God, and the distractions of worldly interests; twenty years of interior conflict before the beginnings of mystical experience or of sanctity were to show themselves.

Teresa's health was never good, and in 1538 she was taken seriously ill. It is impossible for us to assess today the precise nature of her illness, but it seems that it was certainly aggravated, if not caused, by nervous tension and interior conflicts. She suffered from fainting fits and some form of heart trouble, as well as other complaints. The local doctors could not help, and so Teresa's father arranged for her to be sent to Becedas, a small village where a woman healer famous throughout Castile was accomplishing wonderful cures. On the way she stayed with her married half-sister at Castellanos de la Cañada and also with her uncle, Don Pedro Sánchez y Cepeda, already mentioned. On this occasion Don Pedro gave Teresa a copy of a book that was to influence her greatly – Francisco de Osuna's *Third Spiritual Alphabet*, a treatise on contemplative prayer. Teresa had been trying to follow a good religious life and had been practising 'vocal prayer' – that is to say, reciting set liturgical prayers aloud. Later, as her mystical life developed, she was to become adept at 'mental prayer', recollection, and contemplation – all forms of mystical prayer in which there is a communion with God without words, in the interior of the soul. (Today we might call it meditation, though this word actually has a different meaning in the context of sixteenth-century Christian spirituality.) The astonishing thing about Teresa's progress is that she found no one to guide her along this spiritual path for many years; her confessors, as we shall see, frequently insisted that the visions and raptures which she received came from the devil, and she constantly had to fight for her conviction of the value and validity of her own experiences. In her *Life* we see how she was entirely transformed by her profound personal spiritual experiences, and how she gradually grew, almost unaided, to understand and evaluate her experiences.

But this is to run ahead of ourselves. Teresa did not find a cure in Becedas; if anything, the remedies prescribed for her made her feel worse. She did, however, find temptation in the form of a young priest who was her Confessor while she was staying in the village:

> . . . he became extremely fond of me. . . . There was nothing wrong in his affection for me, but being excessive it ceased to be good. He clearly understood from me that nothing would induce me to commit any grave offence against God, and he gave me the same assurance for himself. So we had many conversations. . . . I never thought that there was anything wrong in it [their affection], though it might have been of a purer nature. Moreover there were occasions when, if he had not kept himself in the near presence of God he might have committed very grievous sins.[14]

The impression one receives from reading Teresa's account of this episode in her *Life* is that the pair fell in love and sublimated their feelings. Eventually, this priest confessed to Teresa that he had been living with a woman for seven years, but had been continuing to say Mass. He had lost his reputation, for the fact had become publicly known. Teresa does not condemn either the priest or the woman in her account, but her developing spirituality and aspirations for the Divine, and her relationship with the priest, must have had a profound effect on him, for as a result of her influence he broke off relations with the woman, giving to Teresa an amulet which his lover had apparently given him as a love-charm; Teresa promptly threw it into a river, for it was believed that the power of this magical object could be broken by depositing it in water. (The amulet was of copper, believed to bring down the influence of Venus, and interestingly enough Teresa assumes that anyone would know that.)[15]

Teresa was always a woman of strong affections and (as seems to be the case with a surprising number of mystics) had a well-developed sensuality in spite of the fact that her sights were set ultimately on the supersensual. Her relationships with her male confessors and spiritual co-workers are interesting in this respect. She was particularly close to Gracián (Fray Jerónimo de la Madre de Dios), who joined Teresa's Reform in 1572 and was later made Provincial of the Discalced Carmelites. Many of her confessors, too, shared a spiritual intimacy with Teresa that gave rise to gossip, and scandals about the love affairs that Teresa was said to have with them pursued her until she was 60. I cannot see that there is any reason to believe these slanderous accusations, which are exactly the type of allegation from which a woman like Teresa might have expected to suffer: beautiful, successful in a man's world, a self-confessed 'sinner' in the past, and of somewhat doubtful reputation for her visions and raptures, she was, I am afraid, exactly the sort of woman likely to fall prey to such accusations. Apart from Gracián and a number of her confessors, we should mention here, as men to whom Teresa was close, St Peter of Alcántara, an ascetic old Franciscan who helped Teresa greatly in spiritual matters, and St John of the Cross, who had a close friendship with Teresa in spite of the fact that the pair were so unalike that I suspect they never quite understood each other. No suggestion is being made here that anything that would have been considered sinful by the standards of the time (or even anything improper) passed between Teresa and any of these men. Indeed, John of the Cross and Gracián were both some thirty years younger than Teresa, and her feelings for them might be seen as coloured by maternal rather than erotic elements. (On one occasion she even went so far as to ask Gracián outright in a letter, whom he loved more, his mother or herself!) But against this type of evidence we have to set the patently sensual vision of Gracián – one of two, in fact, that might qualify for such description – of which Teresa gives us her own account: 'I suddenly became recollected, and saw a great light within me, so that I thought I was in another world, and my spirit found itself inwardly in a most delightful rustic garden, so lovely that it recalled to my mind those words in the *Songs* "Veniat dilectus meus in hortum suum" ["Let my beloved come into his garden", Song of Songs 5:1].' Then, Teresa says, she saw Gracián there, having a strange beauty about him, with a garland of precious stones on his head, and walking before him were maidens with palms in their hands, while all around was delightful music made by birds and angels. The vision was so lovely that she could not take her eyes from it. She felt that she loved Gracián more as a result of this vision, and adds 'I have had my fears that it might have been a temptation.'[16]

Victoria Lincoln, as previously mentioned, is quite frank about Teresa's emotional life. Lincoln interprets the evidence as suggesting that Teresa had an affair at 16, hoping to marry the man with whom she was involved. Her seclusion in Our Lady of Grace was intended to let the scandal die down and keep her out of harm's way. Teresa's resistance to the idea of marriage, Lincoln claims, was due not only to her observation of her mother's unhappy life, but also because Teresa knew what sort of marriage she could now get, at 18 and with her honour very badly damaged, her own description of herself at this time. (In sixteenth-century Spain, marriages for girls were usually arranged in their early teens.) I am not sure that the evidence for Lincoln's reading of Teresa's life is conclusive, but it is a challenging interpretation and not one that we should dismiss out of hand. Then, at the Incarnation, a certain nobleman became Teresa's *devoto*. She became very fond of him and attracted to him, so much so that she says he 'disturbed her soul'. With her growing love for Jesus Christ, she came to feel that this was a kind of spiritual adultery, but she found it extremely difficult to break off this relationship. Lincoln's reading of the evidence – again, not conclusive, but worthy of consideration – is that Teresa followed the example of so many other nuns at the Incarnation and had an illicit affair with this man.

Lincoln continues to tell us of Teresa's friendship with Doña Guiomar de Ulloa, a young widow whom we shall mention again shortly. On one occasion their mutual Confessor, Juan de Prádanos, fell ill and went to stay at one of Doña Guiomar's country properties, where the two women nursed him. By this time, Teresa was wholly reformed from her 'sinful' past, and while she felt a great spiritual love for many people – including many men – she kept to her vows of chastity. But she was never careful enough to avoid scandal. Her relationship with de Prádanos was misconstrued and he became the first of many men who were 'persecuted' for a 'great false witness' as Teresa cautiously puts it – that is, unjustly slandered as having been her lover.

Interpretation of the evidence is made extremely difficult by the fact that many of Teresa's letters have been 'censored' by later copyists or keepers: large chunks are blacked out and deleted, including many passages dealing with Teresa's feelings for Gracián and for her confessors. But Teresa admits in her *Life* that she has known the problem of becoming too attached to some of her confessors so that her mind was quite taken up with thinking about them.[17] She interprets these feelings as 'loves in Christ' but nevertheless admits that she finds it almost impossible to tell whether a love is entirely spiritual. My own feeling is that if her love were *wholly* spiritual, Teresa would not have had her mind taken up all the time with thoughts of the men in question; furthermore, a wholly spiritual love would bring greater love of the Divine, and not only greater love of a particular man, which Teresa mentions as the only effect of her vision of Gracián. Nevertheless, to admit that Teresa's 'loves in Christ' had something this-worldly about them is not to join forces with her persecutors. My belief is that these men fulfilled an emotional, rather than a sexual, need. Teresa had a nature that longed for love and affection. She needed someone to 'understand her soul' as she put it; and she needed someone to love. Lincoln comments that notwithstanding Teresa's adherence to her vows of chastity, 'The fact remains that one cannot think of any time in her life except for its lonely last weeks when Teresa was not emotionally dependent upon some man: some man whom she felt to be responsive to her spirit.'[18]

At the same time it is true, I think, that Teresa's need for love came to be transposed onto spiritual levels. From childhood she had been fascinated by the concept of a love that lasted 'for ever and ever'. Disillusioned, perhaps, by her teenage experiences of human love – for there is more than a hint of bitterness in her analogy of love as 'false dice' which can deceive[19] – she was later to find eternal love in her passion for the Divine, and in particular for Christ her Heavenly Spouse, who is clearly responsible for drawing Teresa away from her earthly loves. This transposition of emotional yearnings is seen quite clearly in a number of passages, such as the following:

> A very serious fault of mine which led me into great trouble was that
> if I began to see that someone liked me, and I happened to take to that

person myself, I would become very fond of him. Then my memory would be drawn to dwell on that person, although I had no intention of offending God. But I took delight in seeing him and thinking of him, and in considering the good qualities that I saw in him; and this was such a harmful thing that it was ruining my soul. But once I had seen the Lord's great beauty, I could find no one who seemed handsome to me by comparison, and no one to occupy my thoughts. For merely by turning the eyes of my mind onto the image that I carry in my soul, I become so entirely free that from that time forward everything I see has appeared nauseating to me in comparison with the excellencies and glories that I have glimpsed in the Lord.[20]

I do not by any means wish to imply, here, that Teresa's religious experiences were simply a sublimated substitute for an unfulfilled sexuality; we have had too many Freudian interpretations of mysticism. Rather, she discovered that her romantic ideals and dreams could never be fulfilled on the ever-changing plane of material reality, but only in the realm of the changeless, which I take as being a Reality in its own right. But Teresa continued to puzzle over the precise relationship between spiritual and sensual love. Writing of spiritual love she says that those who love in this way do not love less than others, but more so, with a more genuine love; 'that, in a word, is what love really is.' If they love anyone it is not for their outward appearance or for any of the 'externals': they 'look right beyond the body [and] fix their eyes on the soul.' If they see there even a glint of gold they will think nothing of the labour of digging in search of more.[21] Elsewhere Teresa writes that love, in its most exalted form, can be purely spiritual, but more often than not there is an element of sensuality in it; and as we have noted she admits that she finds it almost impossible to tell whether love is wholly spiritual or not. But in any case, she says, love that has an element of sensuality can itself be turned into a virtue. If a nun imagines that she is developing too great an affection for her confessor, there is no need to feel guilty and to go searching for someone else, only to find the same thing happening again. Here, as on so many occasions, Teresa demonstrates her intuitive understanding of human nature, drawn partially from reflection on her own experiences. Provided the confessor is leading a nun to greater perfection, she should not worry about being fond of him, as long as there are no wrong intentions involved.[22] Clearly, Teresa had known the depths of communion that are possible between two souls in close spiritual relationship;

and she had also known how easily the spiritual and the sensual can sometimes become confused when those two persons are of the opposite sex. Many mystics have had to confront this problem, but few have described it with such candour.

It is, no doubt, significant (in view of the emotional conflicts that one can imagine she had undergone) that when Teresa returned from Becedas her illness worsened. She was in agonising pain, debilitated, and unable to eat; the doctors gave her up as incurable. In August of 1539 she had an attack, apparently of catalepsy, which left her unconscious for almost four days. She was pronounced dead and her grave was dug – indeed, when she finally recovered consciousness, her eyelids were stuck together by the wax of the funeral tapers. She was paralysed to a greater or lesser degree for almost three years after this incident, and suffered terribly. Although her health improved to some degree in later life, it was never good, and we have to remember, in considering her achievements, that they are all the more remarkable for the fact that they were accomplished by a sick woman in a world dominated by strong men.

Of the period in Teresa's life from 1543 to 1555 we know relatively little. Although she had tried for a little while to follow 'mental prayer' as outlined in Francisco de Osuna's *Third Spiritual Alphabet*, she had soon given up this practice, excusing herself on the grounds of her severe ill health. But she knew very well that her health was not the real problem. Although Teresa continued to have feelings of religious aspiration, and even intimations of the presence of God within her – and although her 'miraculous return from the dead', as some saw it, had caused quite a stir in Avila and made people gossip about whether the Convent of the Incarnation housed a saint – Teresa knew that she was far even from putting her most basic spiritual yearnings into practice.

> On the one side God called me, and on the other I followed the world. All divine things gave me great pleasure; yet those of the world held me prisoner. I seem to have wanted to reconcile two opposites as completely hostile, one to another, as the spiritual life and the joys, pleasures, and pastimes of the senses. . . . When I was among the pleasures of the world, I was saddened by the memory of what I owed to God, and my worldly affections disturbed me when I was with God.[23]

And she admits frankly to a problem with which most meditators will be familiar: '. . . very often over a period of some years I was more occupied with the wish that the time I had assigned myself for prayer would end, and with listening whenever the clock struck, than with other and better thoughts.'[24]

A severe oscillatory conflict of this type, between the realm of the Divine and the world of matter and the senses, is a frequently observed phase of spiritual development which most mystics have to conquer. In traditional Catholic terminology this is known as the Way of Purgation. The rigid dualism between 'God' and 'the world' implied in Teresa's statements, although perhaps foreign to the ears of some today, is very much a feature of medieval Christianity; although for many mystics this conflict between the divine and the material realms seems to be overcome at a later phase in their progress.

During this period of her life, then, Teresa felt acutely and painfully conscious of all her failings, shortcomings, and 'sins'. She had begun to receive what she calls 'graces' – spiritual experiences of various kinds – and it is at this time that she mentions her first vision of Jesus Christ. She felt completely unworthy of these blessings:

> A single fault, I am sure, troubled, shamed and distressed me more than many illnesses and severe trials put together. For these I knew that I deserved, and they seemed to be a partial payment for my sins, though all my sufferings were but small and my sins were great. But to find myself receiving fresh graces when I had shown so little gratitude for those already received, is a kind of torture that is terrible to me, and to everyone, I believe, who has any knowledge or love of God.

Of this stage of her experience, Teresa regrets not having found any 'kindred souls':

> It is a dreadful thing for a soul to be alone among such perils, and I think that if I had had anyone with whom I could have spoken of all this, it would have helped me not to fall again. . . . I do not know why those who are beginning truly to love and serve God should not be allowed to discuss their joys and trials with others. . . . those who serve Him must back one another up if they are to progress. . . . I had plenty of friends to help me fall. But when it came to picking myself up I found myself completely alone.[25]

It was around 1555–56 – there is some disagreement as to the exact date – that Teresa experienced what is often known as her 'second conversion', the full awakening of her spiritual life that placed her firmly upon the mystical path. A sudden peak of religious experience occurred when she came upon an *Ecce Homo* (an image of the wounded Christ; such images, in Catholic Spain, are intensely lifelike) in the oratory. She was profoundly moved by it and by a sudden realisation of the meaning of the crucifixion which it awakened in her, and threw herself on the ground before the image in tears, imploring Jesus to give her strength not to offend him again. From that time forward, she says, she improved greatly. She studied St Augustine's *Confessions* and apparently found much in them with which to identify, since Augustine had also been a worldly man and a 'sinner' before his conversion. She avoided the parlour, resumed mental prayer with fervour, and found herself to be grow-ing in ethical virtues. She often experienced the 'Prayer of Quiet', as she called it, a state of interior peace and joy in which the inner self of the mystic is absorbed in contemplation of God; and occasionally the 'Prayer of Union', a high state of contemplation which is a foretaste of the ultimate mystical goal which Teresa calls the 'Spiri-tual Marriage'.

Teresa's writings on the various types of prayer and stages of mystical experience will be examined in more detail in the next chapter. We reserve for the next chapter, too, a fuller discussion of the visions, voices (locutions), raptures and mystical ecstasies which now became part of Teresa's normal experience. Suffice it to say here that Teresa was intensely subject to visions and locutions of varied kinds from this point on, as well as to rapture and ecstatic trance shortly afterwards. But unlike the many mystics who are extremely wary of such phenomena, she emphasises the great value that these experiences had for her. They left her with a new degree of love for the Divine, with peace and inner consolation, and issued in a life of increased psychological integration, heightened ethical awareness, and unremitting perseverance in pursuit of her high reli-gious ideals. In fact, Teresa's testimonies with regard to the worth of these experiences necessitate a re-evaluation of such experiences for Christian thought. But Teresa had to go through much inner turmoil and conflict because of those who told her she was deluded, or that her visions and voices came from the devil. These persons included some of her own confessors and superiors, so during this period of her life Teresa certainly had to work out her own path with no other guide than her own interior light and conscience. Many visionaries and ecstatics in her lifetime were being persecuted by the Spanish Inquisition: women who claimed marvellous spiritual experiences were especially suspect. Some had been imprisoned, even tortured or burnt at the stake. Teresa did have several brushes with the Inquisition during her lifetime: they came to little in the long run, but make the attitude of caution betrayed in her writings only too understandable. (As we shall see later, the fact that Teresa was from a Jewish family background was a further reason for extreme caution.) Partly, no doubt, because of this, and partly to satisfy her own inner need to be sure of the validity of her experiences, Teresa goes to great lengths to explain how we can tell whether a vision or locution comes from God, whether it is the work of one's own imagination, or whether it comes from the devil. This point will be taken up again in due course.

Teresa refers on a number of occasions in her writings to the problems that can be encountered if one is not able to find a spiritual director (a confessor and guide in prayer) who understands the nature of one's particular spiritual path. Directors who are not spiritually minded themselves, who do not understand the different types of spiritual experiences, who are not learned enough, who are inexperienced – all can block the progress of a soul and cause it real torment. It is obvious that Teresa speaks from bitter experience here, and equally evident that she must have had a tremendous battle to fight in convincing others of the worth of her experiences. As a woman in a strongly male-dominated culture she was denied the theological learning which might have enabled her to argue out fine points of doctrine with her persecutors. She had nothing but her trust in her own experience to guide her. 'Women', she warns, '. . . should be advised to keep their experiences to themselves, and their advisers should keep them secret too. I speak as one who has suffered grave trials from the indiscretions of certain persons with whom I have discussed my prayers.'[26] On occasions, Teresa becomes positively subversive, so that we are astonished (as we shall also have cause to be for other reasons) that she did not in fact encounter more trouble from the Inquisition. Many men, she says, make the mistake of supposing that they can understand spirituality without experiencing anything of it; while such a man can direct those souls in his charge as far as conduct goes, or on matters of the intellect or points of teaching found in the Scriptures, he should not think that he can understand what he cannot, 'or quell spirits which are being guided by another Master greater than he . . . the Lord is perhaps giving to some little old woman a deeper knowledge of this science than to himself, learned man though he is. . . . I say once more that unless he has experience . . . he will gain little, and the people he deals with will gain even less.'[27] It was precisely such claims to direct knowledge of God without the mediation of the hierarchy of the Church that the Inquisitors were on the alert for, among other heresies. A case in point were the *alumbrados* – literally 'those who are lit' (by an inner light) – the 'Illuminists' or 'Enlightened Ones'. They advocated direct, ecstatic, personal contact with God for lay people, and rejected many of the tenets of outward popular devotion: for example, they held that it was unnecessary or even idolatrous to venerate images, and that fasts and similar outward practices were useless in the quest for salvation. It is possible to see certain parallels between the *alumbrados*, and Teresa and her teachings. There are, too, some important differences, the most notable perhaps being that Teresa was more orthodox than the *alumbrados* as regards outward devotions, and did not advocate the sexual licentiousness which was an aspect of the *alumbrados'* practices. Nevertheless, her accusors, as we shall see in Chapter 4, believed that her teachings on mental prayer, raptures, visions and revelations were identical to those of this heretical sect. St John of the Cross, Teresa's co-worker, was denounced to the Inquisition as an *alumbrado* on no less than three occasions, and Teresa had to live with the almost constant rumour of being an *alumbrada*, perpetuated by those who sought to oppose her.

All mystics emphasise the importance of personal spiritual experience as the only way in which one can fully know divine truth; but Teresa does so on so many occasions and with such force that one feels that this must be in part due to the trials caused her by spiritual directors who had no such experience. 'I am speaking the language of spirituality. Anyone with experience will understand me. But if I have not made myself plain, I can say no more.' 'However clearly I may wish to explain this matter of prayer, it will be very obscure to anyone who has not the experience.' '. . . it is strange what a difference there is between understanding a thing and subsequently knowing it by experience.' 'I know by my own experience, which is my only means of knowledge.'[28] Again and again Teresa makes this

point, throughout her writings but especially in her *Life*, and it
would be tedious to list the extremely numerous other examples. She
takes a very firm stand on the authority of her own experience: '. . .
as I have had these experiences for so many years, I have been able to
make my observations, and so can speak on the subject very defi-
nitely.'[29] One is amazed contemplating just how dangerous it was for
a woman in her position to make these kinds of statements.

So when she began to experience visions and other 'graces',
although deep within herself she was convinced that they came from
God, Teresa was, she says, very much afraid, since there had
recently been cases of women who had been judged to be deceived
by the devil, and burnt at the fires of the Inquisition. Accordingly
she began to search diligently for spiritually minded people to whom
she could talk. The first few men whom she consulted considered
that she was being deluded by the devil and, needless to say, this
caused Teresa great distress, alarm and suffering. Quite possibly,
her own lack of learning so intimidated her in the presence of these
theologians (*letrados*) that she could not find words with which to
dispute their verdict. She says that she did not dare to contradict her
critics, as they would then imagine that she, a 'mere woman', was
trying to instruct them. 'I had no one to discuss matters with, since
they were all against me. When I spoke to them about my experiences, I thought they were mocking me, as if it were all my fancy.
. . . This continued for about two years. . . . I was utterly disquieted
and exhausted, and did not know what to do. . . . I had enough
troubles to drive me out of my mind.'[30] The theologians decided that
Teresa ought to consult the Jesuit fathers, who had founded a college
in Avila in 1554, for they were held to be great experts in spiritual
matters; apparently the thought that was uppermost in the minds of
these men was that the Jesuits might perform an efficient exorcism!
As it happened, Teresa had been greatly attracted to the Jesuits,
simply through what she knew of their way of life and methods of
prayer, and some consider that she had had some contact with them
already, but apparently she had considered that it would be too
presumptuous of her to consult them specifically on this matter. At
this stage in their history the Jesuits were not as wary of visions or
mystical experiences as were many other Orders, and they approved
of the practice of 'mental prayer'. The Jesuit father to whom Teresa
talked disagreed with the former verdict: her experiences he held to
be quite patently the work of God. He gave Teresa instruction in

prayer, and other forms of spiritual guidance. 'This . . . led me along paths that seemed to turn me into a very different woman. What a great thing it is to understand a soul!'[31] From this time on, Teresa's inner life was firmly based on Jesuit methods of prayer or meditation, and most of her confessors were Jesuits. This did not mean that her trials were over: there were always some who were sceptical of her experiences; for example, one confessor ordered her to scorn and resist her visions. But she also began to meet people who understood her. Peter of Alcántara came to Avila in 1560:

> . . . the Lord was pleased that he should feel love for me, and stand up for me, and encourage me at a time when I was in great need. . . . Almost from the beginning, I saw that he understood me from experience, and that was all I needed. . . . I needed someone who had gone through it all himself, for no one else could both understand me and explain to me the nature of my experiences. He gave me the greatest enlightenment, particularly in regard to the visions. . . . He used to say that women made much more progress on this path than men, and he gave excellent reasons for it, which there is no reason to repeat here, all in women's favour.[32]

Teresa was in fact introduced to Peter of Alcántara by a friend who had supported her all along, and with whom she was staying at this time, Doña Guiomar de Ulloa, the young widow mentioned earlier. Dona Guiomar had also had some spiritual experiences of her own and Teresa therefore says of her that she was enlightened where learned men remained in the dark. The fact that it was this woman alone who supported Teresa at this time, and indeed throughout her early attempts at Reform, and who arranged for her to meet Peter of Alcántara, is highly relevant to the issue of 'women's spirituality', as indeed, it will be clear, are many of the points that have been raised with regard to Teresa and her experiences. This issue will be discussed in Chapter 5.

It was not until 1560, then, at the age of 45, that Teresa began to see her vocation and the fulfilment of her spiritual life open out before her. By this time she had had many visions and revelations, and the so-called 'Transverberation of her Heart', the vision of an angel piercing her heart with a fiery spear, is believed to have occurred in 1559. She had reached the high stage of mystical apprehension which she was later to call the 'Pain of God' or the 'Wound of Love', a time of purification through suffering and eventually of spiritual rebirth through the 'death' of the lower aspects of one's nature. She had experienced powerful raptures and ecstasies, which embarrassed her when they occurred in public, not least because on several occasions of rapture she was, we are told, seen to physically levitate several inches above the ground! Some thought her a saint, but there were an equal number who thought her an impostor, or who believed her to be possessed and wanted to see her investigated by the Inquisitors. In fact, later, Teresa was indeed denounced to the Inquisition, which, it seems, was always there, haunting her, in the background, throughout her life. (The details of Teresa's dealings with the Inquisition will be recounted in Chapter 4.) For so many years she trod such a thin line that we are astonished at how lucky she seems to have been that the weight of public and learned opinion always seems to have come down in her favour. This seems to have been more as a result of her political shrewdness and personal charm than because of her religious orthodoxy, for as we shall see in Chapter 3, if the Inquisition had only known the full extent of the Jewish influences on Teresa, she would surely have encountered a good deal more opposition, and might even have gone to the stake.

It seems that most mystics eventually reach a point of creative tension where the divine energies that they feel coursing through them must be made manifest in some outward and more or less concrete manner. It is at this point that they begin to accomplish observable things in the everyday world and make ideals into realities. Teresa's accomplishments, from this point on, were marked by a determination, courage and strength remarkable for a woman in sixteenth-century Spain who had to contend against the 'system'. The source of her ability to accomplish so much was the rooting of her inner life in the Divine, which gives to all those who know it, boundless energy and creative power. However badly she was persecuted or misunderstood, she always persevered in her calling, and this in spite of her chronic ill health, which made many of her activities extremely difficult.

For some years – perhaps since 1558 or even earlier – Teresa had been musing over and discussing the possibility of founding a convent which would follow the original 'Primitive Rule', as it was known, of the Carmelites. The relaxed 'Mitigated Rule' at the Incarnation allowed too many distractions to intervene for one who now truly wanted to dedicate her whole life to loving and serving the Divine. For several years she had not translated her ideas into action, for she saw that to do so would mean great labour and anxiety; and would the reality, even supposing she managed to achieve it, live up to her imaginings? But Christ himself, she believed, commanded her in a vision to go ahead with the plan. There is also a tradition that Teresa had a further vision which persuaded her to undertake the Reform, whilst praying before an icon of Nuestra Señora de la Soterraña – 'Our Lady of the Underworld' – which can still be seen in the Basílica de San Vicente, Avila (see pl. 3). In Teresa's time the image was in the crypt, but it has now been moved to the side-chapel in the south aisle. Some, however, place this incident a little later in her life, just after St Joseph's, her first reformed convent, had been founded, and it is then said that Teresa took off her shoes before Nuestra Señora before entering her new convent 'discalced' (shoeless). In any case, after discussions with various of Teresa's superiors, the Provincial (who has overall jurisdiction for religious houses in a given province) eventually gave his sanction to the proposed foundation. A great movement for the reform of the religious Orders was sweeping through Spain; in this, Teresa was doing no more than follow a major spiritual current of the time. The 'Primitive Rule' of the Carmelite Order dated from the twelfth century, when Carmelite friars still lived by Mount Carmel itself and saw themselves as the spiritual heirs of the Prophet Elijah. In later centuries a series of mitigations had made the Rule considerably less austere. Indeed, decadence and laxity had affected all the religious Orders – an episode known as the *claustra* in Spanish ecclesiastical history, the reaction to which was the reform of the Orders in the fifteenth–seventeenth centuries, together with the creation of new Orders. Teresa's Reform was actually a return to the observances of the ancient Order of Our Lady of Mount Carmel. She re-introduced fasting, perpetual abstinence from red meat (though not from fish and poultry), and the wearing of a coarse habit. Vows of seclusion, enclosure and silence were taken. The houses of the Reform were founded in poverty, living on alms plus what could be gained from the nuns' own handicrafts such as spinning and weaving. The term 'Discalced' referred to the fact that the nuns wore rope-soled sandals (some of the friars at first went barefoot, but Teresa, who was not in favour of exaggerated forms of asceticism, discouraged this. Since 1876, leather-soled sandals have been worn.) Silence and prayer did not mean a gloomy atmosphere: Teresa was always a lively, bright woman ('God deliver me from

frowning saints!' she used to say).[33] There was music, song and
dance, poetry and stories at times of recreation, and singing and
dancing even in church. Simplicity, a joyful atmosphere, and tranquil devotion to God; no supercilious piety or excesses of bodily
mortification: these were the qualities Teresa sought to cultivate.

But as soon as the proposal for the foundation became known in
Avila it caused a storm of opposition: '. . . there fell upon us a
persecution so severe that it would not be possible to describe it in a
few words . . . they laughed at us, and they declared that the idea
was absurd.'[34] As far as her persecutors were concerned, Teresa was
a heretic who was possessed by devils and had affairs with her
confessors! There was so much fuss and uproar that the Provincial
withdrew his backing and there was talk of denouncing Teresa to the
Inquisition as an *alumbrada*.

By this time Teresa had already bought a house for her reformed
convent and the deeds were to be signed the very next day. She had
to let it drop. Her Confessor at the time – one of those who
remained sceptical of her visions – ordered her to do so, venturing
the condescension that one day she would come to see that all this
was only a dream. '. . . the Lord knows what great labours and
afflictions it had cost me to bring it so far. Once it was discontinued
and abandoned, people were even more certain that it had all been
an absurd feminine whimsy, and gossip at my expense increased.'[35]
She was even denounced from the pulpit while sitting in the Church
of Santo Tomás with her sister: the preacher began to speak out
against those who leave their monasteries to seek only their own
liberty, under the pretext of founding religious orders.

But still Teresa would not let go of the project entirely. Astonish-
ingly, she in fact continued with it in secret with the support only of
a handful of sympathisers: she had to arrange everything herself. A
house was found: 'It was very rough and ready, and no more was
done to it than was necessary to make it healthy to live in.'[36] Teresa's
brother Lorenzo sent her some money. Then suddenly an order
came from the Provincial that Teresa was to leave for Toledo. A
noble lady, Doña Luisa de la Cerda, in great grief at the death of her
husband, had heard good reports of Teresa and hoped to find comfort through a visit from her. She could not refuse to go, and in the
end she had to stay several months: a complication that she could
have done without at the time, although in fact Doña Luisa became
Teresa's friend and later helped her greatly. But while she was there,

Nuestra Señora de la Soterraña, the 12th century icon of 'Our Lady of the Underworld' in the Basilica of St. Vincent, Avila: an icon of importance in Teresa's life (see p. 21).

Teresa also met a *beata* – a woman following an independent religious vow of her own – who had entered a Carmelite Convent of Mitigated Observance but had left before being professed. This woman, known as María de Jesús, had also conceived the idea of founding reformed Carmelite convents (we are told that she received a command from God to do so on the very same day as Teresa!) and had walked barefoot to Rome to get a patent. From her Teresa learned that the original Carmelite Rule forbade religious houses to have any regular income. So Teresa consulted various people on the practicability of founding a convent in this way, trusting that God would provide. No one would countenance such an idea. Teresa's ironic wit is at its best in her description of their reactions. She sent her suggestions to a certain Dominican friar who so far had been in sympathy with her:

> . . . he answered me with two sheets of refutation and theology, in which he told me that he had considered the matter carefully and urged me against it. I replied that I had no wish to resort to theology and could feel no gratitude for his learning in this matter if it meant that I was not to follow my vocation. . . . Some people began by telling me that they approved of my plan, but afterwards, when they looked into it further, they found so many drawbacks that they strongly urged me once more to give it up. I told them that, in view of the speed with which they changed their opinions, I preferred to stick to mine.[37]

The only person who continued to support Teresa was Peter of Alcántara; but his support meant a great deal to her, and finally, commands which she received in a rapture and believed to come from God sealed the matter.

In July of 1562 Teresa returned to Avila. God brought her back just at the vital moment, she writes, for on the very night of her arrival the Papal Brief and patent for the convent (official documents authorising the foundation), which had been secretly applied for, arrived from Rome. The Bishop of Avila eventually gave his permission for the founding of the convent. Teresa acknowledges her great debt to Peter of Alcántara here: sadly, he died soon afterwards. The convent, which was named St Joseph's (San José), was finally founded and in August Teresa gave the habit to four nuns. But all was still being done in secret, for neither the Provincial nor Teresa's Prioress at the Convent of the Incarnation had been told anything of it. When the secret became known there was, of course, great commotion. Teresa also had her moments of doubt as to the practicability of the whole affair. The City Council and the Cathedral Chapter insisted that the house should be closed, but the Prioress at the Incarnation and the Provincial, although they rebuked Teresa sternly, seemed to give in to this *fait accompli*. A lawsuit ensued. Those who supported Teresa sustained (in her own words) 'a good deal of persecution' and 'everyone condemned' her.[38] The dispute dragged on for two whole years, Teresa gaining ground little by little. In the end she was to spend only four and a half years at St Joseph's, apart from brief periods later in life, for she was to return to the Incarnation as Prioress as well as travelling all over Spain founding many more convents. But those few years in the small, simple convent of just thirteen nuns were the most restful and tranquil of her life:

> The founding of Saint Joseph's comes into Teresa's story like a burst of sunlight. All at once she seems to be liberated from her past. The emotional tension is relaxed; she is no longer a victim of heart-searchings, doubts and fears. At forty-seven she has left her spiritual adolescence behind her; found the purpose of her life, scope for her gifts and an outlet for her creative energy.[39]

The convent is still enclosed today, but its seventeenth-century church can be visited, as can the *iglesia primitiva*, the original church, small and simple, used by Teresa and her nuns when the convent was founded. There is also a museum containing relics, early manuscripts of some of Teresa's works, and other exhibits.

Little need be said, then, of Teresa's time at St Joseph's, since the spiritual teachings which the tranquillity there doubtless allowed her to develop will be discussed separately. It will suffice to mention here that Teresa wrote her *Life* (in two drafts) between about 1561 and 1565, and began her *Way of Perfection* soon after finishing the second draft of the *Life*. Her autobiography therefore covers only the first fifty years or so of her life; biographical material from later years is found scattered throughout her later works, particularly in her *Spiritual Relations* and *Book of the Foundations*.

In 1567 an event occurred which was to dramatically change the course of Teresa's life once more, uprooting her from that peace and simple serenity for which she longed so much. Padre Rubeo

(Giovanni Battista Rossi), General of the Carmelite Order, came to Avila and accepted Teresa's Reform into the Order (for in leaving the Incarnation and setting up on her own she had made her position *via-à-vis* the existing Carmelite Order ambivalent, and this issue had not yet been resolved). Furthermore, he authorised Teresa to found further convents of the Reform, and also two monasteries for men.

Over the rest of her active and stressful life Teresa was to found a further sixteen convents and two priories over almost the length and breadth of Spain (in addition, she helped with the organisation of one other convent which had been founded by María de Jesús, the *beata* whom Teresa had previously met in Toledo). In 1567 Medina del Campo was founded and María de Jesús' house at Alcalá de Henares received Teresa's assistance. In 1568 Malagón and Valladolid were founded, as well as the tiny priory at Duruelo. In 1569, Toledo and Pastrana (the latter comprising both a convent, and the second of Teresa's houses for men). In 1570, Salamanca; 1571, Alba de Tormes. From 1571 to 1574 Teresa was called back to the Incarnation at Avila, where she was Prioress. Just before the end of her office here, in 1574 came the foundation at Segovia; in 1575, Beas de Segura and Seville; 1576, Caravaca. No foundations were made during the period 1577–79, which was a time of great conflict and persecution for the Discalced. In the two and a half years before her death Teresa managed to make five more foundations: Villaneuva de la Jara (1580), Palencia (1580), Soria (1581), Granada and Burgos (both 1582).

Teresa, of course, had no money or property with which to begin her foundations, and the long journeys were made in uncomfortable covered mule-carts. The *Book of the Foundations* gives some graphic accounts of the experiences that Teresa and her travelling companions (a few nuns and a chaplain or friar, plus the mule-drivers) had to endure: '. . . if I were to describe them in detail, it would be very wearisome,' Teresa writes. 'I mean, for example, the state of the roads, the floods, the snowstorms, the losing of our way, and, above all, again and again, the ill health which has troubled me. . . . Then there were other things which were no small trials to me, such as having to put up with people of so many different temperaments in each place we visited, and leaving my sisters and daughters when I went from one place to another.'[40] A full catalogue of all her journeys, as Teresa herself says, would be wearisome, but we may give a few examples of the hardships the nuns encountered. At Medina del Campo the house was so dilapidated that it was almost falling down. Having unloaded the carts, the party walked through the streets in the dark carrying vestments and hangings, looking for all the world like gypsies who had been robbing a church, and only narrowly missing being chased by bulls:

> We arrived at Medina del Campo at midnight on the eve of the festival of Our Lady in August. . . . It was a great mercy on the part of the Lord that we met no one, for it was just at that time that they were shutting in the bulls which were to take part in the next day's bull-fight. . . . The walls [of the house intended for the convent] seemed to me in a very tumbledown condition and by day they appeared worse still . . . there were holes in the roof; and the walls were not plastered. The night was nearly over and we had only a few hangings. . . . These, in view of the length of the porch [which they had decided to use as the church] were of no use at all. I did not know what to do, for I saw that it would not be seemly to put an altar there. But it was the Lord's will that it should be done at once, for by His providence the lady's steward [the lady in question being the one who was selling the house to them] had a great deal of tapestry belonging to her and also a blue damask bedspread. . . . We did not know what to do for nails and it was not a time at which we could buy any. So we started to look round the walls; and at last, after some trouble, we collected a sufficient number. . . . we all worked so quickly that, by daybreak, the altar was set up and the bell hung in a gallery, so that Mass was said immediately.[41]

Duruelo, the first house for friars, was no better:

> Although we set out early in the morning, we were unfamiliar with the road and so went astray . . . we could find no one to direct us. We travelled all that day in the greatest discomfort, for the sun was very strong. When we thought we were near the village, we found we had as far again to go. I always remember the fatigue of that long round-about journey. We arrived only a little before nightfall. When we entered the house, we found it in such a condition that we dared not spend the night there, so dirty was it . . . It had a fair-sized porch, a room divided into two, with a loft above it, and a little kitchen: that is all there was of the building which was to be our monastery . . . my companion . . . could not bear the thought of my founding a monastery there. 'Mother,' she said, 'I am certain that no one, however good and spiritual, could endure this.'[42]

Another foundation that Teresa found particularly trying was at Seville. She was unaccustomed to the heat of southern Spain: 'Though we did not travel during the siesta hours, I can assure you, sisters, that, when the sun beat down on the carriages with all its might, going into them was like entering purgatory.' Teresa became ill. They were accommodated along the way in a most unpleasant inn:

> They gave us a little room roofed like a shed and without a window, into which the sun streamed whenever the door was opened. You must remember that the heat there is not like our Castilian heat but is much more trying. They made me lie down on a bed, but it was so full of ups and downs that I would rather have lain on the floor: I cannot think how I endured it – it seemed to be full of sharp stones. What a troublesome thing illness is! It is easy enough to bear anything if one is well. In the end I thought it best to get up, so that we could go on our way, for I preferred to endure the sun in the open air than in that little room.[43]

Two days later the carriages in which the nuns were travelling were carried away by the current in the process of trying to cross the River Guadalquivir, and were only stopped by the providential positioning of a sandbank. At their next overnight stop the room was crawling with vermin and seemed to have previously been inhabited by pigs. When they arrived in Seville, destitute of resources and nearly 400 miles from home, problems were raised over the issue of founding the convent without an endowment. (Teresa had allowed some of her foundations to have endowments, but only in small places where there would have been no other way of providing for their upkeep. Not surprisingly, she encountered a good deal of opposition from those who thought it the height of folly to try to found convents without any material resources.) Then there was a great deal of trouble and delay over finding a house, involving a lawsuit and many other difficulties.

All the time that Teresa was building up and guiding her new movement over these last fifteen years or so of her life, she was also leading a most demanding interior life (as those who have attempted to practise meditation or contemplative prayer and self-improvement will know, the demands of such inward discipline and self-searching are indeed great). In addition, she was writing books and occasional shorter reflections and maxims (*Exclamations of the Soul to God* probably in 1569; *Conceptions of the Love of God* between 1571 and 1575; the *Book of the Foundations* between 1573 and 1582; the *Interior Castle* in 1577. This is apart from minor works and poems. The *Spiritual Relations*, being accounts of her mystical experiences addressed to her confessors, span the years 1560 to 1581.) She still found time, too, to give spiritual advice and counsel to all who asked for it – and towards the end of her life this must have been fairly time-consuming, as the fame of Teresa's virtues and good works spread and her popular following grew, although there were always those in authority who opposed her.

It was at the beginning of these strenuous activities, in 1567, that Teresa first met St John of the Cross (San Juan de la Cruz; then Fray Juan de San Matias). John of the Cross was a completely different character from Teresa: well-educated and of a sublimely metaphysical turn of mind, otherworldly, more rarified and abstract in his own descriptions of mystical contemplation, wary of visions. A full account of their spiritual relationship and of the similarities and contrasts between them would merit a study in its own right, though we shall say a little more on this subject in a later chapter. John joined the Discalced Reform and lived at the tiny priory at Duruelo. When Teresa became Prioress of the Incarnation, she called him there as Chaplain and Confessor, a role which he held from 1572 to 1577. He must have been a tremendous comfort and a good companion to Teresa during this time, for it was an awkward and tense period of her life. She had left the Incarnation because its ideals were not hers; she was appointed Prioress because the Provincial considered that the Incarnation badly needed to be raised from the spiritual corruption into which it had fallen, not because she wished to undertake this task. The nuns there, many of whom had no wish to be reformed, feared the severity of her rule and received her with open revolt. Teresa responded with a beautiful symbolic act: she put a statue of Our Lady in the Prioress's stall, the keys of the convent in her hands, and sat herself at her feet. (To this day, the statue of Our Lady still occupies the chair originally intended for the Prioress, in memory of this event.) Teresa respected the right of others to choose a different path from her own, and knew that she would have to govern nuns of the Mitigated Observance differently from her own Discalced. Under her the nuns of the Incarnation became more disciplined and devout and renounced many of their excesses. While Teresa was there she continued to observe her own Discalced Rule.

Fountain with belltower of the Incarnation in the background. Teresa is fond of the image of a fountain of living water in which the soul is planted like a tree of life. "We must all journey to this fountain, my daughters. . . . . though we may not all do so in the same way." (WP, CW (II) 91).

© *Keith W. Ray*

But it will be understood how much it must have meant to Teresa to have John of the Cross there. He was probably the only person at the Incarnation with whom she could really communicate on the deeply spiritual and mystical matters which were her lifeblood, and after the peace and serenity of her own small convents she found it turmoil at the Incarnation. In 1574, after travelling to various of her houses and founding another at Segovia, she returned as Prioress not of the Incarnation, but of her beloved St Joseph's, but spent only brief periods there, travelling almost constantly.

Gracián, as we have seen, was another younger man whom Teresa admired greatly. They met in 1575, although he had already joined the Reform at Pastrana two years earlier. Later, when Teresa succeeded in gaining the autonomy of the Discalced from the Calced Carmelites, he was made Provincial of the Discalced. Gracián was a great support to Teresa in her later years and she always had the greatest of respect for him. 'With him she was able to take an easy tone and give rein to her vivacity, without feeling obliged to keep back some amusing retort or spontaneous expression of affection.'[44] He was very learned, eloquent, charming and kind, as well as being a man with whom Teresa felt a strong rapport spiritually. Unfortunately her absolute trust in him blinded her to his faults; but that is a story that would lead us too far from our theme. Teresa needed his help in the years that followed their meeting, for this was a time of great conflict. The friars and nuns of the Reform began to suffer serious persecution from the Calced Carmelites. Gracián had been made Visitor to the Calced in Andalusia and also began more foundations in that province. The Calced Community protested violently. 'In May 1575, a General Chapter of the Carmelite Order, held in Piacenza, decreed the suppression of the Reformed houses founded in Andalusia on the ground that the General's licence had been valid only for Castile. In this measure Teresa saw the germ of a strife which, as she believed, could not be ended save by the partition of the Order.'[45] His Catholic Majesty Philip II had previously given Teresa a special patent for her most recent foundation but one, at Caravaca. Teresa now wrote to King Philip asking him that the Discalced should be made into a separate Province, with Gracián as Provincial – the first step towards becoming a separate Order with their own General, which was accomplished after Teresa's death. Autonomy from the Calced was not, in the end, fully achieved until 1580; in the meantime Teresa was ordered by the General to leave

Andalusia for Castile, where she was virtually imprisoned at Toledo. Gracián was excommunicated for trying to make foundations in Andalusia and for attempts at separatism from the Calced.

Early in 1576 the conflict worsened. The Reform was further suppressed and condemned. John of the Cross was kidnapped from the Incarnation by the Calced friars and imprisoned under tortuous conditions at Medina del Campo. (The following year he was kidnapped again and imprisoned at Toledo; it is thought that parts of his beautiful mystical poem 'The Spiritual Canticle' were written in the dreadful conditions of this prison.) He contrived first to tear up Teresa's letters to him so that she might not be incriminated; the most important ones he is said to have swallowed! The Inquisition searched St Joseph's and the Convent of the Incarnation. Teresa was suspected of being an *alumbrada*. Gracián was accused of sexual misdemeanours with all the nuns and in particular with Teresa. The publicity caused a scandal. The Discalced were forbidden to take in any further novices or found any more houses. These events are investigated in more detail in Chapter 4. Teresa's letters from this period make use of a secret code, with members of the Mitigated Rule being referred to, for example, as 'cats' or 'owls' (because, metaphorically, they lived in darkness) while those of the Reform are 'butterflies' (an image of which Teresa was apparently fond, for she uses it in the *Interior Castle*), 'doves' or 'eagles'. The Inquisitors, with grand irony, she calls 'the Angels', while Jesus' pseudonym is 'Joseph'.

Teresa fought this persecution for four years, using her influence both with the King and with the Pope. Eventually Philip II intervened and succeeded in ending her troubles. The Reform was made a separate Province with Gracián as Provincial. But this was not before many troublesome vicissitudes had been conquered, the details of which it is not possible to recount here. It was during these years of persecution that Teresa wrote (at Gracián's request) her masterpiece of the mystical life, the *Interior Castle*. She herself considered it her best book; it will be discussed in Chapter 3.

Teresa left Avila for what was to be her last journey in January 1582. She had to put up with severe persecution on most of her later journeys, for the scandals from which she had recently suffered never died down in her own lifetime. She was headed for Burgos, staying at various of her foundations along the way. It was an exhausting journey, for she was old and ill and to travel north at that time of the year meant severe travelling conditions. The roads were frequently flooded and the carriages had to be dragged out of bogs. It is of this journey that the story is told that, when her mule-cart had got stuck in the torrent of the flood, and Teresa was feeling that this was the last straw, she heard one of the divine voices that by now had been part of her experience for years. But this time the message was less consoling than usual: 'Do you not know, Teresa, that this is how I treat My friends?' To which Teresa, who always had a gift for repartee, replied, 'Well, if that's so, then it's not surprising that You don't have many of them.' The story may be apocryphal, but even if this is so, for those who recounted it, it illustrated both Teresa's sense of humour, and her belief that suffering is something to be valued, because it shows us that God is working in us; suffering is to be embraced, because to experience suffering is a way for the mystic to imitate Christ.

On arrival at Burgos Teresa was too sick to do any more than remain lying down and speak to those who came to see her. Then there were problems over the foundation at Burgos which was the purpose of the journey. But eventually, after a delay of several months, the convent was completed. On 26 July Teresa left Burgos for Avila, but never reached her home town. On the way she stayed at her convents at Palencia, Valladolid (where her illness detained her for nearly a month) and Medina del Campo. She was now not so far from Avila; but then she received an order to go to Alba de Tormes in order to visit the Duchess of Alba, whose daughter-in-law was expecting a baby and who had asked that *la santa Madre* – 'the holy Mother', as some now called her – might be present at the birth and bless the child. 'Unfit though she was for further travelling, and longing to reach her desired haven, Teresa silently obeyed.'[46] They reached Alba de Tormes on 20 September. The child had already been born and Teresa had been feeling progressively worse. We are told that some of the nuns at Alba de Tormes had received supernatural signs that Teresa was to die there (no doubt an example of the hagiographical embroidering which attaches itself to the biography of every great religious leader; there are other examples of this in popular accounts of Teresa's life).

Over the next few days Teresa continued to work at matters that needed to be seen to, but was soon confined to bed. Her last Mass two days before her death brought the exclamation: 'My Lord, it is time to set out; may the journey be a propitious one and may Thy will be done.'[47] It was an otherworldly journey for which she was preparing now. When asked if she wanted her body to be taken to Avila, her sense of humour had still not left her: 'Won't they give me the charity of a little earth here?'[48] When the nuns saw that she was dying they begged her to say something to them which should be to their profit: she simply entreated them to keep to their Rules and Constitutions. After that she said little more, except to repeat again and again a verse from the Psalms: 'A sacrifice acceptable to God is a broken spirit: a contrite and humbled heart, O God, Thou wilt not despise.'[49] What did she mean by choosing to refer to herself as a broken spirit? Much would be written in idealised hagiographical commentary on her passing; the more realistic facts of the matter are that she died in great pain, worn out by persecution and by the internal strife that had sadly begun to poison her own Reform. It has been suggested too that her deathbed exclamation, 'After everything, Lord, I die a daughter of the Church,' can be read as a sigh of relief after her troubles with the Inquisition.

She died on 4 October. Her face was apparently calm and radiant and we are told that her body gave forth a wonderful fragrance (the so-called 'Odour of Sanctity' which is said to emanate from the bodies of saints). Later, many testimonies were received (from doctors as well as members of Teresa's Reform) to the effect that her body was incorruptible. This was seen to be the case, if we are to believe these accounts, when Teresa's body was moved to Avila and on other occasions when the coffin was opened. The incorruptibility of the body was regarded as a proof of sanctity. It is repugnant to us today to relate that her body had already fallen prey to the relic-hunting of her own associates only nine months after the interment; Gracián himself severed Teresa's left hand which was deposited in a sealed casket at Avila, and carried about on his person Teresa's little finger. Eventually the body was entirely dismembered, with parts scattered all over Spain and even in Rome and elsewhere. Distasteful as this is to us, we have to remember that in the Spain of Teresa's time there was an unshakeable belief that the relics of a saint were a source of healing and also that they gave protection to the church in which they were housed.

The reputation for sanctity which Teresa attracted in her lifetime grew rapidly after her death, aided by the rather hagiographical testimonies of members of the Discalced Carmelites. Reports were received of instances of healing brought about through contact with

Teresa's relics, and of other miracles which, it was believed, came about through her intervention. In 1614, Teresa was beatified (that is, she became officially known as Blessed Teresa of Jesus). In 1622, she was canonised (becoming St Teresa). She was even nominated as Patron Saint of Spain – almost depriving St James (Iago) of this honour. Much more recently, in 1970 Pope Paul VI pronounced her a Doctor of the Church. She thus became the first woman to be granted this title, having been popularly known during her own lifetime as the 'Holy Mother' and the 'Mother Foundress' and soon after as the mystical doctor or doctor of mysticism, *doctora mística*.

A few aspects of Teresa's character that have not already been touched on above may be quickly outlined, for it is no doubt true that her personality is a major reason for the breadth of her appeal. Her determination, strength and resolve are obvious; no doubt, as some of those who knew her observed, these qualities could sometimes give way to a headstrong stubbornness. She was an intelligent and shrewd woman who showed good business sense in the managing of her convents, and she was eminently practical, efficient, energetic and hard-working. With her strong mental and nervous energy and her tendency to pay attention to every small detail (even to the point of being fussy or fastidious) it is likely that she would have been a 'worrier' and would have suffered from nervous tension (which in turn might have affected her health). It has often been observed that she perfectly fuses realism and idealism in her character: a blend of the otherworldly and the down-to-earth which is perhaps not as unusual as it at first seems, for it has been said that the greatest mystics are essentially practical, their inspirations by no means nebulous.

She hated being criticised, and craved approval as much as she craved affection. At the same time she was highly self-critical:

> Whenever I think of myself I feel like a bird with a broken wing and I can say nothing of any value. . . . Beseech His Majesty, my daughters, always to live within me, for otherwise what security can there be in a life as misspent as mine? And do not let it depress you to realize that I am like that. . . . the reason it affects you in that way is that you would like to think I had been very holy.[50]

There are many strands of relevance bound up together in these constant statements that Teresa makes of her own sin, wickedness and unworthiness. Certainly, she had perfected the virtue of humility. Certainly, too, she had genuine feelings of guilt and repentance over what she saw as her 'mis-spent youth'. But a further point concerns the advisability of making these kinds of statements under the watchful eye of the Inquisition.

> Teresa's self-reproach is excessive. . . . This is something that goes beyond the humility of the saints. . . . Teresa, the saint, had this humility – but there is much, besides, which is part of Teresa the girl and the woman and is independent of her sanctity. Her self-reproach must be seen against the background of her country, her times and her upbringing. . . . To use self-depreciatory language was the surest defence against carping clerics – especially the Inquisitors, who were always waiting to swoop on anyone guilty of what they were pleased to regard as a lack of humility, particularly a woman who, in any case, was by divine dispensation (so they thought) a witless and unstable creature.[51]

To this must be added a final factor: that when we are travelling on the 'Way of Perfection', nothing but perfection will do. Our smallest faults continually torment us like a burning fire. Here we touch upon one of the greatest paradoxes of the mystical life – that the mystic must strive for perfection and yet that perfection seems ever unattainable in this life. By virtue of the very fact that 'we are not angels and we have bodies' as Teresa puts it[52] – by virtue of the fact that we are incarnated human beings – we can never be fully perfect. Some monistic mystical traditions (for example, the Advaita Vedānta system of India) differ on this point, but all theistic systems agree. (The issue of the contrasts between monistic and theistic forms of mysticism will be taken up in the next chapter.)

Yet Teresa's honest and critical self-analysis and her account of her gradual growth to spiritual maturity are, as many writers have observed, heartening to the ordinary reader. One of the most marvellous things about Teresa's writings is that they reveal her to us much as she was, with her imperfections as well as her virtues. She tells us in great detail about her attempts at self-improvement and about the earlier stages of the mystical path, and her painfully honest self-criticism makes us remember that sanctity is grounded in humanity and that the mystical path can be followed by us all. 'Everything she writes is based upon her own experience, and so penetrating is her insight and so diaphanous her language that her

Statue of Teresa, in front of the belltower of the Incarnation. We can imagine her striding forth like this to found her convents and priories.
© Keith W. Ray

readers can see themselves mirrored in her and interpret her experiences in terms of their own.'[53] Furthermore, Teresa's writing is so direct, simple, unpretentious and straightforward that she rarely fails to 'hit a point home'.

It is this same natural simplicity that caused one of Teresa's nuns to remark that there was something fundamental about her which made even those who spoke ill of her realise that she was a saint without making any claim to be. 'Something fundamental: affections deeply rooted, a life firmly centred, a heart surely fixed' reflected one great Teresian scholar.[54]

Sadly, she was a lonely woman, a fate that perhaps befalls anyone who has such singular vision: 'I find such loneliness in spiritual matters. . . . Indeed, I feel lonely everywhere.'[55] The desire for individual communion with the Divine and the degree of inner solitude that this implies can often be tinged by a feeling of loneliness with regard to one's fellow women and men, and certainly with a sense of lack of deep spiritual communication with any but a few.

Other aspects of Teresa's character will unfold as we proceed with our investigations in the following chapters. Teresa, of course, would have disliked the thought that her personality would shine through her words, for she wished not to draw attention to herself, but to act and write only for the glory of her God. Even her books were written under command from her superiors rather than out of any desire for self-aggrandisement. It is, indeed, a delicate matter to say much of the personality of one who lived so close to the Divine: her ability to stand firm through such terrible trials, her capacity to bear such intense suffering and still radiate peace and joy, her depth of illumination in spiritual matters – were these of her, or of the divine power that animated her? 'I see clearly,' she wrote, 'that all I gain comes to me through these revelations and raptures: it has nothing to do with me; I am no more than a *tabula rasa*.'[56] 'If Our Lord had not bestowed on me the favours He has, I should not, I think, have had the courage to perform the works I have, nor strength to endure the trials and oppositions and criticisms that I have.'[57] This sense of being worked on by a power greater than herself is something of which we are aware throughout Teresa's account of her life.

CHAPTER 2

Teresa as Mystic and as Mystical Teacher

As much as I desire to speak clearly about these matters
of prayer, they will be really obscure for anyone who has
not had experience. . . . These things I'll say from what
the Lord has taught me through experience and through
discussions with very learned men and persons who have
lived the spiritual life for many years.[1]

It is the purpose of this chapter to outline Teresa's accounts of her
own mystical experiences and the spiritual teachings which are so
intimately related to these experiences and to her reflection on them.
We shall begin by sketching the various 'stages' of the mystical path
according to Teresa, the growth of the soul towards experiential
knowledge of the Deity, as revealed to Teresa in her own experience.
We shall then examine Teresa's accounts of her visions and locutions, raptures and ecstasies, and her evaluation of these types of
phenomena. Our approach is phenomenological rather than theological: we will be looking primarily at what Teresa says about her
own experiences, letting them 'speak for themselves' rather than
bringing to them preconceived frameworks of doctrinal interpreta-

tion, assumptions about the truth or falsity of particular beliefs or the divine or delusory nature of certain experiences. In this way we hope to enter into the inner dynamic of Teresa's accounts of her experiences, to appreciate empathically or intuitively what Teresa's experiences meant *for her*, rather than for later theological commentators. It is, furthermore, my firm belief that in order best to understand mystical experiences we must not divorce intellectual study from our own intuitive and experiential understanding. The scholar of mysticism should herself or himself have at least some practical knowledge of mystical experience at first hand.

Such an interweaving of intellectual and experiential perspectives is beginning to gain ground in scholarly studies of religion, while in the area of women's studies (touched on in Chapter 5) it is an established methodological principle. It challenges previous scholarly assumptions that the researcher who adopts a detached, unconcerned stance with regard to his or her subject matter, removing himself or herself from personal involvement, can attain an 'objectivity' which is inaccessible to the researcher who has personal commitment to or involvement in the object of study. Such assumptions are fast fading as we come to realise that there is no single 'objective', totally value-free standard by which we may understand reality. All structures of thought and modes of interpretation necessarily rest upon certain assumptions, and traditional methods of Western rational-empirical analysis are no more 'objective' than other methods. In the area of studies of mysticism, then, personal experience is a prerequisite for understanding some aspects of mystical description, while it does not imply that our analysis of mysticism will be any more 'subjective' or 'biased' than that of one who tries to maintain a 'detached' attitude, provided adequate methodological guidelines are employed.[2] This book, then, is in some ways a result of my own interweaving of perspectives: I have made a point, for example, of meditating on the *Interior Castle* as well as looking at it in a more traditional academic manner.

Towards the end of this chapter we move on to look at the fact that, unlike many mystics, Teresa is a convinced theist: that is, she is a firm believer in the supreme value of meditation on a personal deity (in her case, Jesus Christ), in the reality of God with form, God portrayed under a specific image, even in the very highest stages of mystical experience. In this, Teresa breaks with one of the most important intellectual strands composing Christian mysticism in her day, the *Via Negativa*, the tradition descending from Pseudo-Dionysus (Dionysus the Areopagite) which emphasises formless awareness and 'unknowing', as will be explained later. The contrast that is brought out here between theistic and monistic forms of mysticism is explored and discussed in the broader context of comparative studies of mysticism.

We begin, then, with Teresa's scheme of mystical progress, which is in fact not entirely self-consistent. In the two major writings dealing with this theme (the *Life* and the *Interior Castle*) she uses different classificatory schemes and different ways of subdividing the various types of experience. This has caused some consternation among Teresian scholars, many of whom have tried to correlate the two schemes. But it must be remembered that fifteen years elapsed between the writing of the *Life* and the *Interior Castle* – fifteen years which were, for Teresa, a time of great spiritual development, and during which time she refined her thoughts on the matter of the landmarks along the road to God. In the *Interior Castle* she herself admits: 'It may be that in writing of these interior things I am contradicting what I have myself said elsewhere. This is not surprising, for almost fifteen years have passed since then, and perhaps the Lord has now given me a clearer realization of these matters than I had at first.'[3] Furthermore, it is in the final analysis impossible to confine the richness of a lifetime's mystical experiences within the limitations of any set formula. In the end, then, it matters little into how many 'stages' we divide the mystical Way: the mystics do not intend to reify such formulae. Any dividing lines will be fluid, and any scheme of use only in that it helps us to understand the mystical life (whether from without or from within). We shall therefore content ourselves with discussing the spiritual experiences described by Teresa according to the fluid outlines of a generally accepted plan.

Contemplative prayer is the pivot of the spiritual life, though naturally the full expression of spirituality must also comprise love for others, dedicated work in the service of God, selflessness, detachment from material things, perfection of the virtues. It is prayer, however, that is the door leading into the sevenfold castle which is Teresa's most vivid symbol of the soul: not 'vocal prayer' (recitation, out loud, of set liturgical formulae) – though Teresa does not advise us to leave this behind altogether – but unspoken 'mental prayer' in which there is a communion and loving dialogue with God within the innermost recesses of the soul. (This type of prayer, as we shall see later, was automatically suspect so far as the Inquisition was concerned.) The first stage or degree of prayer is 'Meditation', a word which has a different meaning in the context of sixteenth-century Christian spirituality from that which it has acquired for many of us today. For Teresa, meditation is made up of 'reflection' or reasoning upon a particular subject – most often, some episode in the life of Jesus – and 'affection' or opening our heart to the divine being after having thought about the truths encapsulated in our chosen subject. This affective element, this love of and opening of one's heart to the divine, takes precedence over reasoning, both in the context of Meditation and, it might be said, in Teresa's outlook on the mystical life in general.

Meditation 'shades over' (there is no hard and fast dividing line) into Recollection (*recogimiento*), whereby '. . . the soul collects together all the faculties and enters within itself to be with its God.'[4] Teresa holds on the basis of her own experience that God, while present in all things, is to be found in particular within the soul. In Recollection, we detach ourselves from outward stimuli and sense-perception, turning away from exterior things, stilling the surface mind so that it is calm and tranquil, and fixing all our 'faculties' (explained below), every ounce of our attention and dedication, on one point – the centre of the soul where the Deity dwells. The activities of the 'faculties', or powers of the soul, are withdrawn into the inner self to concentrate upon God (but they are not at this stage 'suspended': the 'suspension of faculties' is a type of transcendence of normal consciousness of which Teresa speaks, which we shall examine shortly). According to the Scholastic philosophy then current, the human soul was regarded as divisible into two parts: the higher part or spirit was composed of the three 'higher faculties' of memory, understanding and will; and the lower part, the 'animal soul' or seat of sensory perception, consisted of the five 'exterior senses (sight, hearing, touch, taste and smell) and the 'interior senses', namely the imagination and the fancy. These last two are closely linked in their operation, but the imagination for Teresa is literally 'the power of imaging', the ability to create inner pictures in the mind's eye from data given us by sense-perception. The imagination thus plays an important role in the visualisations that are part of Teresa's meditative methods. The use of the term does *not* imply (as it does to many modern readers) that the images are illusory, 'figments of the imagination' as some would say today: they are quite 'real' on their own level, though this is not the level of physical reality. The term 'fancy', on the other hand, is used to denote these meanderings of the mind which do not possess the same kind of power or importance for the spiritual life.

Aspects of this 'faculty psychology' may seem artificial and stilted to us today, but it is necessary to bear in mind when reading Teresa's works that she writes from within the framework of reference presupposed by this view of the human person, and it is in the context of these philosophical presuppositions that her references to understanding, will, imagination and so on must be understood. This is not to imply, though, that Teresa was learned in Scholastic theology: like all Spanish women of her time she was denied all possibility of formal intellectual training, and so her use of the Scholastic terms is not always precise.

In Recollection, then, to continue with our central theme, the senses are withdrawn from exterior things so that the inner, spiritual sight of the soul may become clear. We begin to develop a relationship with the Deity within. 'Remember how important it is for you to have understood this truth – that the Lord is within us and that we should be there with Him. . . . Those who are able to shut themselves up in this way within this little Heaven of the soul, wherein dwells the Maker of Heaven and earth, and who have formed the habit of looking at nothing and staying in no place which will distract these outward senses, may be sure that they are walking on an excellent road, and will come without fail to drink of the water of the fountain. . . .',[5] writes Teresa (employing one of her favourite similes, that of God as a fountain of living water). She advises that we can cultivate Recollection by trying to remain aware of the presence of God within ourselves; by resigning our self-will and giving ourselves wholly to him; and by retiring within ourselves to interior reflection even during our everyday tasks and occupations. Recollection will probably require much effort and inner toil at first, and our success in it depends upon the degree of control that we can exercise over the body and senses.

In traditional Catholic terminology, what is known as the Way of Purgation often takes place at around this time, its effects often diminishing as we become gradually more proficient at Recollection. We have mentioned the stage known as Purgation in our account of Teresa's life: it is a time of conflict between our attach-

Part of the patio at the Incarnation. Behind these windows is the parlour where Teresa used to talk to John of the Cross on spiritual matters. On one occasion it is said that they were caught up to such heights of ecstasy that they were observed actually to levitate!

ment to the world of the senses and passions and material things, and our aspirations towards the realm of the divine, the spiritual life which is slowly opening out. The senses and imagination must be purified, mastered, and trained to follow the will of the spirit. But although Teresa speaks of such feelings and developments within herself, she does not use the traditional Catholic terminology to describe them. Indeed in many ways, as we shall see, she forges her own path and breaks with traditional terminologies and classifications.

When we have become proficient in Recollection, we enter a state which Teresa calls the Prayer of Quiet (*Oración de Quietud*). She does not always clearly differentiate between Recollection and Quiet, as, again, the dividing line between the two is not rigid, and perhaps they should not be seen as separate phases of the spiritual life so much as a method and its resultant effect. In the Prayer of Quiet, we experience an interior peace, joy and delight, which cannot be understood rationally. There is a receptivity, stillness and inner silence in the depths of the soul and a new knowledge of God which is not a rational understanding but a conviction springing from the experience itself. The will, detached from its own selfish ends, cleaves in intention to God's will – Teresa says that it is 'united' with God's will, but her rather untechnical use of terms should not be taken to imply the more advanced mystical state commonly referred to as union with the divine. As for the other 'higher faculties' (memory and understanding) they sometimes fall into line with the activity of the will, but at other times are quite distracted, so that despite our sense of a certain consciousness of God, the mind may flutter around aimlessly, or the imagination may wander off on all manner of subjects, threatening to disturb the quiet that the will is experiencing.[6] Teresa insists that we cannot induce the Prayer of Quiet by our own efforts: like all the forms of prayer of which she speaks from this point on, it is a type of what she calls 'supernatural' prayer, that is, it is given by the grace of God alone. 'We can no more control this prayer than we can make the day break, or stop night from falling'[7] – though we can, of course, prepare ourselves to receive it by cultivating humility and virtue and practising meditation. Teresa describes the Prayer of Quiet as follows:

> Both the inward and the outward man seem to receive comfort, just as if into the marrow of the bones had been poured the sweetest of

ointments, resembling a fragrant perfume, or as if we had suddenly
entered a room where there was a perfume coming not from one
place, but from many, so that we cannot tell what or where the
perfume is – we only know that it pervades our whole being. Just so
does it seem to be with this sweet love of our God. It enters the soul
with great sweetness, and brings it such joy and satisfaction that it
cannot understand how or in what way this blessing is entering it. So
anxious is it not to lose this love that it would fain stay still without
moving and neither speak nor even look anywhere lest it should
vanish. . . . Great truths are communicated to it. . . . When
experiencing this joy, it is so deeply inebriated and absorbed that it
seems to be beside itself and in a kind of Divine intoxication.[8]

The next 'stage' of experience of which Teresa speaks is the Prayer
of Union (*Oración de Unión*). In the terminology of most mystical
writers, 'union' denotes the final, ultimate achievement of oneness
with God, but it is important to understand that Teresa does *not* use
the term in this sense: when speaking of the final mystical goal she
talks instead of the Spiritual Marriage. The type of 'union' of which
Teresa speaks now is not so exalted an experience, but it is, nevertheless, a foretaste of the Spiritual Marriage (in one place, Teresa
describes it as being like the Betrothal which precedes the Marriage),
or even a fleeting glimpse of it, a high state of contemplative prayer
in which the mystic enjoys a deep and intimate experience of God's
presence. This state approximates to that known as 'Illumination' in
traditional Catholic mystical theology, but 'Illumination', like the
'Purgative Way', is a term which Teresa does not actually use herself. The soul begins to experience a transformation within itself;
now not only the will, but also the other faculties, are 'asleep to the
world', lifted above everything earthly, and absorbed in the divine.
This is an overpowering experience which is even less explicable by
the rational mind than the states we have previously described. The
soul is beginning to go through the spiritual 'death and rebirth' of
which so many mystics speak. It is looking directly at divine reality
but seems incapable of expressing what it sees, analysing what is
happening to it, or understanding the experience discursively.
(These statements of ineffability need not be taken absolutely at face
value, for, of course, Teresa provides us with a wealth of analysis
and description of her experiences; nevertheless, she feels like all
mystics that the essential core of the experience, or its most intimate
aspects, cannot be fully expressed in words.) The Prayer of Union is of

brief duration (it is never experienced for more than half an hour at any one time, Teresa says) but once known it is never forgotten, nor its reality doubted.

It is from this stage onwards that one may experience 'suspension of the faculties' (*suspensión de las potencias*) or 'sleep of the faculties' (*sueño de las potencias*). What this amounts to is that the mystic has so completely surrendered herself or himself to the Deity that a suspension of normal consciousness results, and the use of the faculties is momentarily lost. (So, for example, 'If the soul has been meditating upon any subject, this vanishes from its memory as if it had never thought of it. If it has been reading, it is unable to concentrate upon what it was reading.'[9]) The soul is so absorbed in God during the actual experience (which is always brief) that 'it can neither see nor hear nor understand'.[10] But on return to everyday consciousness, we know beyond doubt, says Teresa, that we have been with God – temporarily united to him – and the experience brings great spiritual benefits.

> This state is a sleep of the faculties, which are neither wholly lost nor yet can understand how they work. . . . This seems to me to be nothing less than an all but complete death to everything in the world and a fruition of God. . . . This state is a glorious folly, a heavenly madness, in which true wisdom is acquired. . . . The faculties retain only the power of occupying themselves wholly with God. . . . Here we are all asleep, and fast asleep, to the things of the world, and to ourselves (in fact, for the short time that the condition lasts, the soul is without consciousness and has no power to think) . . . the soul appears to have withdrawn so far from the body that I do not know if it has still life enough to be able to breathe. . . . even if any consciousness remains to it, neither hands nor feet can move. . . . The faculties rejoice without knowing how they rejoice; the soul is enkindled in love without understanding how it loves.[11]

Certain aspects of Teresa's description of this state are reminiscent of her descriptions of her ecstasies and raptures (which will be discussed shortly) and in fact on one isolated occasion Teresa declares that raptures and suspension of the faculties are the same thing, though she contradicts this elsewhere. It is certain, however, that they can often occur simultaneously. Even allowing for mystical paradox and the inadequacy of rational language, Teresa describes the suspension of faculties in the most bewilderingly contradictory

of terms; and it is true too that there are certain philosophical problems attendant upon the type of experience she describes. Teresa
herself muses over some of these: how can the soul be said to see or
understand *anything* if its inner sight and understanding are suspended? And if the memory is suspended, how can we later recall
the experience to mind?[12] Teresa confesses that she cannot understand this, and sees it simply as an indication of God's mystery and
greatness. The problems that philosophers raise about mystical
experiences are very often raised by the mystics themselves, who
make no secret of their difficulties in remembering the more sublime
of their experiences, bringing them through to everyday consciousness, and expressing them in words. But Teresa insists that after our
return to rational understanding from such an experience, we have a
sure feeling that we have been with God. Some of these experiences
can be described after the event, some cannot, she says; but even
those that cannot be described are so clearly imprinted in the depths
of the soul that they are never forgotten, and they work great benefits, increasing our virtue, selflessness and detachment. The only
way in which we can understand these experiences of the 'suspension of faculties', it seems to me, is by assuming that the *surface-
consciousness only* of the mystic is inhibited; normal consciousness
may cease, so that specific mental contents, images and ideas are
eliminated, but this is not an unconscious state, rather a super-
conscious one. Although Teresa says that the soul is 'without
consciousness', it is clearly not without *all forms of* consciousness,
for it is aware of enjoying delight and love and of being close to God.
Perhaps we can understand this state and its aftermath by saying
that a seed is planted, as it were, in the deeper consciousness during
the experience and, although we cannot be conscious of it at the
time, our surface-consciousness will become aware of it later on;
subsequently this seed will blossom forth in our outward life and
everyday actions.

Teresa next speaks of a type of experience which may follow on
from the Prayer of Union or may occur intermittently with it; an
experience characterised in particular by the 'Pain of God' or the
'Wound of Love'. Here there is an acute awareness of our separation
from the Deity, and of our sins, shortcomings, and failings, combined with an ever greater love and yearning for him, producing
desolation, pain, loneliness and anguish as the mystic realises that
no earthly thing or person can ever fulfil this love. It is the pain of the

finite that would be infinite, the bittersweet pain of insatiable love. Teresa speaks of a grief that reaches to the depths of our being and seems to tear the soul to pieces and 'grind it to powder'.[13] Those who are familiar with the writings of St John of the Cross will recognise parallels with his 'Night of the Spirit'. Like St John's 'Dark Night', this is a time of purification through suffering and eventually leads to the 'inner death' that the mystic must undergo in order to live more fully in God; the death of the 'lower self' or a death to all our selfish, hedonistic attitudes and attachments and limited, contingent ways of relating to the world; a death which is simultaneously a rebirth into a new life of free and creative love for all things. Teresa speaks of this experience in terms of a burning inner fire which refines and purifies the self – a very widespread symbol in theistic mysticism – and says that the soul, through its suffering, is refined like gold in the crucible. She also speaks of the heart being pierced by a fiery arrow or spear, an experience described in one of her most celebrated visions:

> It pleased the Lord that I should sometimes see the following vision. I would see beside me, on my left hand, an angel . . . not tall, but short, and very beautiful, his face so aflame that he appeared to be one of the highest types of angel who seem to be all afire. They must be those who are called cherubim. . . . In his hands I saw a long golden spear and at the end of the iron tip I seemed to see a point of fire. With this he seemed to pierce my heart several times so that it penetrated to my entrails. When he drew it out, I thought he was drawing them out with it and he left me completely afire with a great love for God.[14]

Because of this vision, Teresa is often depicted in ecstasy with an angel piercing her heart with an arrow or spear, as for example in Bernini's sculpture *Ecstasy of St Teresa* (see pl. 7). Teresa says that she had this vision on several occasions. Catholic dogma, however, holds that the angel came only once, and that his spear did not plunge 'several times' into Teresa's body, but pierced her heart with a single thrust. The episode, held to be a miracle, has become known as the Transverberation of the Heart, and the heart itself is now in a reliquary in Alba de Tormes, with the hole purportedly made by the spear displayed. The vision has even led to the establishment of The Feast of the Transfixion in the Catholic calendar, celebrated on 27 August, for it occurred (for the first time, if we accept Teresa's testimony that it actually took place on several occasions) on or near 27 August 1559.

Male commentators on this vision almost invariably assume that there is something highly erotic about it, an attitude, apparently based on a simplistic identification of the burning spear as a phallic symbol, which I find unconvincing.[15] So often we are told that certain experiences of the mystics, particularly those that are expressed in romantic or sexual imagery, are simply a substitute for or a sublimation of unfulfilled sexuality; we might be forgiven for wondering whether it is the commentator, not the mystic, who has sexual problems! Of those women with an interest in mysticism to whom I have spoken, I have not yet found one who sees Teresa's vision as self-evidently erotic. Nevertheless, it cannot, I think, be denied that certain aspects of Teresa's imagery and forms of religious expression, indeed of her very personality, are highly sensual: 'sensual' here being meant as possibly including the erotic in some respects but by no means being confined to it. I do not see that there is any good reason to try to disguise these sensual aspects of Teresa's experiences: nor do I see that they constitute evidence for denigrating her experiences as those of a frustrated or 'hysterical' celibate. They simply show that Teresa was a whole woman, a fully fledged personality with a complex sexuality. While certain similarities (of paradoxical emotional expression, for example) can be observed between human sexuality and the love of the mystic for the divine, this by no means implies that mystical experience can be wholly explained in terms of sexuality.

Teresa says of this experience that '. . . the soul has been wounded with love for the spouse'; it is

. . . conscious of having been most delectably wounded . . . it is certain that this is a precious experience and it would be glad if it were never to be healed of that wound. It complains to its Spouse with words of love, and even cries out aloud, being unable to help itself, for it realizes that He is present but will not manifest Himself in such a way as to allow it to enjoy Him, and this is a great grief, though a sweet and delectable one.[16]

Note here the ambivalent emotive tone of both agony and ecstasy, both suffering and joy. Paradoxically, there is a joy in suffering itself for mystics like Teresa: firstly because suffering allows us to 'imitate Christ', modelling ourselves on his exemplary life; secondly because

Bernini's 'Ecstasy of St. Teresa' (Cornaro Chapel, Santa Maria della Vittoria, Rome) depicts Teresa's celebrated vision of the angel with the fiery spear (see p. 45).

suffering is something we have to 'work through': if we can learn to accept suffering, and to empty ourselves of worldly attachments, we will find that our suffering is transmuted to joy and love, and that we become transformed, filled with the divine life. '. . . the soul sees opening before it the gates of another world – a world of new horizons of divine love in which it advances ever onward until it loses itself completely in a flame of love and pain.'[17] The arrow of fire '. . . makes a deep wound, not, I think, in any region where physical pain can be felt, but in the soul's most intimate depths. It passes as quickly as a flash of lightning and leaves everything in our nature that is earthly reduced to powder.'[18]

Of this phase of the spiritual life Teresa says that the mystic '. . . thinks of herself as of a person suspended aloft, unable either to come down and rest anywhere on earth or to ascend to Heaven.'[19] We are stuck between two worlds: that of the divine, and that of the mundane; the former seems out of reach, and the latter cannot satisfy. In the *Interior Castle* Teresa elaborates on this experience of living between two worlds, using the analogy of a silkworm turning into a butterfly to depict the spiritual 'death' and the emergence of the transformed soul. But the butterfly, once it has emerged from its cocoon, '. . . knows not where to settle and make its abode . . . everything it sees on earth leaves it dissatisfied.'[20] No consolation can be obtained, either, from prayer or the interior life of the soul in God, for the burning inner fire continually torments us for our faults and failings and shortcomings, so that we have to live all the time with a painfully acute awareness of our wretched helplessness and unworthiness. We then become conscious of a strange solitude; other people, and all earthly things, seem like mere shadows. Teresa says that this state involves peril of physical death, and it is certain at the very least that the intensity of the spiritual death to the limited self undergone by the mystic can be such as to make one *feel* that one is near physical death. According to Teresa, the soul at this time also has longings for actual death, because it is so anxious to attain complete union with God, and yet it knows that this can never be achieved in this world. This point leads us naturally to Teresa's view of the ultimate mystical goal that can be obtained in this life, which is the next level of experience of which she speaks.

Teresa holds, in fact, that we cannot *fully* know God in this life; in this she is typical of the majority of Christian mystics, for whom the 'Beatific Vision' of full union with God occurs only after death.

She constantly contrasts the glory of God with our own sin and wretchedness. It is not possible, she says, to be in a continual state of absorption in God in this life: '. . . though angelic spirits, freed from everything corporeal, may remain permanently enkindled in love, this is not possible for those of us who live in this mortal body.'[21] Nevertheless, the Spiritual Marriage (*matrimonio espiritual*), the marriage of the soul and the divine lover, comes very close to the Beatific Vision in its wonder and sublimity and in the depths of transformation worked upon the soul. Teresa does not describe it directly in as much detail as she lavishes on other stages of her experience, no doubt precisely because it is, she says, quite ineffable: words could never do it justice. The mystic has now 'died' to his or her limited self-consciousness and lives in and through the Divine. Whereas in the previous stages of mystical experience, periods of separation from God still occur, in the Spiritual Marriage the mystic is continually united with God in the deepest centre of the soul. She or he experiences almost continual inner tranquillity, being completely at one with the divine will, longing only to make this will manifest in her or his life. This does not, of course, mean that we no longer experience any difficulties in life; there may well be many outward trials, and the faculties and passions may not always be at peace; but the centre of the soul remains unruffled and at one with God, and we are able to dwell in this centre continually. 'They have no lack of crosses, but these do not unsettle them or deprive them of their peace.'[22] Furthermore, whereas before we may have understood little of what we were going through, now the scales are removed from our eyes, and we *see* what we before held by faith and trust in our experience alone. In describing the Spiritual Marriage, Teresa uses an image well-known to many mystical writers and most notably to the Vedāntic tradition of India:

> It is like rain falling from the heavens into a river or spring; there is nothing but water there and it is impossible to divide or separate the water belonging to the river from that which fell from the heavens. Or it is as if a tiny streamlet enters the sea, from which it will find no way of separating itself.[23]

The use of this imagery would initially *seem* at face value to imply that Teresa feels that there is no difference at all between the perfected soul and God; that the two become absolutely one, rather than simply sharing a loving communion in which a distinction between God and the soul remains. If this were so then it would be surprising, for the latter belief is more typical of the theistic mysticism of which Teresa is, on the whole, an outstanding example; the motif of 'rivers running to the sea' denoting final liberation is actually more typical of the monistic mystical traditions. (The distinction between these two types of mysticism will be explored more fully later.) Probably, the explanation lies in the fact that Teresa is not using imagery in a systematic way here. Elsewhere she in fact states in passing that she does not believe that the question of whether or not there is any difference between the soul and God in the final state of union can be settled by means of the understanding,[24] a position with which many non-intellectual mystics would agree, though those mystics of more metaphysical persuasions, like John of the Cross, appear to differ.

But although Teresa cannot describe the full glory of the *experience* of the Spiritual Marriage or confine its mysteries within rationalistic formulae, she does speak of the practical *effects* of this experience, the results it produces in the soul, which are for her perhaps even more important than the experience itself. She emphasises that the mystic will wish now to work for God's glory and to try to fulfil the divine will on earth. We no longer wish (as before) to die in order to be with God, but rather to live, if by so doing we may fulfil God's will. We do not retreat into a solipsistic enjoyment of our own spiritual experience, but engage ever more fully with life in all respects:

> The interior part of the soul works in the active life, and in things which seem to be exterior; but, when active works proceed from this source [Spiritual Marriage], they are like wondrous and sweetly scented flowers. For the tree from which they come is love of God for His own sake alone, without self-interest; and the perfume of these flowers is wafted abroad, to the profit of many.[25]

The mystic now acts in a pure pouring-out of love and service, without thought of reward, personal reputation, or personal credit. Teresa herself, in her tireless activities of reform, is a prime example of the astonishing strength, courage, and energy to accomplish what one would think impossible, shown by the greatest mystics; the

reception of divine power gives the will and ability to work with
unflagging dedication and perseverance.

A few more general comments on Teresa's conception of the mystical life may be in order. She always emphasises the need for a solid
basis of humility, prayer, virtue and meditation: 'We must not build
towers without foundations.'[26] Her writings certainly show her own
deep humility and consciousness of her imperfections, and give us a
picture of a woman always deeply questioning herself and analysing
her experiences so as to grow in self-knowledge. She also stresses the
necessity of selfless love, and of detachment, both from created
things and from our own self-will. Indeed, in the *Way of Perfection* – written for her nuns as a treatise on prayer and not addressed
specifically to mystics nor even to those who had aspirations to the
mystical – love, detachment and humility are numbered as the three
most important virtues in the religious life. It is unfortunate that the
insistence of great spiritual writers on these themes is so often
misunderstood today – for example, detachment is often confused
with contempt for worldly things, and humility with being a
'doormat' – but a full exploration of the significance of these terms
would take us too far outside the scope of this study. Suffice it to say
that humility can be seen as a sincere facing-up to, and acceptance of
responsibility for, our numerous shortcomings and faults which
alienate us from the life of the divine. Love – that all-embracing
spiritual love for which Teresa was so sadly misunderstood –
should be impartial and untainted by selfish emotion or passion.
Detachment means not to set any store by things of this world in that
we do not expect them to bring us ultimate fulfilment and do not
hanker after what we do not have, fixing our sights on the transcendent reality beyond.

It should not escape our notice, too, that Teresa's shrewd intuitive
understanding of psychology – not to mention her common sense
and realism – give rise to much apposite teaching on the nature of
spiritual growth and the pitfalls for which one must be alert, such as
self-deception in its various forms, self-will, attachment to material
things, and self-love. Teresa is well aware of the illusions which can
so often hide under the surface even of what may seem to us to be
sublime and truly spiritual experiences. This is a further reason for
her concern to establish the distinctions between the true and the
false with regard to visions, raptures and other such phenomena.
But self-deception can be found not only in such experiences, but in

almost any aspect of the spiritual life: in our imagining that we are virtuous, in our inclination to spend time in contemplation rather than helping our neighbour when the latter needs to be done, and so on.

Central to Teresa's view of the mystical life – though those who have been concerned to defend her orthodoxy have often tried to argue otherwise – are the visions, locutions or auditions (voices), raptures and ecstasies of which she had such rich and plentiful experience. These phenomena do not correspond to any one of the 'stages' in Teresa's scheme: visions and locutions may occur at almost any stage along the mystical path, except that we cannot experience them when the faculties are 'suspended', for here there is no seeing or hearing, whether of the inner or outer senses. Certain types of vision tend to fall off, too, Teresa tells us, right at the end of the path. As for raptures and ecstasies, according to Teresa we do not usually begin to experience these states until we are reasonably accomplished in contemplation, though there can be exceptions to this rule. It is certainly true that (in common with most other mystics) Teresa tells us we should not seek after such phenomena; she does not see visions, raptures and other such experiences as being of such great importance, in themselves, as our awareness of God, our conformity to his will, and our cultivation of virtue. I do not wish to deny the validity of this observation, which has been amply illustrated by previous writers, but rather to suggest that it shows us only part of the picture. For when this point is over-emphasised, as it is by many dogmatically inclined writers, it detracts from and even belittles Teresa's own evaluation of her visionary and ecstatic experiences, and makes a mockery of the considerable amount of time she considers worth devoting to her descriptions and analyses of them. An accurate assessment of the nature and significance of such experiences has been hindered by writers who disregard visions and related phenomena as being unworthy of attention, or as not being examples of 'true' mysticism.

Visions and locutions have traditionally been divided by mystical writers into three categories: corporeal, imaginary, and intellectual. Corporeal visions are those that are seen with the physical eyes, called by Teresa the 'eyes of the body' (*los ojos del cuerpo*); very few mystics actually experience this kind of vision except perhaps on one or two isolated occasions. Where they do, they are usually extremely wary of them, arguing that it is difficult to be sure that they are not merely hallucinations, or (in the context of Christian mysticism) sent by the devil (although theoretically it is always *possible* for a corporeal vision to be genuine and to come from God). Teresa claims that she has never experienced corporeal vision[27] although her account of the famous 'Transverberation' is ambiguous here, for she says that she saw the angel with the fiery spear 'in bodily form – a type of vision which I am not in the habit of seeing, except very rarely'.[28] Early in her spiritual development, however, before she came to have greater experience and understanding, Teresa was perplexed by the fact that she supposed she *ought* to be receiving corporeal visions: she did not realise that there were eyes other than those of the body with which one could 'see'.[29] Teresa says little more on the subject of corporeal visions other than to concur with the standard judgement of them as being the lowest kind of vision and the most susceptible to delusion. As for corporeal locutions (where words are heard with the physical sense of hearing) Teresa reports only one insignificant instance of this.[30]

Imaginary visions or auditions, which form the second type, contain distinct images or words, but are apprehended not with the physical senses but with the inner eye, the 'eyes of the soul' (*los ojos del alma*), or with the 'inner hearing'. The term 'imaginary' does not imply that these experiences are illusory, nor, confusingly, that they are produced by the imagination. The word is here used in a technical sense to denote a vision that presents itself in the form of a picture (*imago*). In Teresa's terminology, imaginary vision is always spontaneous, coming upon her without foreknowledge or forewarning; that is to say, a mental picture or visualisation deliberately induced by the imagination for the purposes of meditation, would not count as a vision. Teresa does used willed visualisation in meditation (a technique which she probably learned from the Jesuits) – here images (for example, of scenes from Jesus' life) are called up in the imagination, kept under the control of the mind, and dismissed at will. But a true vision cannot be dismissed when it comes upon us, nor can it be conjured up by the will and imagination. Genuine visions have a life, reality and 'depth' which a visualised image does not usually possess; in Teresa's descriptions, divine figures in visions are often seen to shine with a soft white light of unearthly radiance. The visions are seen with the eyes of the soul more clearly, if anything, than we see with the eyes of the body, and will be remembered even in detail many years afterwards. Mystics vary in their attitude to imaginary visions, some granting them greater importance and validity than others. John of the Cross disagreed with Teresa on this point, but Teresa was convinced that '. . . after each favour which the Lord granted me, whether vision or revelation, some great gain accrued to my soul'; 'if there is anything good in me, it is they that have been the source of it.'[31] She advised her nuns, then, that 'Some people seem to be frightened at the very mention of visions or revelations. I do not know why they think a soul being led in this way by God is on such a dangerous path. . . . the good or evil is not in the vision, but in the person who sees it.'[32]

Nevertheless, it was obviously important for Teresa to formulate some guidelines by means of which she might hope to distinguish genuine visions from delusions; we will examine these guidelines shortly. We give below some accounts of imaginary visions in her own words.

When Our Lord is pleased to bestow greater consolations upon this soul, He grants it, in whatever way He thinks best, a clear revelation of His sacred Humanity . . . and although He does this so quickly that we might liken the action to a flash of lightning, this most glorious image is so deeply engraven upon the imagination that I do not believe it can possibly disappear until it is seen where it can be enjoyed to all eternity. I speak of an 'image', but it must not be supposed that one looks at it as at a painting; it is really alive, and sometimes even speaks to the soul and shows it things both great and secret. But you must realize that, although the soul sees this for a certain length of time, it can no more be gazing at it all the time than it could keep gazing at the sun. . . . The brilliance of this vision is like that of infused light or of a sun covered with some material of the transparency of a diamond, if such a thing could be woven.[33]

On one occasion, when I was reciting the Hours with the community, my soul suddenly became recollected and seemed to me to become bright all over like a mirror: no part of it – back, sides, top or bottom – but was completely bright, and in the centre of it was a picture of Christ our Lord as I generally see Him. I seemed to see Him in every part of my soul as clearly as in a mirror. . . . This, I know, was a vision which, whenever I recall it, and especially after Communion, is always of great profit to me. It was explained to me that, when a soul is in mortal sin, this mirror is covered with a thick mist and remains darkened so that the Lord cannot be pictured or seen in it, though He is always present with us and gives us our being.[34]

(We may note in passing that the mirror is a fairly widespread mystical symbol of the soul or self: John of the Cross uses the image in a manner very similar to Teresa, and we can find parallels even in Zen Buddhism.[35] It is possible, too, that Teresa's use of mirror symbolism here owes something to her Jewish ancestry, a point to which we shall return.) As the reader may have gathered, many of Teresa's imaginary visions were of Jesus, and she speaks of them as experiences of great beauty, beauty sometimes so intense and awesome that it is hard to bear. We give one final example of an imaginary vision, this time of the Virgin Mary, which occurred while Teresa was undergoing ridicule and persecution over her proposed foundation of St Joseph's in Avila. In a rapture, she seemed to see herself clothed in a white robe by Our Lady and St Joseph. Mary then told Teresa that she was giving her great pleasure by serving St Joseph and promised that the plans for the convent would be fulfilled.

> She said that they would watch over us and that her Son had already promised to be with us; and that as a sign that this would be so she would give me a jewel. Then she seemed to hang round my neck a very beautiful gold collar, from which hung a cross of great value. The gold and stones were so different from those of this world that there is no comparing them; their beauty is quite unlike anything we can imagine here. Nor can the imagination rise to any understanding of the nature of the robe, or to any conception of its whiteness. . . . The beauty that I saw in Our Lady was wonderful, though I could make out no particular detail, only the general shape of her face and the whiteness and amazing splendour of her robes, which was not dazzling but quite soft.[36]

Of imaginary locutions, Teresa says that 'The words are perfectly formed, but are not heard with the physical ear. Yet they are received much more clearly than if they were so heard; and however hard one resists it is impossible to shut them out.' In the midst of great disturbances and trials, a few simple words, 'Be not troubled', will be enough to calm the soul. Or (here Teresa obviously recalls her personal experiences) a soul is distressed because its confessor tells it that its experiences are of the devil; yet the short locution, 'It is I, fear not' takes all fear from it.[37]

The third type of vision or locution, the intellectual type, is more abstract, indeed some might consider intellectual vision a rather broad use of the term 'vision'. It is a type of inspiration, intuition or revelation which has no form and is seen neither with the eyes of the body nor with the eyes of the soul. Christian mystics are more or less unanimous in granting the greatest importance and the least possibility of delusion to this type of vision or audition, although some are wary even of these. Teresa describes one such experience as follows:

> One day when I was at prayer . . . I saw Christ at my side – or, to put it better, I was conscious of Him, for I saw nothing with the eyes of the body or the eyes of the soul . . . He was speaking to me . . . All the time Jesus Christ seemed to be at my side, but as this was not an imaginary vision I could not see in what form.

Teresa then tells of the difficulty she had in explaining and justifying this experience to her Confessor. Struggling for comparisons by means of which to illustrate her experience, she continues:

> . . . if I say that I do not see Him with the eyes of the body or the eyes of the soul . . . how then can I know and affirm that He is beside me with greater certainty than if I saw Him? If one says that one is like a person in the dark who cannot see someone though he is beside him . . . There is some similarity here, but not much . . . He appears to the soul by a knowledge brighter than the sun. I do not mean that any sun is seen, or any brightness, but there is a light which, though unseen, illumines the understanding so that the soul may enjoy this great blessing. . . . though He is unseen He imprints so clear a knowledge on the soul that there seems to be no possibility of doubt. . . . It is easier to doubt one's eyes. . . . It is the same with another of God's methods of instructing the soul, that by which He speaks to it without words. . . . He uses so celestial a language that it is difficult to explain. . . . He introduces into the innermost parts of the soul what He wants it to understand, presenting it not in pictures or in the form of words, but in the manner of this vision that I have described. Consider carefully this way in which God reveals to the soul not only His wishes, but also great truths and mysteries.[38]

Teresa argues at some length regarding how we can be sure whether or not a vision or locution is genuine. This is not only because she wanted to protect others from the possibility of falling prey to illusion, or to auto-suggestion – of which power she was well aware, though naturally she did not call it by this name. It is also certain that it is partially because she had so often to defend the value of her own experiences before confessors, theologians, and the

Inquisition's investigators. In her accounts of her visions she anti-cipates possible criticism by a caution which is often quite trans-parent, painstakingly spelling it out that she wishes her experiences to be interpreted so as to be in conformity with orthodoxy.

It was commonly believed in sixteenth-century Spain that visions, auditions and similar experiences could come from one of three sources: God, the devil, or a wandering mind. Teresa puts forward the following tests by which we may know whether or not a locution is genuine, that is, coming from a divine source.

A genuine locution has a sense of power and authority, so that if, for example, one is experiencing great inner disturbances and trials, a single word, as we have already noted, will be enough to calm the soul and bring a great light to it. A genuine locution also produces a tranquillity, recollectedness, and desire to praise God. Auditions that come from the devil, on the other hand, leave the soul in restlessness, turmoil and confusion. The words of a true locution do not vanish from the memory for a very long time, and we have an inner certainty that what we are told by these words will come to pass, even if realistically it may seem impossible. A series of tests can furthermore be applied to the nature of the locution itself. A genuine locution is clear and distinct, whereas those created by the mind are imprecise, like something heard half in a dream. Secondly, the voice comes unexpectedly and refers to things of which one would never have thought of one's own accord, so that the imagination, Teresa believes, cannot possibly have invented them. In genuine locutions, moreover, '. . . the soul seems to be hearing something, whereas in locutions invented by the imagination someone seems to be com-posing bit by bit what the soul wishes to hear.' Again, '. . . there is a great difference in the words themselves: in a genuine locution one single word may contain a world of meaning such as the under-standing alone could never put rapidly into human language'; so that through locutions we can quickly grasp things which it might take us a very long time to work out for ourselves. Furthermore, 'much more can be understood than the words themselves convey.' In retrospect, too, we can tell that a locution comes from God if what is revealed in it does in fact come true. On many occasions, Teresa tells us, she was told things in locutions which were fulfilled several years later. Finally, if what is revealed by an audition is in conformity with the Scriptures, we may trust it; otherwise we should suspect that it comes from another source.[39]

Clearly, some of these criteria are more satisfactory than others. The test of conformity to Scripture is standard for Christian mystics, but formal and unoriginal, and would carry no weight for someone who was not already predisposed to believe in the Christian Scriptures. Furthermore, as we shall see, Teresa could interpret Scripture in some surprising ways and thus cause some challenging personal realisations to appear to conform with it. Again, in the light of modern psychology, much of what Teresa says about locutions could easily be explained without reference to the idea of God; for example, the fact that many of her locutions came true could simply be seen as proving that she had well-developed psychic or intuitive powers of precognition. But a full-scale investigation of the psychology of mystical phenomena would lead us too far astray from our theme. If the modern reader is willing to take Teresa's accounts of her *experiences* at least, at face value – leaving aside for the moment the question of their ontological source – one of the strongest impressions received is, I think, of pity for her in her persecution and her attempts to justify the value of her experiences to often arrogant theologians, in an ecclesiastical climate that was one of fanaticism and mania where any suspicions of heresy were concerned. Underhill comments:

> St Teresa's mystic life was governed by voices: her active career as a foundress was much guided by them. They advised her in small things as in great. Often they interfered with her plans, ran counter to her personal judgement, forbade a foundation on which she was set, or commanded one which appeared imprudent or impossible. They concerned themselves with journeys, with the purchase of houses; they warned her of coming events. As her mystical life matured, Teresa seems to have learned to discriminate those locutions on which action should properly be based. She seldom resisted them, though it constantly happened that the action on which they insisted seemed the height of folly: and though they frequently involved her in hardships and difficulties, she never had cause to regret this reliance upon decrees which she regarded as coming direct from God, and which certainly did emanate from a life greater than her own.[40]

In treating of the genuineness of *visions*, Teresa puts forward one additional very important criterion: a true vision is known by its effects. Although she does not explicitly mention this criterion in the context of *auditions*, it would seem more than likely that she intended it to be applied to them too. This seems to be the most important criterion for Teresa as far as visions are concerned: visions are known 'by their fruits'. Speaking of the interrogations to which she was submitted by the theologians who tried to persuade her that her visions came from the devil, she writes:

> I once said to the people who were talking to me in this way that if they were to tell me that a person whom I knew well and had just been speaking to was not herself at all, but that I was imagining her to be so, and that they knew this was the case, I should certainly believe them rather than my own eyes. But, I added, if that person left some jewels with me, which I was actually holding in my hands as pledges of her great love, and if, never having had any before, I were thus to find myself rich instead of poor, I could not possibly believe that this was delusion, even if I wanted to. And, I said, I could show them these jewels – for all who knew me were well aware how my soul had changed . . . the difference was very great in every respect, and no fancy, but such as all could clearly see . . . it was quite clear to me that these experiences had immediately made me a different person.[41]

True visions, then, issue in a life of improved ethical quality and increased psychological integration. They inspire the soul with love for God and give strength, fortitude and inner peace. The test of visions as being known 'by their fruits' is one that many mystics cite as being a reliable criterion of the validity of spiritual experiences. (Indeed, one of the reasons – though not the only one – that Teresa's confessors doubted her earlier visions and raptures was because they held that such 'favours' could not possibly be granted by God to someone who was as 'sinful' as Teresa felt herself to be.) A moment's thought here will show to us that the value of spiritual truths is not conveyed only by the words spoken of them. It is conveyed also by the integrity, ethical worth and inner depth of the person who gives voice to them: by the person's self-harmony, integration, constructive attitudes, ability to love and to give. If our observation of a person convinces us that they live up to their spiritual ideals, that they are at peace with themselves, that they have profundity of character, we feel, rightly I think, that extra weight is added to their statements regarding spiritual truth (although this is not to say that we should consider this criterion to be sufficient in itself).

A further point concerning the difference between true and false visions, according to Teresa, which we have touched on already, is that genuine visions cannot be called up at will, nor can they be resisted when they occur. They come upon us irresistibly, when they will, and apparently from without. We cannot alter them, add to or subtract from them. They are quite different from a picture which we have consciously built up bit by bit with the mind: 'The soul is very far from expecting to see anything and the thought of such a thing has never even passed through its mind. All of a sudden the whole vision is revealed to it.'[42]

Teresa's concern to justify her experiences, the intimidation which learning induced in her, and the danger she was in because of the social and ecclesiastical climate of her time, can be inferred from the following passage with which we may conclude our account of her visions and auditions:

> . . . when I am in prayer, and on days when I am enjoying quiet and my thoughts are fixed on God, all the learned men and saints in the world might unite in tormenting me with all imaginable tortures, and, even if I wanted to believe them, they could not make me believe that this is the devil's work, because I cannot. When they did try to make me believe this, I was afraid, seeing who they were that spoke to me in that way, for I thought that they must be speaking the truth, and that I, being who I was, must be mistaken. But the very first word I heard, or the very first moment of recollection or vision, was sufficient to destroy the effect of all they had said to me; and I found it impossible not to believe that my experiences came from God. Nevertheless I can believe that the devil may sometimes take a hand in them. . . . But the effects which he produces are different and I do not believe he will ever deceive any person of experience. . . . though I certainly believe myself to be led by God, I would never on any account do anything which my director did not think was for the greater service of Our Lord. . . . I am given warning when anything I am doing is leading me, or may lead me, into danger.[43]

A brief comment may be in order here on Teresa's view of the devil and evil, for her rigidly dualistic opposition of God and the devil, and in particular her apparent belief in the devil as a physical reality, rings strange to many modern ears. Yet Teresa is in many ways more 'modern' than we might expect here. She had 'imaginary' visions of hell and of the devil, and of demons, which caused her great distress. She tried at first to banish the devils and demons by various means, but came eventually to the conclusion that the best course of action was to ignore them; '. . . every time we pay little heed to them, they lose much of their power and the soul gains much more control over them.'[44] On certain occasions, she tells us, she saw a multitude of devils around her, yet she was protected by a divine light which enveloped her, and she realised that the demons have very little power to harm the mystic who is surrendered to God. Here, as on so many other occasions, Teresa shows herself possessed of a shrewd psychological insight. (It is possible too, we shall later argue, that her concern with demons can be traced to the importance of demonology in medieval Jewish thought.) Whether the demons had an objective reality or, as many would prefer to argue nowadays, were the product of Teresa's own unresolved conflicts, they were certainly real to her. But more to be feared than these demons was '. . . the unseen devil . . . the personification and source of all evil both in the world at large and in her own life'[45] who waits in hope of ensnaring the soul at every stage of the mystical journey. He is able to conjure up false visions and take on the appearance of an angel of light. Above all, he is persistent, working ceaselessly, like a noiseless file (to borrow Teresa's marvellous analogy), working on the mind, emotions, nerves or imagination to unbalance the soul in one way or another and turn it astray from its path.

Related to her visions and auditions is the inspired writing to which Teresa, in common with some other mystics, was subject: writing in an absorbed, contemplative, almost 'entranced' condition in which the pen seems guided by some other power and the writer often does not fully understand until later the meaning of the words that appear on the paper. It is said that the *Interior Castle* was written in just such a condition; Teresa's nuns testified that while working on this book she was seen to be radiant, writing with great rapidity, completely absorbed in her writing.

We may now consider the accounts that Teresa gives of her raptures and ecstasies and her teachings concerning them. She is not alone among mystics in granting importance to these experiences, which are often seen by mystics as a higher form of spiritual perception than vision, but as one which must nevertheless be scrutinised for the possibility of delusion. But although Teresa is not alone in her evaluation of these experiences, she is certainly a pioneer among mystics in the detailed firsthand account that she gives us of her experiences of ecstasy and rapture.

There are a number of terms which Teresa uses here for the same basic state of consciousness: rapture (*arrobamiento*), transport (*arrebatamiento*), elevation (*elevamiento* or *levantamiento*), flight of the spirit (*vuelo de espíritu*), ecstasy (*éstasi*). Although she occasionally dwells on slight distinctions between some of these terms, she says in at least one place that they are all different words for the same experience, and clearly sees any minor differences that there may be as of no importance.

Rapture, ecstasy, or whichever word we choose to give to it, then, is a brief state where the soul is transported or caught up to God. The physical effects are often those of trance, perhaps similar to that induced in some yogic trances. Teresa speaks of immobility, a slowing-down and quietening of the breath almost to the point of inaudibility, coldness of the extremities or of the whole body, a feeble pulse, and inability to feel pain, as the main observable symptoms.

> While seeking God in this way, the soul is conscious that it is fainting almost completely away in a kind of swoon, with a very great calm and joy. Its breath and all its bodily powers progressively fail it, so that it can hardly stir its hands without great effort. Its eyes close involuntarily, and if they remain open, they see almost nothing.[46]

The use of the senses and the surface-consciousness may be partially retained, or (particularly at the height of the experience) momentarily lost, with somatic repercussions, as in the 'suspension of faculties':

> The subject rarely loses consciousness; I have sometimes lost it altogether, but only seldom and for but a short time. As a rule the consciousness is disturbed; and, though incapable of action with respect to outward things, the subject can still hear and understand, but only dimly, as though from a long way off. I do not say that he can hear and understand when the rapture is at its highest point – by 'highest point' I mean when the faculties are lost through being closely united with God. At that point, in my opinion, he will neither see, nor hear, nor perceive; but . . . this complete transformation of the soul in God lasts but a short time.[47]

In rapture, Teresa says, '. . . the Lord gathers up the soul . . . and raises it up till it is right out of itself . . . and begins to reveal to it things concerning the Kingdom that he has prepared for it.'[48] The soul is carried away like a bird set loose from its cage, to another world, and there is often the sensation of leaving the body. Teresa also speaks of several occasions when she was seen by others actually to levitate physically, the great force lifting her up from beneath her feet. The physical effects of such raptures embarrassed Teresa (and, no doubt, made her fear that she was attracting the wrong type of attention to herself so far as her relations with the Inquisition were concerned!) and she often tried (in vain) to resist such 'flights of the spirit'. But nowhere does she disparage such experiences as being unimportant or as necessarily coming from an ungodly source. The present writer's opinion is that such phenomena are realities, though one might wish to argue that some of them come under the domain of parapsychology rather than mysticism. Teresa, in common with many mystics, sees such 'psychic powers' as levitation as being incidental to spiritual progress, as phenomena which often accompany true mystical growth but are not essential to it. Nevertheless, she values rapture or ecstasy so highly that she declares that it is of a much higher nature than, and more beneficial than, the Prayer of Union (remembering, of course, that 'union' for Teresa does not denote the highest state of mystical achievement).[49] This is a fact which some theological commentators have tried to ignore, wishing to confine Teresa's teachings within the bounds of a more orthodox line of thought which insists that all trances and raptures are potentially dangerous and a sign of disequilibrium. Teresa in fact sees rapture or ecstasy as a great gift from God; during the experience there occur revelations and visions of divine secrets, which enrich and strengthen the inner life and bring many spiritual advantages.

> . . . often it comes like a strong, swift impulse, before your thought can forewarn you of it or you can do anything to help yourself; you see and feel this cloud, or this powerful eagle, rising and bearing you up with it on its wings . . . you are being carried away, you know not whither. . . . the soul, when enraptured, is mistress of everything, and in a single hour, or in less, acquires such freedom that it cannot recognize itself. It sees clearly that this state is in no way due to itself, nor does it know who has given it so great a blessing, but it distinctly recognizes the very great benefit which each of these raptures brings it. Nobody will believe this without having had experience of it.[50]

> He [the mystic] feels as if he has been in another world, very different from this in which we live, and has been shown a fresh light there, so

much unlike any to be found in this life that, if he had been imagining it, and similar things, all his life long, it would have been impossible for him to obtain any idea of them. In a single instant he is taught so many things all at once that, if he were to labour for years on end in trying to fit them all into his imagination and thought, he could not succeed with a thousandth part of them.[51]

When we descend to everyday consciousness again from a rapture, we feel enchained and imprisoned in this world; but we are filled with greater humility and love of the divine:

> . . . ecstasy has the effect of leaving the will so completely absorbed and the understanding so completely transported – for as long as a day, or even for several days – that the soul seems incapable of grasping anything that does not awaken the will to love; to this it is fully awake, while asleep as regards all that concerns attachment to any creature.[52]

This state of detachment is experienced both physically and spiritually, says Teresa: there is felt a pain which manifests itself interiorly as loneliness and weariness of spirit, and physically in the form of various bodily pains.

The rational mind cannot fathom the experience of rapture; the understanding is often so completely transported, and the experience so intense, that the mystic has no power to think about what is occurring. The length of a rapture varies, usually being very brief at first, perhaps of greater duration as one progresses; it often seems to be of shorter duration than it actually is, an example of the experience of time seeming to contract which is well-known to mystics and meditators of all traditions: 'I thought I had been there only a very short time,' writes Teresa of one such instance, 'and I was astounded when the clock struck and I found that I had been in that state of rapture and bliss for two hours.'[53]

Laski, in her study of ecstatic experiences, found that they were tumescent experiences usually of momentary duration; that they could not be voluntarily induced; and that they were followed by a period of up to an hour or so, which Laski calls 'ecstatic afterglow', during which the experience is interpreted and normal faculties and perceptions gradually restored (as I have suggested is the case following Teresa's 'suspension of faculties'). She notes that most

ecstatics agree, as does Teresa, that these experiences are to be
valued not so much for the delight they give as for their beneficial
results.[54]

Just as she is well aware that visions can sometimes be deceptive,
so Teresa recognises that raptures and ecstasies are not always what
they seem and that there are similar experiences which are no more
than 'frenzies', illusions. Until one has had a good deal of experience
of rapture, one can afford to be doubtful; but in genuine ecstasy, one
is united with God, and upon return one cannot possibly doubt the
truth of this. In order to ascertain whether a particular case of
rapture is genuine, Teresa again advances her test that such phenomena are known 'by their fruits'. True raptures leave us with peace,
tranquillity, knowledge of God's greatness, self-knowledge, humility, increased detachment from material things. (This might seem to
contradict Teresa's assertion that the after-effects of rapture include
both physical and spiritual pain. Doubtless Teresa would reply that,
as is so often the case in the later stages of the mystical way, we can
paradoxically experience both pain and peace.) True raptures reveal
great and divine secrets and mysteries. Teresa warns that we must be
careful to distinguish such genuine ecstasies from mere imaginings,
or from a kind of physical weakness or languor which can come over
people of poor health when they receive spiritual experiences. She
speaks in particular of nuns who allow themselves to be carried
away by false raptures and abandon themselves to irrational inertia
and mere physical swoons which are not accompanied by any spiritual enlightenment.[55] Genuine raptures, Teresa declares, must be
differentiated from the imaginings of weak women.

Time and again we will see how Teresa's necessity to defend her
experiences is bound up with her position as a woman in sixteenth-
century Spain. In her time and culture not only were visionary and
ecstatic experiences regarded as evidence of possible heresy, but
furthermore women, and also those of Jewish ancestry, were held to
be particularly prone to such experiences. Unfortunately for
Teresa's reputation, visions and raptures were also seen as going
hand-in-hand with sexual laxity. It is a thorny problem to dis-
entangle the genuine inspired visionaries from the hysterics who
were also rife in medieval Spain, not least because of the tendency of
the patriarchal, misogynistic, and antisemitic Church authorities to
denounce prejudicially the majority of visionaries and ecstatics who
were either female or from Jewish family backgrounds. (We speak of

Jewish 'family backgrounds' and 'ancestries' because officially, as it were, there were not supposed to be any actual Jews in Spain in Teresa's time: those who wished to remain true to their faith had been expelled in 1492. Nevertheless, many Jews had in fact converted to Christianity as a mere cover and had continued to live in Spain. This issue is explored more fully in our next chapter.)

We have remarked that Teresa is a firm believer in the value of contemplation of the personal Deity (Jesus), God with form, even in the highest stages of mystical experience. It is ironic that it is partially for this reason that she has come to enjoy the reputation of being one of the more orthodox of Christian mystics. The irony is due both to the fact that, as this book attempts to show, Teresa was very far from being 'orthodox' as far as her visions and raptures and the Jewish influence found in her writings are concerned; and also because in advancing this view regarding contemplation of Jesus Christ, Teresa was in fact going directly *against* the dominant Scholastic mystical tradition of her day, and putting forward a challenging new viewpoint; '. . . by presenting a mystical system which is independent from Scholasticism, she is undermining the way of thinking that enjoyed greatest authority in the Church.'[56] Scholastic mysticism emphasised an ascent to contemplation of the formless Divinity by means of renouncing the objects of the senses, intellectual ideas, and all symbols and images – including the image of Jesus' humanity. Contemporary exponents of this form of spiri tuality included John of the Cross, and Francisco de Osuna, whose *Third Spiritual Alphabet* made such an impression on Teresa. But, in spite of her respect for both these men, Teresa parts company with them regarding the role of Jesus and of meditation on his image and figure. She feels that the path which keeps always before us the image of Jesus' human form is the safest, and the most appropriate for incarnated human beings. Although she admits that we may have short periods of ecstasy where we rise above all forms and images – for in the 'suspension of faculties', any awareness of Jesus' humanity or of any specific idea or image must necessarily be briefly lost – Teresa feels that the soul is 'left in the air' on such occasions. As usual, she speaks from experience: when she began to have a little experience of the Prayer of Quiet, she says, she did in fact try to follow the method of contemplation generally advocated by the Scholastics. At that time, '. . . no one could have made me return to my meditations on the Humanity, which seemed to me to present a positive hindrance.'[57] But she soon came to disagree with this approach, in spite of the fact that there were those who told her that she did not understand the matter, and who criticised her for writing of it. While we live as human beings, it is very important for us to keep Jesus' humanity before us and to approach God through this humanity, Teresa declares insistently. 'We are not angels and we have bodies. To want to become angels while we are still on earth . . . is ridiculous. As a rule, our thoughts must have something to lean upon [*tener arrimo*, which might alternatively be rendered "a support to hold onto"]'.[58]

Teresa explains that she does *not* mean that we do not need to withdraw from corporeal things once we reach a certain stage along the mystical path. 'What I should like to make clear is that Christ's most sacred Humanity must not be reckoned among these corporeal objects,' she writes.[59] For those who took the Scholastic point of view, contemplation of the humanity of Jesus – picturing scenes from his life and so on – was relegated to the level of 'discursive meditation', roughly equivalent to the early stage of prayer which Teresa speaks of as 'meditation'. John of the Cross found it extremely important to pass *beyond* discursive meditation – and hence beyond the image of Jesus. (We shall look at his position in more detail shortly.) Teresa challenges this: for her, spiritual exercises entailing meditation on the person of Jesus can continue also onto the level of 'infused' or 'supernatural' contemplation, the higher stage of mystical prayer which is given by the grace of God. The mysteries represented by Jesus' person are then apprehended not discursively, but 'in a more perfect way'[60] – by which Teresa appears to mean through an advanced form of mystical intuition.

O'Donoghue therefore argues that Teresa does not mean that we should not rise above meditation to contemplation. Rather, the contemplative experience, however high-flying, should always be 'anchored in the Word made flesh'; representations of Jesus, or of key episodes in his life, are used as a 'launching pad of the mind's journey into the world of Divine Mystery'. O'Donoghue distinguishes three strands in Teresa's understanding of the Divine humanity: Christ as object of meditation, Christ as friend or companion, and Christ as 'a support to hold onto' as I have rendered it above, allowing the mystic to scale the heights of contemplation without feeling 'left in the air'.[61]

We have seen that Teresa had instruction in Jesuit methods of prayer and meditation: the object of Jesuit exercises was not to attempt to rise above symbols and images so much as to use and develop them by means of visualisation, so perhaps these teachings played a part in developing Teresa's ideas here. It is true that in her 'suspension of faculties', Teresa does pass beyond all form and image, and it is possible (though a full discussion of this cannot be embarked upon here) that her suspension of faculties may represent the same *experience*, though differently *interpreted*, as the heights of 'unknowing' or formless vision sought by John of the Cross and others. But it is clear that even if these experiences are the same, Teresa does not evaluate the experience in anything like the same kind of way as does John. That is, even though she has known moments of formless awareness possibly like those spoken of by John, and even though she has tried the form of prayer recommended by those of his persuasion, Teresa values more highly what is a supremely theistic experience, an experience of *relationship* with Jesus, not of oneness with the formless Godhead. Even at the time of the experience which she regarded as the culmination of her 'Spiritual Marriage', she had a vision of Jesus in human form (though in her description of this vision she readily admits that 'To other people the experience will come in a different way').[62] Through this experience '. . . she realized that the "soul never ceases to walk with Christ", even if no longer through analytic thought and the incessant use of the imagination, factors rightly regarded as keeping the soul from attaining full enlightenment.'[63]

We can understand this in fuller context by looking at the teachings of John of the Cross in more detail, and also at those of the great German mystic Meister Eckhart. Both are representatives of the 'Dionysian' mode of Christian mysticism, that is to say, the stream of mystical philosophy whose origins can be traced ultimately to the works of Dionysius the Areopagite, now known as Pseudo-Dionysius[64] and which represents one application of the *Via Negativa* (Way of Negation). The mystic, according to this system, must pass beyond all particular, limited ideas, all specific apprehensions or illuminations, all images and symbols, however spiritual or sublime they may seem, to enter an ineffable state which is beyond rational comprehension. This state, described (or, rather, hinted at) only by means of paradox or by designating it as a darkness, emptiness, nothingness, etc., is seen as an experience of union with the Divine. Specific intellectual formulations, particular images,

personal revelations or visions, all these are obstacles to this
ineffable realisation because they are all relatively limited and
narrow, circumscribed by the finitude of our human nature, and as
such will obscure the vision beyond.

For John of the Cross, the use of images and visual aids to devotion, and the use of discursive reasoning to attempt to understand
what is inwardly revealed in meditation, are not repudiated for
those on the earlier stages of the mystical way. Indeed, for beginners
on the path these things are necessary: they are valuable means to an
end. But in the more advanced stages of mystical endeavour, a
reorientation is necessary: the mystic must then pass beyond
meditation on specific concepts and images, to contemplation,
which is a formless and passive awareness of, or an absorption in,
the Deity, in which God is known by direct perception, without the
need for apprehensions to be channelled through particular forms or
images. In this state, there is no place for meditation on Jesus'
humanity, contemplation of his image, or visualisation of scenes
from his life. The more we advance in spiritual understanding, the
more we will cease to identify *any* such particular images or conceptions with Divine Reality. If we can empty ourselves of all limited
ideas and images, rising above the dichotomies and dualisms of
rationalistic thought (which can never hope to penetrate these
mysteries), we will apprehend all things as One, that is, we will see
all things in and through that single principle which is the ground
and basis of all and which we call God. St John calls this higher form
of apprehension which is a living awareness of Divine Reality,
'unknowing'.[65] In this divine dark, this nothingness which is also
All, it is clear that the image of Jesus as a man, the meditation on
particular episodes in his life and so on, which Teresa values so
highly, must be transcended along with all other limited symbols or
particular ideas.

Meister Eckhart (*c.* 1260–1328) articulates even more uncompromisingly the *Via Negativa*. Beyond the triune God, for Eckhart,
is the Godhead (*Gotheit*), which is the One, absolute unity, eternal
and unchangeable, beyond all names, concepts, attributes and
images. The mystic must pass beyond God as he is conceived under
particular names and forms – and this will obviously include passing beyond the figure of Jesus – to become one with the undifferentiated Godhead, the 'Nothing', 'wilderness' or divine 'darkness'.
Although Eckhart certainly acknowledges the value of devotion to

the personal God – and, indeed, expresses such devotional religious feelings of his own with warmth and fervour – it remains true that his real goal is unity with the One, which entails surpassing all particular human conceptions of the Deity. Jesus is seen primarily as a messenger from God to humanity and as the ideal or perfected human being. For both John of the Cross and Eckhart, we must be attached to no specific ideas, images or conceptions of God if we are to enter into the dark 'nothingness' in which God works. We must pass beyond all forms to the Formless, rising above all particular apprehensions, however 'good' or 'spiritual' they may seem, to uncover the naked essence of truth which is free from our limiting, personalised ways of conceiving things. Then we see what God really is, independent of our particular human conceptions of God.[66]

This type of mysticism can be seen as the more monistic branch of Christian mystical thought. For monistic mystics worldwide, the spiritual Absolute (the highest Godhead) is transcendent, ineffable, beyond all opposites, beyond all particular conceptions and images. It is often described, as we have said, by means of negative terminology or paradox. The personal Deity or anthropomorphic god (or, in some instances from outside the Christian tradition, goddess) may be seen as being manifested from out of this Absolute, as a symbol for the Absolute, a messenger from it, a making actual of its powers, or a means of attaining to it. But the formless, impersonal aspect of divine reality is always emphasised: the mystic must pass beyond God as he, or she, is conceived by us under various forms and guises, to the formless Absolute. To attain to this vision in 'unknowing' (to use the Christian terminology), all symbols and particular concepts must be transcended; so too must the limiting messages of emotion, sense-perception and rational comprehension. Thus the mystic hopes to reach a state of immediate, direct apprehension of divine reality by being united with this reality, or even, as some mystics (including Eckhart) intimate, by becoming absolutely one with it.

Such examples of monistic mysticism can be contrasted with theistic mysticism, where the focus of the mystic's attention is on the personal God conceived more or less in anthropomorphic form. Theistic mystics typically emphasise devotion, love of God, and the importance of the grace of the Deity in granting the soul progress. They often express themselves in romantic, emotional, even passionate language, culminating in what is perhaps the crowning symbol of theistic mysticism, the Spiritual Marriage: the union of lover and Beloved in which the two nevertheless remain distinct. Theistic mystics, unlike those just discussed, do not usually advocate the transcendence of all particular ideas, images and forms. Typically, they strive for enjoyment of a loving relationship with the personal Deity, rather than absorption into an undifferentiated Absolute. Teresa fits more squarely into this pattern than into that of monism, and in this respect can be compared, to give just one typical example, with Richard Rolle of Hampole (born in Yorkshire, c. 1300). Rolle's goal is to be transformed into and made one with God through Jesus by the power of love. He is a 'romantic' writer, pouring out depths of feeling rather than expressing himself according to a clearly defined rationalistic scheme. His highest experiences are expressed in terms of the soul's participation in the divine harmonies which he hears as an invisible melody, as spiritual music, and in terms of the pouring out of his heart in joy and love. He does not speak of 'unknowing', 'emptiness', or radically ineffable experiences: indeed he seems not to have experienced such states of formless or undifferentiated awareness at all. In this respect Richard Rolle differs from Teresa, for she does seem to have had some experience of such states (in her 'suspension of faculties', and perhaps also during the period when she followed the usual Scholastic modes of meditation) but she nevertheless places a higher value on a theistic mysticism of loving relationship. The two are in accord, however, in their estimation of the theistic experience as the summit of the mystical life. Unlike the monists, Rolle and Teresa do not find it helpful or necessary to pass beyond the image of the personal God as manifested in Jesus.[67]

Until recent years, many scholars tended to assume that all mystical experiences were basically the same, an assumption which is still reflected in much popular thought. This belief usually takes the form of some variation on the argument that, whereas the images, symbols and doctrines by means of which the mystic expresses his or her experiences are determined by cultural and theological factors, the realm of being or the ontological reality experienced by mystics of different times and places is one. Descriptions or interpretations of experience may differ, but an underlying similarity can be found which transcends the divergences of religious doctrine or culture. In contrast to this viewpoint, more recent studies have recognised a

number of basic types of mystical experience, claiming that differences can be perceived not only at the level of *interpretation* of the
experience but at the level of the *experience* itself. Some writers have
gone further still and have argued for the recognition of a wide
variety or plurality of types of experience, each of which can only be
understood from within its own cultural context.

I have undertaken elsewhere a full discussion of the philosophical
and methodological questions involved in this issue[68] and do not
propose to repeat this rather technical discussion here. But it is at
least worth adding that in our attempts to unravel the question of
whether different types of mystical experiences are at bottom the
same or not, among our most valuable informants are those mystics
who appear to have undergone both theistic and monistic types of
experience and who go to the trouble to explain what, in their view,
is the relationship between them. Teresa is one such mystic, and so
her testimony regarding her experiments with the recommended
Scholastic forms of contemplation, and how she came to reject these
for her own Christocentric path, is of great interest for studies of
mysticism in general. Other mystics can be mentioned briefly here
who also seem to have known both types of experience. Eckhart
certainly seems to have done so, but in stark contrast to Teresa, he
elevates the monistic way above the theistic. In the Hindu tradition,
we might cite Śankara, discussed later in the present chapter, a
monist who, like Eckhart, affords strictly limited value to theistic
experiences. Rāmakrishna, to give another example, was a
nineteenth-century Bengali mystic who spoke with fervour both of
his devotion to the Goddess Kālī, and of his experience of oneness
with Brahman, the formless, impersonal Absolute. Rāmakrishna
sees the theistic and monistic experiences as two sides of the same
coin, and does not elevate either one to a position of pre-eminence,
but he does not see the nature of the experience of each as identical: they are, we could say, equal but different. In this respect,
Rāmakrishna's teachings represented a new perspective in Hindu
tradition, in which the theistic and monistic streams of thought had
flown parallel to each other down the centuries, often intermingling
but never before being thoroughly synthesised.

But Teresa, as we will remember, tells us that she has experienced
both monistic and theistic experiences, that the two are *not* the
same, and that it is the latter, she believes, which provide the
greatest potential for spiritual growth. (I should perhaps add that, as

a person of monistic persuasions, I do not entirely agree with her here; so these remarks are by no means intended to suggest that I myself believe theism is superior to monism, but simply to illustrate that Teresa believed this.) She tried the recommended Scholastic methods of contemplation in which the humanity of Jesus was to be transcended at a certain stage along the path, and found these wanting. She also, it would seem, continued to have formless experiences in her 'suspension of faculties', which may possibly represent the same *experience* as St John's 'unknowing'. Possibly Teresa's suspension of normal consciousness in which the use of the senses, memory, understanding and other faculties is lost, the soul being absorbed in love of God, is the same essential *experience* as the 'unknowing' in which, for John, the faculties are emptied of all particular ideas or images so that we may rise above them to receive direct knowledge of the Divine in darkness and emptiness. But even if this is the case, Teresa's evaluation of her experiences is nowhere near as positive as St John's estimation of 'unknowing', nor do these experiences play so central a role in Teresa's mystical system as in John's. This is not to say that she considers them unimportant, but she does not strive after them in the same way as does John of the Cross: for him, they are a supreme goal to be attained, for her they come largely unsought and do not shake her belief that the soul needs something to hold onto (as she puts it) in the form of an anthropomorphic deity. Furthermore, Teresa does not interpret her experiences in terms of the intellectual framework of Scholasticism. She breaks with the Dionysian tradition of 'unknowing', the *Via Negativa*, and formless awareness, that has played so important a part in mystical Christianity, forging her own terminology and her own interpretative framework. In all these respects her attitude is the direct reverse of that of Eckhart and John of the Cross.

This should not be taken to imply that there are not also important parallels and similarities between the writings of the various Christian mystics, and indeed, looking beyond the confines of Christianity, between Christian mystics and mystics of other religious traditions. Common to both monistic and theistic mystics are certain basic techniques such as the turning within oneself to find the still centre (called by Teresa 'recollection') and certain methods of meditation following from this; the cultivation of ethical qualities such as detachment, selflessness, compassion, integrity and so on; the belief in our essential unity with spiritual reality (however that reality is conceived); the distinction between the true self or deeper spiritual self or soul, and the empirical personality. Both monistic and theistic forms of mysticism are concerned with a radical change of focus, one's attentions and energies being drawn away from the world of multiplicity and relativity, towards the realm of the eternal and absolute – even where, as is often the case, the latter is found *in* the former, the eternal seen in everyday life. Each is a quest for spiritual illumination in which the ego or limited personality is transcended, giving rise to a realisation of one's true or deeper self and of the essential connection of this self with God or the spiritual Absolute. Through penetration to the still, pure, inmost centre of the self, the mystic uncovers a type of apprehension which is free from the strictures of our usual dualistic, rationalistic thought-patterns and from the disruptive fluctuations of our emotions: a type of apprehension which is a direct, immediate, intuitive awareness, and through which the mystic will come to know divine reality. In discussing similarities between different forms of mysticism one could also point to interesting parallels of mystical symbolism; or to certain common reported components of mystical experiences, such as a sense of oneness and unity, feelings of joy and peace, of paradoxicality or ineffability, and so on.

Yet to acknowledge the existence of these common characteristics is not to negate the fact that it can be helpful to classify mystical experiences into distinct categories for the purposes of a more focused understanding of particular examples of mysticism. Doubtless mystics of most traditions would regard the common characteristics outlined above as true, but as too abstract or incomplete as descriptions of their experiences. For example, Teresa would doubtless agree that at the height of her mystical experience she is united with spiritual reality and has feelings of great joy and peace; yet she would wish to add to this description certain additional points about the nature of this spiritual reality, assertions which would bring us back to the more particular cultural, doctrinal and religious context in which her experiences took shape, and to specifically theistic and Christian claims.

Several scholars in recent years have in fact proposed a threefold categorisation of mysticism in which experiences are subdivided into monistic mysticism, theistic mysticism, and nature-mysticism. (The latter lies outside the scope of the present study, but can be briefly summarised as a revelation of the divine in nature or of

nature as divine, in which sense-perception is heightened so that the
mystic sees inward meaning in every detail of the external world,
and sees the unity, harmony and beauty given it by one indwelling
'life-force'.) In order to set Teresa's mysticism in a broader context it
may be helpful to look briefly at representatives of the monistic and
theistic traditions in India, where similar patterns of mysticism can
be observed.

As an example of the former we choose Śankara, born probably
around CE (AD) 788, a great metaphysician and the major exponent
of Advaita Vedānta, the philosophy of non-dualism. Śankara
acknowledges the value of both theistic and monistic approaches to
the divine, and judging by the various writings attributed to him he
seems to have known both types of mystical experience himself. But
he sees the theistic approach as only a relative truth, a lower teaching; as a necessary means, advantageous at a certain level of spiritual development, but not the highest truth. The personal deity
(*Īśvara* or *saguṇa Brahman*) is seen simply as a symbol for and an
appearance of the higher, formless reality; a symbol and appearance
which must eventually be transcended. The relationship between
the two is not dissimilar to that between God and the One for
Eckhart. The *relative* truth of theism is not denied; as is so common
in mystical teachings, we have here the acceptance of different levels
of truth, each valid on their own plane of reality, but not all carrying
equal weight or ultimacy.

The higher reality for Śankara, the formless Absolute (*nirguṇa
Brahman*) is absolutely non-dual, changeless, eternal, infinite,
indivisible. It is beyond all determination, unable to be categorised
in terms of finite, limited characteristics. But whereas it cannot be
fully described, it can be realised in mystical insight as one with
oneself, for it is found within us as our inmost spiritual essence
(*ātman*). The cornerstone of Śankara's philosophy lies in this belief
that the primal source of the universe (*Brahman*) is identical with the
inner spirit of humanity (*ātman*). But, deluded by ignorance
(*avidyā*), we fail to realise our true nature and mistakenly identify
ourselves with our ego and body, with our desires and sense-
pleasures; thus we become bound to the wheel of *saṁsāra* (birth,
death and rebirth; also denoting the phenomenal world of half-truth
and constant change) and are reincarnated again and again. The aim
of Śankara's mystical discipline is to enable us to rise above our
narrow, fragmentary view of reality; to remove the false, limiting

conditions of our empirical selfhood so that we realise the true Self (*Brahman/ātman*). This entails leaving behind the limitations of rational analysis and also all symbols and forms, to realise our oneness with the All (a transcendental state known as *nirvikalpa samādhi*), without the intermediacy or sense-perception or mental cognition – just as we find in the 'unknowing' of the monistic Christian mystics.[69]

In India, where claims to union with God or personal experience of the divine have not been suppressed by orthodoxy as has sadly been the case in the West, both the theistic and the monistic streams of mystical thought have enjoyed a rich tradition and heritage. The theistic position is well illustrated by the poems of the *bhakti* saints, many of whom afford more than one interesting parallel with Teresa. From the sixth century onwards in India there arose a wave of devotional movements, flowering first in the south and eventually spreading to cover the whole subcontinent. In contrast to the tenor of most earlier Indian spirituality, the religious position of these movements was uncompromisingly theistic, emphasising a sense of separation between the devotee and the Deity, with a corresponding use of romantic and sexual metaphor to express an impassioned longing for union. *Bhakti* (devotion) was directed either to one of the gods Viṣṇu or Śiva or to Devī, the goddess, in one or other of their forms, the devotee beseeching the Deity to break down through his or her grace the wall that separates lover and Beloved. An emphasis on the unworthiness and helplessness of the human soul again presents a contrast to the monistic viewpoint. This helpless wretchedness of the human condition is to be overcome, so the devotee hopes, through his or her ecstatic adoration of and surrender to the Deity, and through the unbounded compassion of the latter. Thus the mystic may come to enjoy a blissful though bittersweet relationship of love with God: bittersweet because it seems that, in this life at least, the bifurcation between the mystic and God can never be *completely* overcome once and for all. These same basic characteristics can be observed in devotional forms of mysticism in the West, although here they may be rather less intensely and passionately expressed. I have discussed the writings of some of the *bhakti* mystics elsewhere, explicating in greater detail than the present work permits some of the parallels between their mystical beliefs and those of Teresa.[70] For the present, it will suffice to illustrate this theme briefly by reference to one of the most celebrated *bhakti* mystics, Mīrā Bāī, a female devotee of Kṛṣṇa who like Teresa lived in the sixteenth century. Her devotion is expressed in the romantic and sensual terms of the 'Mystical Marriage', very similar in tone to the Song of Songs, by which, as we shall see in the next chapter, Teresa was deeply influenced. Interestingly, a number of close parallels of symbolism can be found between her writings and those of Teresa, pointing to what may be a common experience. For example, Mīrā Bāī's image of the fiery arrow of love that pierces the heart shows a remarkable correspondence with Teresa's celebrated 'Transverberation':

> An arrow from the quiver of love
> Has pierced my heart and driven me crazy . . .
>
> Shyām [i.e. Kṛṣṇa] shot an arrow
> That has pierced me through.
> The fire of longing
> Is burning in my heart
> And my whole body is in torment.[71]

The pain and torment created by the mystic's longing for God, the constant awareness of distance or separation felt by the mystic between herself or himself, and the Deity, is characteristic of theistic mysticism in both East and West, and eloquently expressed by both Mīrā Bāī and Teresa. There is an ambivalent emotive tone, then, to this type of mysticism, containing as it does elements both of suffering, and of joy or religious bliss, both agony and loving illumination.

In the final part of this chapter we have looked briefly at Teresa's teachings and experiences in the light of aspects of comparative mysticism, allowing us to gain a broader perspective on these teachings and an appreciation of them in a more global context. Through this we have attempted both to understand Teresa's uniqueness, and also to see what she shares with other mystics. In the next chapter we look at some revealing similarities between aspects of Jewish mysticism and Teresa's writings.

CHAPTER 3

The *Interior Castle* and Jewish Mysticism

The king has brought me into his chambers
(Song of Songs, 1:4)

The history of the Jews in Spain had been bittersweet. They had first settled there hundreds of years before the period with which we are concerned here, when the Christian Church was still newly established, or perhaps even before the advent of Spanish Christianity. They had made contributions of immense worth towards Spanish culture and civilisation, and Judaism itself had undergone important and productive developments in Spain. There seems to have been no anti-Semitism to speak of in the very earliest times of Jewish settlement in Spain, but as soon as the Catholic Church gained supremacy, Jews became subject to oppression and discrimination. There followed centuries of enforced Christianisation, waves of expulsion or voluntary exile of those who refused to convert to Christianity, and the continual intermingling of Jewish and Christian ideas, as outwardly 'converted' Jews clung inwardly to their ancestral religion. Many remained true in their inner conscience and belief to Judaism, and tried to practise Judaism so far as they were able, whilst ostensibly professing Christianity.

The evidence that has come to light in my research shows that Teresa, although regarded until recently as one of the more orthodox of the Christian mystics, in fact absorbed into her writings elements from the Jewish Hekhalot and Kabbalistic mystical traditions (the main characteristics of which, so far as they touch on our theme, will be outlined shortly). There are two main factors pointing to this conclusion, which will be elaborated on below: firstly Teresa's Jewish family origins; secondly the structure of her work the *Interior Castle* and to a lesser extent other aspects of her writings showing Jewish influence. The *Interior Castle* is also of immense value in its own right, as Teresa's most mature work on the mystical life and the one that she herself considered to be her best book. It is the most mystical of her books, the work in which she speaks most authoritatively of her own inner experiences, and discourses on spirituality with a degree of assurance and maturity not found in the *Life*. We will therefore discuss it in depth, pointing out the parallels it affords with Jewish mystical tradition. Thereafter we shall examine more briefly the other aspects of Teresa's works that have a bearing on the question of Jewish mysticism, including her commentary on the Song of Songs, *Conceptions of the Love of God*.

The revisionist view of Teresa to be advanced here is indebted to the new understanding of Spanish history developed over the past few decades, which has emphasised the importance of the coexistence of Christianity, Judaism and Islam in medieval Spain. It is now generally accepted by theologically impartial scholars that Teresa was of Jewish descent and attempted, like the other members of her family, to conceal her family origins. This has been well documented by Egido[1] while Davies[2] offers some additional insights. Teresa's family on her father's side originated in Toledo, a city characterised in the fifteenth century by its large Jewish population and in particular by its large number of *judeoconversos*, Spanish Jews converted to Christianity, who continued to live in the old Jewish quarter of the city and were stigmatised as converts from Judaism just as they had previously been stigmatised as Jews. Teresa's mother may have been from a wealthy rural Jewish background.[3] Teresa's grandfather, Juan Sánchez de Toledo, was a *converso* who, like many others, lapsed back into the secret practice of Judaism. In 1485 he made public confession of this. It was seven years before the final expulsion of the Jews from Spain, when all those who refused to renounce their religion were driven out of the country. It was also the very year that the Spanish Inquisition had moved its headquarters to Toledo and some of the local *conversos* had plotted to revolt and assassinate the Inquisitors. The plot failed and several ringleaders were hanged. In addition it was a 'grace-period' when either Jews or lapsed *conversos* might expect to receive favourable treatment if they admitted heresy and recanted. It will be seen, then, that there were powerful political and practical reasons motivating Juan Sánchez's decision. A statement of the Holy Office of the Inquisition in Toledo records his formal admission of 'heresy and apostasy against our holy Catholic faith'.[4] Like all new or reconciled *conversos*, Juan Sánchez and his three sons (including Teresa's own father, then probably about 10 years old) had to do public penance. Teresa's father's elder brother, in fact, could not reconcile this with his religious conscience: studying in Salamanca at the time, he changed his name, and continued to profess Judaism – all with Juan Sánchez's blessing. The penitents would have had to go in procession on seven successive Fridays to all the churches in Toledo, wearing the *sambenito*. This was a knee-length yellow tunic marked with crosses; bystanders would be sure to throw stones at or spit at anyone they saw wearing it. It was linked in the minds of the people with a similar garment which heretics wore to the stake along with mitre like hats painted with flames and demons.

The humiliation and emotional trauma of this public penance must have played a significant part in Teresa's father's later feelings about Christianity. No doubt these feelings were instrumental in his opposition to her joining a Christian monastic order, for when Teresa took the habit at the Incarnation, she had to do so against her father's will.

Some time later, the family moved to Avila, where they might perhaps succeed in hiding their origins and building a new life. (It has been suggested that Teresa was not in fact born in Avila, though the dominant view still seems to be that she was.) They lived, like the Toledan *conversos*, in what had been the old Jewish quarter of the town. Various members of the family were suspected of reverting to the Jewish faith. Juan Sánchez's brother Sancho came under the attack of the Inquisition; an uncle of Teresa's was condemned to life imprisonment by the Holy Office; and earlier (in 1482) Teresa's great-uncle had had his possessions seized by the Inquisition.

Davies points out that Jewish connections are also evidenced by

various social tendencies found in Teresa's family, matters to do
with family structure, characteristic Jewish callings and trades (Juan
Sánchez, for example, was a merchant dealing in silk and cloth, and
a rent-collector) and so on. He comments that '. . . if we bear in
mind the intense emotions aroused in sixteenth-century Spain by
questions of orthodoxy and heresy, as well as the intense discrimination suffered by those of *converso* origin, we can well understand St Teresa's probable desire to hide at all costs what her own
origins were. . . . It is as though she herself had conspired to reveal
as little of herself as possible – a strange remark to make in view of
her usual and deserved reputation for frankness and sincerity.'[5]
Teresa had to protect not only herself but also her Order and her
family. Particularly when referring to her family and social
acquaintances, she tells well-intentioned 'lies of omission' or is
vague and prevaricating to the point of ambiguity.

Egido discusses in depth the social rift characteristic of the Spain
of Teresa's time between 'Old Christians', as they were known, and
the oppressed descendants of the *conversos*. A concern over genea-
logy and 'purity of blood' (*limpieza de sangre*) had reached obsessive
proportions, and anyone with a drop of Jewish blood in his or her
veins was liable to be excluded from a number of important positions and opportunities in society, and from the majority of religious Orders. *Conversos* were regarded more or less as Jews by the
Inquisition, and were unfairly accused of various evils such as steal-
ing the host, or practising black magic to bring destruction upon the
Inquisitors.[6] The *conversos*, then, had to face hostility, opposition
and enforced social isolation. They were constantly suspected of
reverting to their ancestral faith and practising Judaism in secret
(and one must add that one feels every sympathy with those who
did, denied full participation in a religion to which they had been
forcibly and humiliatingly 'converted'). Before Teresa's lifetime,
large numbers of *conversos* had begun to enter monasteries so as to
be able (they hoped) to practise their Jewish religion in secret in
greater safety. It was as a result of this that many Orders began to
pass regulations not to admit *conversos*. The question of whether
one was genuinely Christian was by this time hardly at issue; the
problem developed strong racist overtones, so that Jewish ancestry
was enough to exclude one from many religious Orders even if the
sincerity of one's own Christian faith was not doubted. Teresa's own
Order, the Discalced Carmelites, did not accept the statutes of

'purity of blood' (which excluded those of Jewish origin) in her lifetime; in fact almost all the nuns admitted to Teresa's first foundation, St Joseph's, were of so-called 'impure blood' (although this would not have been made openly known) and so the theoretical possibility of practising a form of 'Jewish Christianity' remained. Fifteen years after Teresa's death, however, the friars of her Order succumbed to social pressure and excluded from their ranks those of Jewish and also 'Moorish' ancestry.

Egido emphasises that Teresa, as we have already pointed out, had to fight a genuine battle to ensure that her religious reforms were not denounced by the Inquisition; not only because of the secret of her Jewish ancestry, which would have damaged her reputation and that of her reform if it had come to light, but also because female visionaries or contemplatives were looked upon with suspicion. Teresa had to tread her path very carefully, and, it seems, sometimes to rake over her footprints behind herself; given the religious and social climate of Spain at the time, it is surprising that she did not encounter more opposition. The activities of the Inquisition in Spain had by no means ended with the expulsion of the Jews in 1492; following this there had been a steady stream of trials for heresy, leading (for those found guilty) at best to penalties such as confiscation of goods and loss of any public office, at worst to dreadful tortures and executions including death at the stake. The Inquisition laws were modified under Charles I, but from 1559 were strongly reinforced; and as we have remarked, Teresa herself was investigated by the Inquisitors, a subject which is examined in the next chapter. In fact the *Interior Castle*, the book which is the subject of the present chapter, was itself written while Teresa's *Life* was in the confiscation of the Inquisition and while much of the worst of the persecution that she endured was going on. It was suggested to Teresa that, since her *Life* was currently not available as a guide to the religious life for her nuns, she should write a new book on this theme; thus the *Interior Castle* came to be written. It must have taken a great deal of courage on Teresa's part to produce a book so deeply inspired by Jewish mystical tradition at a time when her *Life* was already being held by the Inquisitors. Furthermore, at the time of writing the *Interior Castle* Teresa was also facing many persecutions from the Calced Carmelites (as mentioned in Chapter 1), with her movement being widely condemned and suppressed, and the Inquisition taking more than a passing interest in the further scandals that were circulating.

Egido sees Teresa's writings as revealing her to be a 'victim of the establishment';[7] her expressions of bitterness and her protests against social presuppositions show that she felt herself to be in some measure an 'outcast'. Because of her social vulnerability, her reputation or 'honour' was constantly open to attack. The concept of 'honour' or 'reputation' (*fama, honra*) was of tremendous importance in sixteenth-century Spain and it is difficult for us to appreciate, from the vantage point of modern values, the enormous impact that it had on social values and codes. It was inextricably bound up with questions of lineage and 'purity of blood', and, for women, with sexual purity (by which was meant publicly proven virginity before marriage, fidelity thereafter). In the Castile of Teresa's time, as Egido shows, 'honour' was 'the very soul of social behaviour'.[8] It is significant, then, that in her own religious reform, Teresa opposes the futilities of this often hypocritical worldly 'honour', the niceties of social etiquette and 'respectability', the obsessive concern with outward appearances, to true spiritual worth. Concern for 'honour' and pride in one's lineage had to be sublimated by followers of Teresa's Reformed Rule, which entailed equality before God and sharing of possessions in common. Her principle, from which she never wavered, of attaching more importance to inner virtue than to lineage, may seem unremarkable to us today, but in her time was little short of revolutionary. Teresa's attitude here no doubt springs from ideals that are essentially spiritual, rather than from political considerations, but spiritual ideals are not conceived in a vacuum, and can usually be related to the social conditions of their milieu. Her contempt for the pompous, hollow displays of wealth, the vanities, and the absurd preoccupation with outward shows of 'honour' that often bore no relation to the real moral worth of the individuals in question, shown by the aristocracy of her time with whom she mingled, is no doubt primarily a response to religious impulses; but these impulses are expressed in the terms of reference of a *judeoconversa* fighting for social acceptance and disillusioned with the 'ways of the world'.

Teresa was always silent about her ancestry, although she must have been aware of the suspected 'Judaising' (as it was known) of some of her family members. Her reticence may have been partially because she objected on spiritual grounds to the social preoccupation with matters of lineage, but she also 'kept a more than suspicious silence'[9] on her own part. Gracián himself alluded to her reluctance to speak of her family origins and her sensitivity when questioned on this point, and once remarked that she was remarkably skilled in keeping things hidden but without ever actually lying![10] Teresa's statements about her family in her *Life* are marked, as Davies says, by 'careful selectivity and omissions', as are her references to the *converso* origins of many of her social acquaintances.[11] It should not escape our notice here that among many *converso* families in sixteenth-century Spain it was taught that it was a sin to talk openly about one's ancestry; the importance of guarding the secret of being a *converso* was paramount.[12] After Teresa's death, witnesses reinforced the presupposition of her 'purity of blood' through a suspiciously stereotyped pattern of response to investigations, which falsified the facts by glossing over them; it was left to hagiography to complete the process.[13]

The *judeoconversos* came to practise a form of Jewish-Christian synthesis. It is known that many possessed Jewish prayer books and observed Jewish dietary laws. As Davies points out, conversion to Christianity was not a simple operation in which the nature of one's religious adherence changed overnight. Judaism had '. . . always accepted the need in practice for a false conversion, under whose cover the Jew might go on believing in his own religion, although practising another.'[14] I am not suggesting that this applied to Teresa, who was brought up as a *conversa* (rather than being born a Jew who subsequently turned to Christianity) and who was obviously a devout and sincere Christian. It certainly, however, applied to some members of her family two generations and even one generation before her. But in any case, as Davies suggests, *conversos*, including those whose family conversions went back a full century, '. . . did not simply slough off one skin to reveal another which now represented their new identity. There must have been a continuum between the one identity and the other, and it would be reasonable to assume that the kind of Christians they became was in many cases different from their Old Christian coreligionists.'[15] What we know of Teresa's father suggests that '. . . he remained hedged about by those strict injunctions, and severe prohibitions, that would have characterised a devout Jew . . . [he] carried over into the new religion certain instincts and practices acquired in a different cultural and religious environment. And, of course, he in turn would have created a particular domestic situation that affected his own sons and daughters.'[16] Certainly there was no doubt in the minds of the officers of the Inquisition or of 'Old Christians' in general, that 'Judaising' was going on extensively among even second- or third-generation *conversos*.

Thus the *conversos* developed a particular brand of Christianity characterised by varying degrees of Jewish influence in custom, symbolism, religious attitudes, and so on, and indeed some merely paid lip-service to the new religion. Others turned to the Kabbalah, which, as we shall see, could be more or less reconciled with either Judaism or Christianity, or with a Jewish-Christian synthesis. Religious persecution like that of the Inquisition may be able to eradicate outward, observable religious practices or rituals, destroy synagogues and burn prohibited books; but it cannot change the fundamental inward attitudes of those who still find some worth in their own religious and cultural heritage.

It is not being suggested that all Jews who converted to Christianity did so without any real belief in their new religion. Some conversions must have been genuine. But it is equally certain that political and social conditions provided the impetus for many conversions, which could be seen in that case as a response to intimidation and a desire to escape discrimination.[17] *Conversos* of this latter type tried to bring up their children according to the Jewish way of life, in the hope that one day they would be able to leave Spain and join Jewish communities elsewhere. The memory of past Jewish communities in Spain lived on in their hearts, and the message passed around these *conversos'* circles was to remain faithful to their ancestral religion and to pray for reunion with those Jews who had left Spain rather than 'convert'.[18]

Davies mentions certain aspects of Teresa's general religious attitudes and use of religious phraseology that are characteristically Jewish. For example, she shows a Judaic sense of the division of objects into 'clean' and 'unclean';[19] she expresses the notion of suffering – often apparently connected in her mind with the discrimination encountered by *conversos* – in images familiar to a medieval Jew, images of the bondage of the People of God or of an exile from God's favour.[20] It is clear that the Old Testament – in particular, the Psalms and the Song of Songs – was a source of great inspiration for her; yet she plays down the extent of her literacy, assuming a cultivated naïvety, particularly in references to texts like the Song of

Songs that might be considered dangerous. (Teresa's own commentary on the Song of Songs is discussed later in this chapter.) She chooses her words carefully so as to avoid possible danger, to the extent that in retrospect, or from the vantage point of history, we can say that '. . . she betrays her social origins by her very desire to protect herself against possible charges that could bring her imprisonment, or even help carry her to the stake.'[21] Davies adds that the Carmelite Order to which Teresa belonged, through its direct connection with the Holy Land and Mount Carmel, '. . . epitomized the specifically Judaic element that had gone into the making of the Christian tradition';[22] the Carmelite tradition gave credence to the notion of the historical continuity of Judaism and Christianity and to the belief in Christianity as the fulfilment of the Jewish law. Teresa's Christianity, in other words, notwithstanding her undoubted depth of sincere Christian devotion, is a Jewish Christianity.

Now while Egido and Davies have noted Teresa's Jewish origins, in addition to certain Jewish elements in her phraseology and so on, prior to my earlier article on the subject[23] the Jewish elements in her book the *Interior Castle* had not been noticed. The argument being put forward here is not that Teresa was a member of some secret Jewish Order, but rather that, in the *Interior Castle*, she made use of symbolism drawn from her own cultural background, which naturally suggested itself to her as a means of expression of her mystical experience; she employed images from Jewish mystical tradition that would explain her experiences to other *conversos*. Whether the use of this symbolism was fully thought-out and conscious, or the result of some inspiration coming to Teresa spontaneously from semi-conscious inner depths, we cannot be sure. Diego de Yepes (who was Teresa's Confessor for a brief period while she was writing the *Interior Castle*, and who was also, as it happens, one of Teresa's first biographers) reports in a letter to Luis de León (the first editor of Teresa's works; he will enter our story again later) that the image of the seven-roomed crystal castle which Teresa uses in her book came upon her suddenly in a vision, which would seem to suggest a spontaneous use of symbolism.[24] But Fray Diego's report was written some nine years after the event and we cannot be sure of its accuracy. Moreover, there are hints here and there that Teresa was consciously aware of the significance of the symbolism she was using, of its links with Jewish mystical tradition, which will shortly be outlined. She had already used, briefly and in a more general manner, the image of a King dwelling in a palace, which is the heart, in her earlier *Way of Perfection*.[25] Fray Diego also reports that she made him promise not to repeat to anyone what she had said about her vision of the sevenfold castle during her lifetime. In her own Introduction to the book, Teresa tries to cover herself, as she so often does, by declaring that 'If I should say anything that is not in conformity with what is held by the Holy Roman Catholic Church, it will be through ignorance . . .';[26] and the book as a whole is not marked by any lack of her usual attempts to 'backtrack' and cover up when she thinks she has said too much or is giving something away. Finally, perhaps the most convincing argument of all for the possibility that Teresa was aware of the significance of her seven-roomed castle is shown by the overwhelming number of very close parallels between her book and the Hekhalot/Kabbalistic tradition utilising the imagery of seven palaces or mansions to express religious experience. These parallels will unfold as we proceed; they seem to me to be too precise and specific to arise out of a simple non-reflective tuning in to a symbol buried in the unconscious.

We know that the Kabbalah, a major system of Jewish mysticism and magic, had flourished in Spain for several centuries prior to Teresa's lifetime. We know too that Spanish Kabbalah perpetuated, with modifications, the older Jewish tradition of Merkavah and Hekhalot mysticism. The relevant features of these two mystical traditions need now to be briefly outlined before we proceed.

Merkavah and Hekhalot mysticism seems initially to have developed from speculations on the prophetic visions of the Tanach (Christian Old Testament), such as those portrayed in the books of Ezekiel and Isaiah, and in II Kings where Elijah's ascension to heaven is described.[27] To abstract a typical example, the visionary is taken up to heaven and sees God sitting on a throne, which is supported by a chariot, in a crystal firmament, surrounded by fire, with the Cherubim and the Four Holy Living Creatures nearby. The first full-scale literary presentation of Merkavah ('Chariot') mysticism is in the Hekhalot ('Palaces') literature; the texts that survive date mainly from the third to the tenth centuries. The Hekhalot literature elaborated on the basic elements of Old Testament prophetic vision, using the biblical descriptions of these visions as a kind of blueprint on which the mystic might model his[28] inner strivings. To this basic model the Hekhalot literature also added the notion of a series of seven palaces, or (as they are often called, particularly in the earlier texts) chambers or mansions, often envisaged like a series of concentric circles, or like seven boxes each one inside the next, through which the mystic must travel:

> Many sages maintain that one who possesses all the necessary qualifications has methods through which he can gaze at the *Merkava* and peek into the chambers on high. One must first fast for a certain number of days. He then places his head between his knees, and whispers into the ground many songs and praises known from tradition. From his innermost being and its chambers he will then perceive the Seven Chambers. In his vision, it will be as if he is entering one chamber after another, gazing at what is in each one.[29]

> TVTRVSY'Y YHVH the God of Israel dwells in seven palaces, one inside the other, and at the gate of each palace are eight Keepers of the Threshold, four to the right and four to the left of the lintel.[30]

The surviving Hekhalot texts (some of which are only fragments of what must originally have been much longer treatises) are fairly heterogeneous, but a number of common elements can be isolated. Doors or gates, guarded by angels, are encountered at the entrance to each of the seven chambers, and the initiate needs to know the special means to be applied to pass through them: this usually entails showing magical seals to the angels, who then guide the mystic on to the next chamber. These seals seem to have had magical names, either of angels or of aspects of the godhead, inscribed upon them. Detailed use is also made of prayer, hymns, invocations, repetition of magical names, fasts, special diets, and ritualised procedures for cleansing and purifying the body. The Hekhalot initiates would have hoped to experience a number of distinct, yet interrelated, levels of what we today might call heightened spiritual awareness, corresponding to the seven levels of reality symbolised by the palaces or chambers. From these inner journeys, they hoped to gain visions of the Deity or of the Divine Throne, revelations of mystical and magical lore, insight into cosmological laws, and understanding of the secret key giving knowledge of the esoteric interpretation of the Torah.

Possibly the most important Hekhalot text is the *Hekhalot Rabbati* ('Great Book of the Palaces'), which describes in detail the mystic's progress through the seven chambers and the wonders experienced in each. The gate of the sixth chamber is seen as a particularly challenging test, and a dangerous ordeal for the unprepared: those who are unworthy to penetrate the secrets of the sixth chamber will be attacked by its guardians. The sixth chamber is described in some depth in Hekhalot texts, and in later Zoharic descriptions of the seven palaces (to be discussed shortly) it seems to be of special importance. Vivid descriptions are given of the awesome, even terrifying, visions of the Hekhalot initiates and the psychic dangers and inner trials to which they were believed to be exposed, analogous to the mystical goal, never attainable without a good deal of effort and suffering. The visions of the seventh chamber, too, as one might expect, can be overwhelming in their naked spiritual power. The mystic who is judged worthy of journeying thus far may stand before the Throne of Glory which is borne by the Holy Living Creatures. God descends to the throne three times a day (corresponding to the times of prayer of the Jewish people) and at other times is seen as residing in a transcendent 'eighth heaven', of which little is said since it is above even the greatest heights of mystical vision and cannot be understood or penetrated. (It should be added that the Hekhalot texts are ambivalent regarding identification of the seven palaces with seven heavens; in many cases such a correspondence does not apply.)

In various Hekhalot texts recurrent elements occur in descriptions of the Divine Throne: streams or tongues of fire may flow from it, its supporting chariot may have wheels shining like the sun, it may emanate dazzling light, it may be of crystal. Sometimes certain of the palaces themselves are said to be of crystal[31] or of sapphire-like diamond; we will see a reflection of this in the *Interior Castle*, with its image of a crystal or diamond seven-roomed castle. The height of the Hekhalot spiritual experience is this vision of the Divine Throne, and not, as in most mystical traditions, union with God or absorption into a non-differentiated spiritual Absolute. The mystic and the Deity remain separate; the mystical aspirant is not called to a loving communion with God or to a merging into his being (although these elements became more pronounced in the later Jewish Kabbalistic tradition). Throughout the Hekhalot writings, the Deity is represented as transcendently majestic, glorious, and 'aweful'. Strictly speaking, it would, in fact, be more correct to call the culminating vision of the Hekhalot initiate a 'numinous' rather than a 'mystical' experience, following established usage of these terms, where a mystical experience entails union or oneness with the immanent Divine Being or Principle, and a numinous experience entails a vision of the Divine as transcendent and 'Wholly Other' than the self. Since the Merkavah/Hekhalot tradition is generally referred to as a form of mysticism, we have, however, discussed it under this category. But in most Hekhalot texts it is held that the initiate, far from seeking union with God, cannot *directly* perceive God at all, not through union with God nor even through a direct vision of God as a Being *separate* from himself. He must see God's glory filtered or reflected through some kind of 'mirror' or mediator, such as an angel who speaks on God's behalf. This is vitally connected with the belief that 'No man can see Me and live';[32] in Jewish doctrine God was utterly transcendent and unknowable, and the vision of God face to face was believed by many mystics to be of such shattering intensity that it could not be borne in this life. In fact some Merkavah and Hekhalot writings, far from giving instructions for obtaining a direct vision of God such as we find in the manuals of other mystical traditions, tell the visionary how to avoid this terrifying experience![33]

The later mystical philosophy of the Kabbalah was eventually to crystallise in Safed (Palestine) during Teresa's lifetime, after the formal expulsion of the Jews from Spain. But before this, and after the early Merkavah/Hekhalot tradition, was a formative period for the creative growth of Kabbalah in Spain and Provence, in the twelfth and thirteenth centuries. This Spanish Kabbalah was epitomised in the enigmatic book known as the *Zohar*. This book was first circulated in Spain in the latter years of the decade 1280–90 by Moses de León, who appears also to have compiled the book although possibly not to have been its sole author. The book is written in pseudepigraphic form and purports to describe the teachings of Rabbi Simeon ben Yohai (who lived in Palestine in the second century); this has caused some confusion as to its real authorship, but it is now generally accepted by scholars that the *Zohar* is a thirteenth-century compilation. The exact relationship of the *Zohar* to earlier strata of Jewish mysticism such as the Merkavah/Hekhalot tradition is still debated, but it is clear that the author (or authors) of the *Zohar* draws on a wide range of sources and that the work does refer back to certain material from the earlier stream of Jewish mysticism, which it re-evaluates and reinterprets. This can be seen to be the case, for example, in the Zoharic allusions to the seven

Gold in the Crucible

palaces or mansions found in the portion of the book known as *Hekhalot*; the author of this portion of the *Zohar*, it seems, was familiar with the Hekhalot tradition. What is revealed here is a system that draws (whether directly or indirectly) on the earlier Hekhalot teachings for its essential symbolism, whilst also showing the influence of the developing Kabbalistic tradition. On the whole, a movement away from the theurgic and occult preoccupations of the Merkavah writings is noticeable, with greater emphasis being placed on prayer, meditation, mystical contemplation, and the development of moral and ethical qualities, which are frequently referred to as prerequisites for understanding the secrets of the seven palaces or for surmounting their thresholds. We are told that the prayers of the righteous and sincere person are carried from one palace or mansion to the next by Seraphim until they are taken before the King of Kings and transformed into gems for his crown.[34]

> Who can utter the mighty acts of the Lord, who can show forth all his praise and teach us the mystery and secret of prayer, but Abraham the patriarch sitting now on the right hand of God? He can tell us, he to whom were revealed in raptured vision the glorious mansions of the Great King. Seven are they in number and each with their entrances, through which the prayers of mankind may ascend up to the throne of the Eternal from the lips of those whose souls are in harmony and union with the Lord of the universe, who embraces worlds above and below with his love and regards them as a glorious whole.[35]

As we shall see shortly, to Teresa were also 'revealed in raptured vision the glorious mansions of the Great King'.

In contrast to the goal of the earlier Merkavah initiates, the mere sight of the Divine Throne now comes to be seen as a relatively preliminary attainment; the ideal or ultimate condition sought by the mystic is now a loving union or communion with the Deity, a blending into a harmonious whole of the human and Divine wills, issuing in ecstasy and symbolised by the 'kiss of love' (*nesheqath rakhunutha*). This 'kiss' which unites the soul to God is usually ascribed to the seventh palace, although sometimes to the sixth, since the symbolic attributes of these two final palaces often intermingle, and it seems that the two can hardly be rigidly separated. The *Zohar* calls the seventh palace the 'Palace of Love', situated in the most secret and most elevated part of heaven. There the profoundest mysteries are; there dwells the Heavenly King, blessed be he, with the holy souls, and is united with them by a loving kiss.'[36] The 'kiss' is said in the *Zohar* to be of such intensity that it may draw the soul out of the body of God, and hence may even cause physical death.[37] (The *Zohar* claims that Moses died in this manner.) We have already seen that Teresa speaks of intense ecstatic experiences in which the soul seems to be snatched away from the body and rapt up to communion with the Deity; and we have seen that she characterises these experiences as being traumatic enough to involve danger of death. As we shall also see shortly, Teresa speaks, like the *Zohar*, of the kiss with which the Divine King consummates the Spiritual Marriage in the seventh mansion of her 'interior castle'.

The descriptions, in detail, of each of the seven palaces in the *Zohar* (or sets of seven, for sometimes there are two or three times seven) will not be discussed here as they will not greatly illuminate our theme. Nevertheless, it is worth mentioning that a number of descriptive images migrate from the earlier Merkavah tradition to the Zoharic writings about the palaces. The palaces may be said to be more splendid and effulgent than precious stones, diamonds or gold, or to be set all over with precious stones, or they may be seen as glittering and shining like burnished brass (a ubiquitous metal in the Jewish mystical landscape). Rivers of fire, dazzling light clear as crystal, and glittering flames are also well-represented in this cosmography. The palaces or mansions are each said to have many gates or entrances (the exact number varies greatly); a point which we also find echoed in Teresa's writings, for she speaks of there being many doors and ways of entry into each of the seven mansions of her castle. Each of the doors or gates to the palaces in the *Zohar* has its angelic rulers, as in the earlier tradition, but no direct reference is made to any system of passing through the various gates by means of the use of magical seals and so on. The seven palaces are usually seen in the *Zohar*, as in the *Hekhalot Rabbati*, as being inside each other, the seventh being the most central. The mystical journey is thus a journey inward to the centre, a penetration to the very core of the self, which entails passing through and beyond successive thresholds as progressively deeper layers of truth are uncovered. It culminates in the dazzling vision of the seventh palace or mansion; in the description of this from the *Zohar* given below, the images of Light and of the ever-flowing fountain are particularly reminiscent of Teresa's mystical symbolism:

The seventh mansion is without visible form, being the highest and most mysterious of all, enshrouded by a veil which separates it from all other spheres and mansions. . . . As the chief priest officiates at the altar of sacrifice and the Levites chant, the cloud of incense ascends on high; so is the ascent of spirits to the higher spheres and mansions, until at length they become unified with the light of light, and abide forever, perfected and wholly divine through the power of prayer. It is then that all spirits like lesser lights are blended with the great divine light, and entering within the veil of the Holy of Holies are overwhelmed with blessings proceeding therefrom as water out of an inexhaustible and ever-flowing fountain. In this mansion is the great Mystery of Mysteries, the deepest, most profound and beyond all human comprehension and understanding, the eternal and infinite Will . . . that through all ages to come will ever act until the human and divine wills are blended together in one eternally harmonious whole, and humanity attains to the Higher and Diviner Life. . . . When perfect union prevails, everything is centred in and proceeds from the Divine Thought or Mind. All forms and ideas give place to and disappear in the Divine Mind, that alone animates, vivifies, sustains and enlightens every human soul.[38]

Now although Kabbalah was essentially and in origin a Jewish mystical system, Christians began to adopt it for their own purposes from as early as the thirteenth century. This 'Christian Kabbalah', as it became known, was *not* generally used (as the modern reader might perhaps suppose) to try to establish a fruitful dialogue and increased tolerance between Judaism and Christianity. On the contrary, 'Christian Kabbalah' was based on the presupposition that Christian truth was the only form of truth, and it was decidedly anti-Jewish. It was used by Christian writers to try to prove the supremacy and superiority of Christianity, to persuade Jews to convert to Christianity, and to re-convert *conversos* who had strayed back to Judaism. For the Christian apologists, Kabbalah was 'good' if it was put to the philosophical service of the Christian religion, 'bad' (and identified with dubious magical practices) if it was Jewish. A significant thread running through the arguments of the Christian Kabbalist apologists was the notion that Jesus Christ's teachings were the true fulfilment of the old Jewish law. Quite possibly, this is how Teresa viewed the relationship between Christianity and Judaism, but this does not exclude her also assimilating into her Christianity, elements derived directly from her Jewish family background.

After the expulsion of the Jews from Spain, Kabbalah was perpetuated not only by *conversos*, but also by Christian apologists,
though with obvious differences in the use made of Kabbalistic
doctrines and symbols. On the one hand, Jewish Kabbalah was
perpetuated orally in *converso* households. In many cases it was a
popularised form of Kabbalah that was thus transmitted, a kind of
'folk wisdom', but what might be called the more esoteric aspects of
Zoharic tradition also survived to some extent. Women may have
been important guardians of Kabbalistic 'folk wisdom' in this process of informal but guarded (and to a large extent secret) transmission of teachings within the home. On the other hand, Christian
Kabbalists continued to adapt Jewish mystical symbolism to their
own purposes and to perpetuate a new form of Kabbalah in this
way.

How much did Teresa know of the Zoharic tradition, or of
Kabbalah in general, through either Jewish or Christian sources? On
the one hand, we have seen that she came from a family of *conversos*
and that many members of her family had been suspected of
'Judaising'. She could have learned about Kabbalah and about other
aspects of Jewish culture from family members; this might have been
especially likely if women did indeed play an important role in the
oral handing-down of such teachings. It certainly seems to me that
Teresa's use of the symbolism of the seven-roomed castle must come
from Jewish, not Christian, Kabbalistic sources, for whereas parallel symbolism is found in the Hekhalot and Zoharic writings, such
symbolism was not used (to my knowledge) by any of the Christian
Kabbalist writers, who tended to concentrate on other Kabbalistic
images, notably the 'Tree of the Sefirot', a mystical diagram setting
out the various powers and qualities of the Godhead. Furthermore,
we find in Teresa's thought no evidence of the influence of Neoplatonism or Hermeticism, which were important ingredients of the
Christian Kabbalistic synthesis, as is explained in more detail in
Chapter 4. Teresa's use of Kabbalistic symbolism certainly cannot
be *directly* attributed either to Jewish works in Hebrew or to the
Latin works of the Christian Kabbalists; she could read no Hebrew
and very little Latin. It is possible that she might have learned something of Kabbalistic imagery through her reading of other Spanish
mystics for whom Latin sources were more accessible – or through
her close relationship with John of the Cross, who was also a
converso and who was a Latin scholar; traces of Kabbalistic influence

can also be found in his works. Again, some Jesuits in Spain were involved with Christian Kabbalah and perhaps certain of Teresa's Jesuit confessors might have told her of Kabbalistic images and themes. But while such possible influences coming from Christian Kabbalah might perhaps explain some of Teresa's more broad, general allusions to Kabbalistic ideas, it does not seem to me that her systematic use of the symbol of the inner castle with its seven mansions can be explained in this way.

That Teresa was familiar with at least one scriptural account of the prophetic visions which were later used as a basis for Merkavah speculations, is shown by her passing reference to Elijah's ascension by means of a whirlwind to heaven, accompanied by a fiery chariot.[39] This allusion may in fact be highly significant, because of the special meaning that Elijah had for members of the Carmelite Order. As previously mentioned, the Carmelites saw themselves as the spiritual heirs of this particular prophet. Just as Elijah's ascent to heaven was one of the scriptural episodes on which the early Merkavah mystics concentrated, so Elijah was held in the utmost esteem and reverence not only by Jews in general but by Spanish Kabbalists in particular, who regarded him as guardian and guarantor of Jewish mystical tradition and invoked his authority to give credence to their spiritual realisations. Later, he became the model for the spirituality of the Carmelite Order; a point of which Teresa was of course aware. Was she aware too of his previous importance in Jewish mysticism?

Teresa, furthermore, speaks in her *Life* of a vision of her own very much like those described in the Old Testament and used as a basis for Merkavah mysticism. Previous commentators have assumed that the symbolism in Teresa's vision can be traced to the Book of Revelation (Apocalypse);[40] but it is highly probable that the symbolism of Revelation is itself derived from Merkavah tradition, and Teresa could have derived her use of the symbolism directly from Jewish tradition:

> I thought I saw, not a door into the heavens, as I have seen on other occasions, but the heavens wide open. There was revealed to me the throne which . . . I have seen at other times, and above it another throne, on which (I did not see this, but learned it in a way I cannot explain) was the Godhead. The throne seemed to me to be held up by some beasts; I think I have heard something about these animals – I wondered if they were the Evangelists. But I could not see what the

throne was like, or Who was on it – only a great multitude of angels. . . . I wondered if they were seraphim or cherubim, for . . . they seemed to be all on fire. . . . the glory which I felt within me at that time cannot be expressed.[41]

More precise and thought-provoking correspondences with Jewish mysticism can, however, be found in the *Interior Castle*, as we shall see, a work which shows parallels to the Merkavah-Hekhalot-Zoharic traditions, not only in its general overall structure, but also in the use of certain specific symbols and images employed by Teresa, and in her descriptions of certain phases of the spiritual journey. It may be informative in this connection to note that when Teresa began work on the *Interior Castle* she was in Toledo, where she had been staying for nearly a year; we might speculate that perhaps she had been in contact during this time with other *conversos* or with distant relatives of her own. We have already remarked on the atmosphere of persecution and of trouble with the Inquisition in the midst of which the *Interior Castle* was written. Teresa had previously suffered great difficulties in Toledo in 1569–70, over the establishment there of the house of her Reform in which she later stayed while writing the *Interior Castle*. The issue of conflict between *conversos* and 'Old Christians' was a significant undertone in these problems, discrimination against *conversos* apparently being particularly invidious in Toledo at this time.[42] Teresa began to write the *Interior Castle* in 1577, and one wonders whether the Jewish influence to be detected in the book might have some connection with remembered bitterness, which would naturally be recalled to Teresa's mind by her staying in her convent at Toledo again.

But it is not necessary to make too much of the Toledan episode. Avila, too, had had its share of contact with Jewish culture prior to the expulsion of the Jews. The *Zohar* originated in Castile and was circulated in part from Avila by Moses de León. It seems that he compiled (or wrote) the work while living in Guadalajara (northeast of Madrid) and circulated the first sections of the book from here. Later he moved to Avila and spent the remaining years of his life in Avila and Arévalo, a village outside the city. From Avila he circulated further sections and copies of the *Zohar*. The area in general became a stronghold of Zoharic Kabbalah, and in later centuries it seems likely that the *converso* families of the district continued to nourish Zoharic traditions. The *Zohar* would still have been known of in Toledo or Avila in Teresa's time, although copies of the book would certainly not have been available – if at all – without the acquisitor exposing himself or herself to a great deal of danger. It is likely, then, that Teresa had heard speak of the *Zohar* and its themes and symbolism. It is impossible, however, that she had actually read the book; even if secret copies were in circulation during her lifetime (which is not known to have been the case), it was written in a form of Aramaic which Teresa certainly could not have read, and although some partial Hebrew translations existed by this time, it had not been translated into Spanish. Furthermore, the traditional prohibition in Judaism against women studying the Scriptures would probably have been carried over into *converso* culture. The circumstances surrounding the appearance and circulation of the various portions of the *Zohar* are not, in fact, known in detail. Rather than having been originally conceived as a single self-contained work, it is a collection of sections united under an all-embracing title. We know that Moses de León first circulated parts of the book – including the 'Hekhalot' portions – nearly three centuries before Teresa lived. But, Scholem points out, 'Complete, well-ordered manuscripts did not circulate, and it is doubtful whether they ever existed. Mystics who took an interest in the Zohar made up anthologies for themselves from the texts they were able to procure; hence the great difficulties in the contents of the early manuscripts.' In the fourteenth century, certain portions were translated into Hebrew; in the fifteenth century some manuscripts containing most of the portions were compiled, but they still omitted certain sections. In the sixteenth century, the French mystic Guillaume Postel (1510–1581) made a Latin translation of certain portions, and shortly afterwards the first printed Latin editions appeared in Italy (1558–60), but it seems unlikely that Teresa would have come across the *Zohar* by this route (and even if she had, she was herself, as we have said, unable to read Latin to any degree). It is significant that, as Scholem points out, the elevation of the *Zohar* to a position of supreme sanctity and importance among the Jews in Safed, Italy and elsewhere '. . . came during and after the period of the expulsion from Spain, and it reached its peak in the 16th and 17th centuries.'[43] So far, however, the status of the *Zohar* in these centuries in the lives of those *conversos* who remained in Spain after the expulsion of the Jews, has only just begun to be documented.

It seems, then, that the correspondences about to be outlined between the Hekhalot portion of the *Zohar* (and the earlier Merkavah mysticism), and the *Interior Castle*, should be traced to the perpetuation of Jewish religious heritage in Spain after the expulsion, a phenomenon which has begun to be documented in recent works. For example, Kottman has argued that Luis de León (1527?–1591), a *converso*, and the first editor of Teresa's works, was strongly influenced by Pico della Mirandola, an Italian Kabbalist and Neoplatonist, and that his commentary on the Song of Songs (which, as we shall see later, Teresa read) is based on the *Zohar*.[44] Swietlicki, likewise, utilising the material brought to light in my earlier article, attempts to show the influence of Kabbalah on Teresa, Luis de León and John of the Cross.[45]

In the *Interior Castle* the determining image, seen by Teresa in vision, is a beautiful crystal or diamond castle, symbolising the soul, with seven mansions *(moradas)*, each with many chambers *(aposentos)*. Teresa did not give the work a formal title and the book is in fact known in Spanish as *Las Moradas* – 'The Mansions' – which seems to highlight its connection with the Hekhalot tradition, which as we have seen speaks of seven mansions, palaces or chambers. The word *moradas* in the Spanish title is taken from the heading of each of the seven main sections of the book. The title *Interior Castle* (*castillo interior*) is taken from a note written by Teresa on the back of the first page of the manuscript. The book is an account of the mystical journey, which Teresa here subdivides into seven stages, as she progresses from the first to the seventh mansions, where she is finally united in Spiritual Marriage with the King of Glory, as we will discuss in more depth shortly. The castle and the palace are often interchangeable symbolically, and indeed Teresa does refer to the castle or to its innermost seventh mansion as a 'palace' on occasion. To begin with, then, we have the same structure of the mystical sevenfold castle/palace/chambers in the *Interior Castle* as in the Hekhalot and Zoharic traditions. Teresa's seven mansions are not only divisions of the castle but divisions of the book; as sections of the book they are further subdivided into chapters, but her initial intention when writing the book was to divide it only into seven 'mansions' without further subdivision.[46] Interestingly enough, Teresa not only divides the *Interior Castle* into seven main sections, she also subdivides her commentary on the Song of Songs, which shows strong Judaic influence, into seven chapters; a way of arranging material which can be

observed in certain Jewish texts such as *Sefer Ha-Razim*, an early
Jewish manual of magic connected with Merkavah mysticism, in
which the seven chapters correspond to seven heavens.

Teresa begins by describing the great beauty that we may discover
in our souls if we understand our true nature and our relationship to
the Divine. But most of us are ignorant of our innate capacity for
spiritual understanding, for 'All our interest is centred in the rough
setting of the diamond, and in the outer wall of the castle – that is to
say, in these bodies of ours.' The outer wall of the castle, then,
represents the physical body; the innermost seventh mansion is the
centre of the soul and the inner temple 'where the most secret things
pass between God and the soul'.[47] The King of Glory dwells in this
central seventh mansion, illuminating and beautifying all the other
mansions by his presence; the nearer one gets to the centre of the
castle, the stronger is the light. Likewise, in Zoharic writings, there
is increasing brightness and light as one penetrates to the seventh
palace, which also sheds its light on the other palaces.[48] In Hekhalot
texts the King, when not in the inaccessible eighth heaven, sits on his
throne in the seventh palace; in *Hekhalot Rabbati* he is called
Zoharariel, 'God of the Shining Light', and another text, *Masekhet
Hekhalot*, describes the effulgent light which emanates from the
throne.[49] Teresa sometimes uses the image of the sun to represent the
God within us at the centre of the soul; thus she augments this image
of divine light, the sunlight penetrating to every corner of the castle.
The representation of God by means of the symbol of light is central
to the *Zohar*; however, it is also widespread in the mystical traditions of most other cultures, so little can be made of this in itself. But
the image of effulgent light at the centre, shining out with decreasing
intensity over a series of seven palaces or mansions, is more specific
and may well be taken as further evidence for the influence of Jewish
tradition on Teresa.

'Now let us return', Teresa continues, 'to our beautiful and
delightful castle and see how we can enter it. I seem rather to be
talking nonsense; for, if this castle is the soul, there can clearly be no
question of our entering it. For we ourselves are the castle: and it
would be absurd to tell someone to enter a room when he was in it
already! But you must understand that there are many ways of
"being" in a place. Many souls remain in the outer court of the castle,
which is the place occupied by the guards; they are not interested in
entering it, and have no idea what there is in that wonderful place,

or who dwells in it, or even how many rooms it has.'[50] Many people, then, have lost the ability to enter within themselves; they have grown accustomed to living in the outer court, where there are many venomous beasts such as toads, vipers and other reptiles; the atmosphere here is foul and dark. Even if these dwellers in the outer court do occasionally manage to enter the first rooms of the castle on the lowest floor, so many reptiles get in with them that they are unable to appreciate the beauty of the castle. The venomous beasts represent aspects of our baser selves that we have to overcome; what Evelyn Underhill, in a commentary on Teresa, calls 'our inclinations to selfish choices, inordinate enjoyments, claimful affection, self-centred worry, instinctive avoidance of sacrifice and pain'.[51] The main focus of the teachings of Teresa's first 'mansion' is on the importance of self-knowledge, which is always held to be of supreme importance in mystical writings. We must enter within ourselves so as to begin to uncover our real natures; and the means of setting out along this road, 'the door of entry into this castle',[52] is prayer and meditation, as we have seen.

Teresa goes on to point out that the mansions of her castle should be imagined as being inside each other:

> You must not imagine these mansions as arranged in a row, one behind another, but fix your attention on the centre, the room or palace occupied by the King. Think of a palmito, which has many outer rinds surrounding the savoury part within, all of which must be taken away before the centre can be eaten. Just so around this central room are many more, as there also are above it. In speaking of the soul we must always think of it as spacious, ample and lofty; and this can be done without the least exaggeration, for the soul's capacity is much greater than we can realise, and this Sun, which is in the palace, reaches every part of it. It is very important that no soul which practises prayer, whether little or much, should be subjected to undue constraint or limitation. Since God has given it such dignity, it must be allowed to roam through these mansions – through those above, those below and those on either side. It must not be compelled to remain for a long time in one single room – not, at least, unless it is in the room of self-knowledge.[53]

We have already seen that in Hekhalot and Zoharic tradition the seven palaces are said to be inside each other, and this is one of the most striking parallels between Teresa's book and the earlier Jewish tradition. Teresa's adjunction that the soul must be allowed to explore all the rooms of the castle denotes that we must come to know and understand every single aspect of ourselves, and that, as Underhill puts it, 'We are required to live in the whole of our house, learning to go freely and constantly up and down stairs, backwards and forwards, easily and willingly, from one kind of life to the other; weaving together the higher and lower powers of the soul, and using both for the glory of God.'[54] One wonders exactly what Teresa has in mind by the notion of the mansions 'above, below and on either side'; perhaps she is thinking of series of two or three times seven mansions such as are described in some Zoharic writings. On the other hand, she may have in mind the many rooms (*aposentos*) of each of the mansions. From her references to the structure of the castle scattered throughout the book, it would appear that she does not see the mansions in terms of a two-dimensional figure (such as might be represented by a diagram of concentric circles); rather, she conflates images of depth (inwardness) and of height, so that one simultaneously penetrates deeper into the centre of the castle, and ascends to its upper rooms and turrets. Like so many meditative images, it seems to me, the castle has a certain fluidity, so that it can be visualised in different ways according to context.[55] But however we see the castle, we must enter by the first mansion, by the room of humility and self-knowledge; 'although this is only the first Mansion, it contains riches of great price, and any who can elude the reptiles which are to be found in it will not fail to go further.'[56] Teresa stresses again and again that we must enter by the door of humility, building our inner life on firm foundations, and must not try to take this citadel of the soul by storm.

Like the Hekhalot mystics, Teresa warns us of the dangers involved in crossing thresholds from one mansion to another, where, she says, the devil has legions of evil spirits stationed to try to circumvent our journey.[57] It is possible to see a limited measure of correlation between these evil spirits, and the gatekeeper-guardians of the chambers in Hekhalot mysticism, although these latter guardians are angelic, and not seen as evil. They simply try to prevent the mystic from penetrating to depths of spiritual reality which he or she is not ready or worthy to experience, acting, so to speak, as a kind of spiritual safety-valve. (It is, however, worth adding in passing that in Gnosticism, which may well have influenced the Hekhalot tradition, we find a similar system of a mystical ascent through seven

spheres or planetary heavens, each of which is guarded by a
malevolent being called an Archon, perhaps showing greater similarity to one of Teresa's evil spirits; the Archons try to prevent the
mystic's passage through the spheres.) For Teresa, at any rate, the
devil and his legions of evil spirits are less successful in barring the
passage of those more advanced mystics who are nearer the King's
chamber; but at this early stage, in the first mansion, we are more
liable to weakness and deception:

> You must note that the light which comes from the palace occupied
> by the King hardly reaches these first Mansions at all; for, although
> they are not dark and black, as when the soul is in a state of sin, they
> are to some extent darkened, so that they cannot be seen (I mean by
> anyone who is in them); and this not because of anything that is
> wrong with the room, but rather (I hardly know how to explain
> myself) because there are so many bad things – snakes and vipers and
> poisonous creatures – which have come in with the soul that they
> prevent it from seeing the light. It is as if one were to enter a place
> flooded by sunlight with his eyes so full of dust that he could hardly
> open them. The room itself is light enough, but he cannot enjoy the
> light because he is prevented from doing so by these wild beasts and
> animals, which force him to close his eyes to everything but them-
> selves. This seems to me to be the condition of a soul which, though
> not in a bad state, is so completely absorbed in things of the world
> and so deeply immersed, as I have said, in possessions or honours or
> business, that, although as a matter of fact it would like to gaze at the
> castle and enjoy its beauty, it is prevented from doing so, and seems
> quite unable to free itself from all these impediments. Everyone,
> however, who wishes to enter the second Mansions, will be well
> advised, as far as his state of life permits, to try to put aside all
> unnecessary affairs and business. For those who hope to reach the
> principal Mansion, this is so important that unless they begin in this
> way I do not believe they will ever be able to get there. Nor, indeed,
> even though it has entered the castle, is the soul free from great peril in
> the Mansion which it actually inhabits; for, being among such poi-
> sonous things, it cannot, at some time or another, escape being bitten
> by them. . . . Remember that in few of the mansions of this castle are
> we free from struggles with devils. It is true that in some of them, the
> wardens, who, as I think I said, are the faculties, have strength for the
> fight; but it is most important that we should not cease to be watchful
> against the devil's wiles, lest he deceive us in the guise of an angel of
> light. For there are a multitude of ways in which he can deceive us,

and gradually make his way into the castle, and until he is actually
there we do not realise it.[58]

Teresa often reminds us, throughout her book, that we have to be
constantly alert for the enemies at our gate who may try to breach
the fortress at some weak spot, and for the venomous beasts who
may try to reassail us.

In the second mansion, we have gained greater understanding and
spiritual awareness, but we also have to endure many severe trials
and inner conflicts. In the third, still more progress has been made in
the spiritual life, but we continue to undergo periods of inner aridity
or barrenness, along with trying experiences and worries. The first
to third mansions are generally taken to correspond to Teresa's first
degree of prayer, the stage of beginners, and to the beginnings of
Recollection. We have already discussed these in Chapter 2, and
Teresa's descriptions of the second and third mansions will not add
anything to our discussion of the parallels between the *Interior
Castle* and the earlier Jewish writings, so we shall pass on to the
fourth mansion. This is generally taken to correspond to the Prayer
of Quiet and heralds the beginning of what Teresa calls 'supernatural' mystical experience, that is, experience that is unattainable
by human effort alone, that goes beyond the bounds of normal
human understanding, and which, it is held, is brought about by the
grace of God. It is to a large degree ineffable, other than to those
who have themselves experienced it:

> As these Mansions are now getting near to the place where the King
> dwells, they are of great beauty and there are such exquisite things to
> be seen and appreciated in them that the understanding is incapable
> of describing them in any way accurately without being completely
> obscure to those devoid of experience. But any experienced person
> will understand quite well, especially if his experience has been con-
> siderable. It seems that, in order to reach these Mansions, one must
> have lived for a long time in the others; as a rule one must have been
> in those which we have just described, but there is no infallible rule
> about it.[59]

The mystic begins to experience a state of absorption in God,
which, since it is different from the operations of discursive reason,
can at first cause some confusion for those who are accustomed to
assess the merits of their state of awareness by exclusively rationa-

listic means, neglecting the messages of their feeling and intuition. They 'fail to realize that there is an interior world close at hand' and that 'the soul may perhaps be wholly united with [God] in the Mansions very near His presence, while thought remains in the outskirts of the castle, suffering the assaults of a thousand wild and venomous creatures.'[60] Great interior trials can develop at this time. We have to learn to withdraw into the castle of our inner self so as to rise above the strictures of excessive rationalism; we must resign ourselves to God's will, in order that we may begin to uncover the hidden treasure which lies within ourselves, or hear the truths which are beginning to be communicated to us in our soul's depths. By now, we should be sure of our direction, although we know that there is still a great distance to travel.

The fifth and ensuing mansions are still more difficult to describe: 'Oh, sisters!', exclaims Teresa to her nuns, 'How shall I ever be able to tell you of the riches and the treasures and the delights which are to be found in the fifth Mansions? I think it would be better if I were to say nothing of the Mansions I have not yet treated, for no one can describe them, the understanding is unable to comprehend them and no comparisons will avail to explain them, for earthly things are quite insufficient for this purpose.'[61] The essential experience of this mansion, though, is the Prayer of Union and the beginnings of the death/rebirth experience of which we have already spoken in the last chapter: the 'dying' to the limited self or lower personality in order to be reborn into the wider life of the spirit. It is in this mansion, too, that we may begin to experience the 'suspension of faculties'. The soul, says Teresa, '. . . has completely died to the world so that it may live more fully in God. This is a delectable death, a snatching of the soul from all the activities which it can perform while it is in the body; a death full of delight.'[62] One feels a stranger to the things of the earth; one can find no resting-place in this world. And the inner transformation, the dying to oneself which the mystic must undergo at this stage necessitates great renunciation, and learning to live with that paradoxical bittersweet pain which is also joy of which we have spoken in the previous chapter.

We have seen that in the Hekhalot and Zoharic writings the sixth palace is of great importance and is described in depth. In the *Zohar* it is said to contain the quintessence of all that is to be found in the other six palaces. Interestingly, Teresa assigns a disproportionate amount of the total length of her book to her description of the sixth mansion. The length of the sixth division of the *Interior Castle* is radically out of proportion with the rest of the book, being three times the length of the second longest sections (which describe the fifth and seventh mansions), and ten times the length of the description given to the second mansion. In the Hekhalot tradition, as we have seen, the gate of the sixth palace is a perilous threshold, entailing spiritual and psychic ordeals which, if not surmounted, could result in extreme danger, even the danger of physical death. Likewise, Teresa speaks of great trials and deep sufferings in the sixth mansion, which is seen as a major threshold reached after the mystical death and rebirth in the fifth. As we have seen, she also holds that these sufferings and tests by which God prepares the soul for the Spiritual Marriage, particularly the 'Wound of Love', may be so intense that they actually involve peril of death. Both in the Hekhalot texts and in Teresa's symbolic scheme, the castle or palaces can be seen as an image of a mystical goal which is not attainable without a great deal of effort. The inner mansions are a well-defended area into which it is difficult to penetrate; those who are unworthy or unready cannot reach the central rooms. The descriptions of the terrifying visions of the Hekhalot initiates, and of the heart-rending trials suffered by Teresa, can be seen as reflections of this. In this sense at least we are dealing here with 'esoteric' forms of mysticism, whose experiences, although (in Teresa's case at least) *potentially* available to all, cannot be attained in *practice* by the unprepared.

The experiences of the mystic in the sixth mansion are indeed extremely complex and intense. The soul has been wounded with love and has an awareness of God's imminent presence and an almost unbearable longing that he may manifest himself more fully to the conscious awareness; yet at the same time there is an acute sense of separation from the Divine. Thus, while there is increased illumination in this mansion, it takes the form of an awareness of an incomprehensible beauty or joy which the understanding cannot fathom and which always seems to be just out of reach. The mystic's awareness of her or his own iniquities, coupled with great yearning for the revelation of the divine reality which is sensed just around the corner, as it were, produces ever greater inner conflict.

In the sixth mansion, moreover, the mystic may experience frequent visions, and ecstatic or rapturous states. Teresa expresses the ineffable nature of these experiences by saying that the Heavenly Spouse, who is in the seventh mansion, orders the doors of all the mansions to be shut, and even those of the castle and its enclosure; all, that is, except for the door to the seventh mansion where he dwells. In other words, the faculties and senses, represented here by the outer mansions, are temporarily dissociated from the centre of the soul, or are in an entirely inactive state (the 'suspension of faculties'), so that the experiences in question cannot be explained rationally or in terms of our everyday modes of perception. Thus, the mystic may not always be able to fathom what is in the sixth mansion, and even if she or he is granted a glimpse of it, it may be extremely difficult to recall it to memory or represent it to the understanding. But at other times, Teresa says, we may have a sudden vision of what is in these rooms, a glorious revelation which engraves itself deeply on the imagination and memory and yet which is terrible in its intensity and majesty, so that we cannot look on it continually. The soul in its unworthiness '. . . cannot endure so terrible a sight. I say "terrible", because, though the sight is the loveliest and most delightful imaginable, even by a person who lived and strove to imagine it for a thousand years, because it so far exceeds all that our imagination and understanding can compass, its presence is of such exceeding majesty that it fills the soul with a great terror.'[63] Teresa's expressions of awe here are not at all unlike the Jewish doctrine that one cannot see God face to face and survive the experience, which has been mentioned in connection with Hekhalot mysticism; the mystical vision is awesome, terrible in its numinosity, rather like the searing spiritual power of the eyes of the angels at the entrance to the seventh chamber in *Hekhalot Rabbati*: each of these angels has 256 faces and therefore 512 eyes, which gaze at the initiate on the threshold with a glance like a flash of lightning, causing him to tremble, feel faint and fall backwards.[64] There are many other similar instances in Kabbalistic and Zoharic tradition of the mystical vision being of such dazzling splendour that it cannot be borne.

We have observed that in Jewish tradition, the symbolic descriptions of the sixth and seventh palaces often seem to mingle into each other, and Teresa also holds that the sixth and seventh mansions cannot be rigidly separated: they 'might be fused in one: there is no closed door to separate the one from the other.'[65] But in the seventh mansion, which represents the Spiritual Marriage, many things are revealed from which we were previously blinded. In the previous mansion, we were conscious of our realisation of God to a high degree, but we understood nothing; now we are illumined with a wonderful knowledge of God and live in constant awareness of his presence 'in the interior of [our] heart – in the most interior place of all and in its greatest depths.' The 'shutters of the understanding' are opened.[66] Teresa says that the King brings us into his own dwelling-place in the soul, his own seventh mansion or chamber, to consummate the Spiritual Marriage: an exact parallel is found with Jewish tradition. Teresa's Spiritual Marriage too is consummated with a kiss which unites the soul to God, just as in the *Zohar* the mystic's union with God is marked by the 'kiss of love'. It is interesting that Teresa, immediately after speaking of this kiss, employs (whether consciously or unconsciously) a plethora of Jewish imagery in describing the inner peace finally found by the soul: 'Here to this wounded hart are given waters in abundance. Here the soul delights in the tabernacle of God. Here the dove sent out by Noe to see if the storm is over finds the olive-branch – the sign that it has discovered firm ground amidst the waters and storms of this world.'[67]

As these preceding words also indicate, Teresa's seventh mansion is the still, quiet, unmoving centre of the soul, the abode of the King, which remains tranquil and at peace beneath the fluctuations of external action, thought and feeling. 'A king is living in his palace,' she says; 'Many wars are waged in his kingdom and other distressing things happen there, but he remains where he is despite them all.'[68] That is, when we are truly at one with ourselves, balanced and centred in the innermost chamber, even though our battles go on, we can retain tranquillity and peace. The innermost mansion, the place where the kiss of union is bestowed, is also compared by Teresa (in another passing reference to Jewish esotericism) to Solomon's Temple and to the 'wine-cellar' or 'banqueting-house' of the Song of Songs.

The Spiritual Marriage, then, takes place in the deepest centre of the soul and gives the mystic a direct perception of God through being made one with him. Teresa expresses this experience of direct perception, in which one's apprehension of God no longer needs to be channelled through the senses, rational mentality, or imagination, by saying that there is no need of a 'door' by which to enter the centre of the soul where God dwells:

I say there is no need of a door because all that has so far been described [i.e. in previous mansions] seems to have come through the medium of the senses and faculties. . . . But what passes in the union of the Spiritual Marriage is very different. The Lord appears in the centre of the soul . . . just as he appeared to the Apostles, without entering through the door.[69]

Teresa concludes her description of the seventh mansion by emphasising that our castle of the soul must be built on firm ground: 'We must not build towers without foundations'.[70] Or as Underhill observes, the ground floor of the soul's house must be put in decent order before we go upstairs: 'The disciplined use of the lower floor and all the rich material it offers is . . . essential to the peace and prosperity of the upper floor; we cannot merely shut the door at the top of the basement stairs and hope for the best.'[71] The foundation of the whole edifice, for Teresa, is humility, together with prayer, contemplation, and virtue; if we do not cultivate humility, our castle will not reach any great height; if it did, it would soon fall to the ground again.

Finally, Teresa reiterates that each one of us is a microcosm corresponding to and mirroring the macrocosm of the heavens. The soul is like 'an interior world [*mundo interior*], wherein are the many and beauteous Mansions that you have seen';[72] the experience of the inner castle, then, is potentially open to us all. The notion of the human being as microcosm reflecting the macrocosmic divine world was a basic Kabbalistic belief. In the *Zohar*, detailed homologies and correspondences are drawn between the human body and soul and the divine world; everything 'below' has its counterpart 'above'. Renaissance Christian Kabbalah adopted this belief in the parallels and correspondences between the human world and the heavenly realm.

Teresa concludes her masterpiece with this advice, at once homely and mystical, practical and transcendental, for her nuns:

. . . considering how strictly you are cloistered, my sisters . . . I think it will be a great consolation for you, in some of your convents, to take your delight in this Interior Castle, for you can enter it and walk about in it at any time without asking leave from your superiors. It is true that, however strong you may think yourselves, you cannot enter all the Mansions by your own efforts: the Lord of the Castle Himself must admit you to them. So, if you meet with any resistance,

I advise you not to make any effort to get in. . . . If you consider
yourselves unworthy of entering even the third Mansion, He will
more quickly give you the will to reach the fifth, and thenceforward
you may serve Him by going to these Mansions again and again, till
He brings you into the Mansion which He reserves as His own and
which you will never leave, except when you are called away by the
prioress, whose wishes this great Lord is pleased that you should
observe as if they were His own. And even if, at her command, you
are often outside these Mansions, He will always keep the door open
against your return. Once you have been shown how to enjoy this
Castle, you will find rest in everything, even in the things which most
try you, and you will cherish a hope of returning to it which nobody
can take from you.[73]

To sum up our argument so far, then, in both the *Interior Castle*
and the Hekhalot/Zoharic traditions we find the image of a crystal
or diamond castle with seven mansions, or a group of seven crystal
palaces, mansions or chambers, all inside each other, each with
many doors or entrances; at the centre dwells the King, from whom
shines forth an effulgent light illuminating the other mansions. The
mystic's journey is one of progression from the circumference to the
centre, surmounting many obstacles along the way, until in the
innermost chamber she or he is united with the King, sealing the
union with a kiss which is so perilous as to involve danger of death.
Other correspondences have also been pointed out regarding, for
example, the ordeal of the threshold of the sixth chamber and the
awesome visions of the seventh.

It is true that sources other than the Hekhalot/Zoharic mystical
tradition have been posited as the origin of Teresa's castle symbolism. For example, it has been pointed out that Francisco de Osuna,
the writer of the *Third Spiritual Alphabet* which influenced Teresa
so greatly in her earlier years, speaks briefly in passing of guarding
the heart as if it were a castle, and of God dwelling within this castle,
which is at the same time a paradise. Crucially, however, Francisco
de Osuna does not associate his castle with sevenfold symbolism in
any way. John of the Cross uses imagery of seven wine-cellars of
love, into the innermost of which the mystic must penetrate, which
some posit as a possible source of influence; but as we shall see in the
next chapter, John was himself influenced by Jewish mysticism,
being a *converso* like Teresa. Other sources that have been proposed
as the origin of the sevenfold castle are as varied as the novels of

chivalry, the architecture of the city of Avila, and Sufi mysticism.[74] With the exception of the final possibility, however, none of these proposed origins of Teresa's symbol explains why Teresa chose *both* to use the image of a castle or palace *and* to organise its contents according to a septenary system of classification. Sufi mysticism does at least offer a parallel to the coexistence of these two aspects of Teresa's symbolism, for it is true that the image of the sevenfold concentric castle of the soul is found in certain Sufi writings. Given, however, that the fact of Teresa's Jewish ancestry is no longer seriously questioned, and that other members of her family had been upbraided by the Inquisition for clinging to aspects of their Jewish heritage, and given that it is not clear how Teresa could have come into contact with Sufi imagery, it seems far more plausible to argue that Teresa's sevenfold castle is derived from Jewish, not Islamic, sources. Furthermore, as we shall now show, this hypothesis is strengthened by the existence of other Jewish elements in the *Interior Castle*, and in others of Teresa's works.

We have already pointed out some of the instances of Judaic symbolism in the *Interior Castle* that are logically independent of its central image of the seven-roomed castle: the seventh mansion is compared to Solomon's Temple; having attained the Spiritual Marriage, the mystic is likened to a wounded hart given water in abundance, to one who delights in the tabernacle of God, to the dove sent out by Noah. To these we may add that Teresa sees the soul as a Tree of Life, planted in the living waters of life, or as an ever-flowing fountain; and that she refers to Jacob's Ladder, Moses' burning bush, and the parting of the Red Sea in connection with the revelation of mysteries and God's greatness.[75] These are all images which are frequently employed and commented upon in Jewish Kabbalistic works. Her liking for symbolism of fountains and wells, and of basins and conduits to be filled with water, is rather reminiscent of certain images in the *Zohar*.[76] It is also possible to argue that Teresa's symbol of the mirror found in her *Life* is derived from Zoharic mystical tradition. As we have seen in Chapter 2, she speaks in her *Life* of a vision in which her soul seems to become like a bright mirror in which Jesus Christ can be seen. When a soul is in mortal sin this mirror becomes dark and misty so that Jesus cannot be seen in it. In Jewish mystical tradition distinctions are drawn between the dull, dark or non-luminous mirror, representing 'lower' or more everyday forms of awareness, and the luminous mirror of higher mystical

insight or direct vision of the divine. It is said, for example, that
Moses saw through a luminous mirror, while all the other prophets
and patriarchs saw through a dull mirror. The *Zohar* speaks of the
righteous seeing God 'face to face' in the luminous mirror after
death, and holds that the mystic can perceive things either in the
luminous or non-luminous glass, depending on the technique used.
The dull and luminous mirrors came to be identified with certain of
the sefirot of the 'Tree' which represented for the Kabbalists the
emanations of the Godhead and their corresponding qualities in
humanity and in creation.[77] It might be added too that Teresa's very
method of interweaving different symbol-systems is highly reminiscent of the *Zohar*, and of Jewish esoteric writings in general, in
which interrelated symbol-systems and mixed metaphors abound.
An initial image such as that of the sevenfold castle is related by
Teresa to new and diverting symbols, different though inter-
connecting metaphors; the soul is now a castle, now a Tree of Life.

In addition, Teresa puts forward a number of interpretations of
Scripture in the *Interior Castle* which are structurally similar to the
type of esoteric scriptural exegesis which has always been an important feature of Kabbalistic tradition. She unreflectively takes it for
granted that incidents described in scripture can be interpreted so as
to refer to the inner life of the soul. For example, the raining of
manna from heaven is seen by Teresa as a symbol of the graces that
God grants the soul in the more advanced stages of mystical endeavour. When the soul is given a foretaste of these graces, they are
compared to the tokens of the nature of the Promised Land brought
back by those whom the Israelites sent on there. The 'wine-cellar' of
the Song of Songs is taken to signify the centre of the soul. The peace
and tranquillity of the communication with God in the seventh
mansion is like the building of Solomon's temple, during which no
noise could be heard. Just as Jesus appeared to his Apostles at the
Last Supper without entering through the door, so, in the Spiritual
Marriage, we gain a direct apprehension of God without the need
for our apprehensions to be channelled through the senses or
faculties.[78] Other similar instances could be multiplied, not only
from the *Interior Castle* but from others of Teresa's works: in her
Life she interprets the 'wings of a dove' of the Psalmist as referring to
the 'flight of the spirit' in ecstasy; in the *Spiritual Relations* the
persecution of the Reform by the Calced Carmelites is, significantly,
alluded to as the Egyptians persecuting the children of Israel.[79]

Davies comments that the way in which Teresa uses biblical texts, and the aura of almost magical reverence which she brings to them, is

> . . . somehow reminiscent of the moment when the scrolls are brought out from their sacred place in the synagogue. They are in some sense, for her, magical texts, which do not have to be understood in a literal sense, yet have the power to move and to inspire. It is impossible in such a context to forget the mystery and magic that the Cabbalists brought to their examination of each dot and tittle.[80]

We look at an example of Jewish Kabbalistic scriptural interpretation later in this chapter, and so defer illustration of this point here.

We have already suggested in passing, too, that Teresa's concern with demons – with the possibility of their interfering in her quest, creating false visions, barring the entrances to the mansions of her castle, and with methods for banishing them or otherwise dealing with them – seems rather Judaic. Some might argue that such beliefs were widespread not only in Judaism but also in Christianity in Teresa's time; but I think we can see similarities with the preoccupation with demonology found both in 'practical Kabbalah', as it was known (in other words the magical side of Kabbalah which was so much a part of the world of medieval Judaism), and in those Kabbalistic concepts that had been absorbed at the level of folk belief among Spanish *conversos*. Teresa's discussion of her battles with demons or 'devils' in her *Life*, her triumphant assertion that 'I have acquired an authority over them, given me by the Lord of all things, and now I take no more notice of them than of flies. . . . I snap my fingers at all the devils; they shall be afraid of me . . .' is as reminiscent of Jewish magic as is her declaration elsewhere that a genuine love of God makes the mystic 'master of all the elements and of the whole world'.[81]

Swietlicki has also suggested that many of the names and attributes that Teresa uses to refer to God are largely Spanish equivalents of Hebraic terminology, and reflect traditional Kabbalistic interest in the many names of God, their values and symbolic meanings and the practical uses to which these names could be put in medieval Jewish magic. The names of angels were equally important, and it is revealing that, in her account of the 'Transverberation' vision, Teresa lets slip in passing a comment that different classes of angels do not tell her their names: such a remark would have little sense or point to one who was not familiar with the more esoteric aspects of Judaism.

To this it might be added too that there is a rather Judaic-mystical ring to the emphasis that Teresà places on the 'secrets' and 'mysteries' that God reveals to the soul in the advanced stages of mystical experience. Alexander considers that one of the three major characteristics of Jewish mysticism is that the Jewish mystics are concerned to penetrate into secrets, mysteries, that which is hidden.[82] This is also in evidence in Teresa's works. Nor is that rather different kind of secrecy, so essential for the survival of Jewish tradition among the *conversos*, absent from her writings. Teresa was apprehensive at the prospect of her *Life* being widely circulated in her own lifetime:

> If the rest [of the *Life*, apart from certain portions that she has just excluded] is shown to anyone I do not wish him to be told whose experience it describes, or who wrote it. That is why I mention neither myself nor anyone else by name and have done my best to write in such a way as not to be recognized. I beg your Reverence [addressing her Confessor], for the love of God, to preserve my secrecy. . . . as I think that you and the others who are to see this book will do what I am asking you for the love of God, I am writing quite freely.[83]

In a similar vein is Teresa's realisation that she had said too much to Diego de Yepes about the vision that caused her to write the *Interior Castle*: Fray Diego reports that '. . . she spoke so freely both of this and of other things that she realized herself that she had done so and on the next morning remarked to me: "How I forgot myself last night! I cannot think how it happened." . . . I promised her not to repeat what she had said to anyone during her lifetime.'[84] It is not necessary to hypothesise some secret Jewish Order to which Teresa belonged in order to explain such statements: they can be understood quite simply as expressions of the inevitable anxiety which any *converso* in sixteenth-century Spain who was in the public eye would have felt as a daily, ongoing social pressure, particularly if that *converso* was also a woman and a visionary. But this issue of what constitutes the 'esoteric' awaits further discussion in the next chapter.

But most revealing of all, perhaps, after the *Interior Castle*, with regard to the question of Jewish mystical influences on Teresa's thought, is her work usually known in English as *Conceptions of the Love of God* (the Spanish title is *Meditaciones Sobre los Cantares,* 'Meditations on the [Song of] Songs'). This was written (probably between 1571 and 1573) as a commentary on certain verses of the Song of Songs and, like the *Interior Castle,* is composed of seven chapters. The Song of Songs was the only scriptural text which Teresa singled out for special attention in this way, and one could therefore argue that the work shows her to have been more deeply influenced by the Song of Songs than by any other single biblical book. Indeed Teresa tells us in her Prologue to the work how deeply the Song of Songs has moved her soul and how God has been enabling her to understand some of the meaning of the text, although she has not dared to write about it previously. This last remark need cause us no surprise, for Teresa was exposing herself to a great deal of danger in writing about this book, which not only makes use of sensual images which the Church found unfitting, but which had also been the mystical scripture *par excellence* for the Jews: many commentaries and reflections on it had been written by Kabbalists and mystically orientated Rabbis. Many Jews believed the scripture to be revealed, spoken by the angels or by God himself; it was viewed with special reverence and awe, and given a highly prominent role in the development of Kabbalism. In the *Zohar,* although no consecutive commentary on the Song of Songs is found, '. . . there exists hardly a page in the entire Zohar in which the Canticle is not in a broader sense discussed. Quotations from this relatively brief Biblical book are everywhere, and even where it is not quoted, its theme remains central to the author's consciousness.'[85] The *Zohar* says that the Song of Songs embraces all that has ever existed, all that is, and all that will be in the future.

The richly erotic imagery of the Song of Songs, based on the vicissitudes of a relationship between Bride and Bridegroom, was taken by the orthodox Jews to be symbolic of the relationship between God and the Jewish people or the 'community of Israel'. Orthodox Christianity developed a parallel interpretation concerning the relationship of God and the Church. For the Kabbalists, however, the imagery of Bride and Bridegroom signified the relationship between the masculine and feminine aspects of the Godhead itself – the 'King' and the *shekhinah,* or God's feminine presence manifest in the world – their estrangement, which had been brought about by the sins of humanity, and the quest for their reunion. In Kabbalah, the Godhead was seen as being both male and female, and the reunion of the estranged masculine and feminine aspects of the Deity was a basic focus of the Kabbalists' spiritual goal. A further variation on interpretation of the scripture, in which it was seen as symbolising the union of the worshipper's soul (the Bride) with God (the Bridegroom), although more prominent in Christian mysticism, is not entirely absent from the Jewish mystical tradition.[86] This more personalised interpretation is adopted by Teresa, who sees the Song of Songs as an intimate allegory of the relationship between the Divine King and the mystic. (The Jewish Kabbalists analysed the scripture in a more detailed manner, identifying particular images of the Song of Songs with particular sefirot on the Tree, which represented for them the workings of the Godhead and the cosmos. It should be emphasised that Teresa does not refer to the Kabbalistic Sefirot at any point in her writings, and her mysticism cannot be correlated with this aspect of Kabbalistic and Zoharic tradition. Swietlicki attempts to equate the upper three sefirot of Jewish Kabbalism with the Trinity (represented by Teresa as a vision granted in the seventh mansion) and the lower seven sefirot with Teresa's seven mansions; but her argument is unconvincing, suggesting greater comparative similarities than can be justified.)

In 1572, Luis de León – a theologian and university professor who, as we have remarked, was also later to become the first editor of Teresa's writings – had been arrested and imprisoned by the Inquisition. Luis de León was a *converso* and well-schooled in both Christian and Jewish forms of Kabbalah. One of the reasons for his imprisonment was that he had translated the Song of Songs into the vernacular. Martín Gutiérrez – one of Teresa's confessors who had also been slandered as having been her lover – lent Teresa Luis de León's translation. It was thus, apparently, that she came to write her commentary on the book. Soon after, a new Confessor, Diego de Yanguas, having been shown Teresa's work, ordered that it should be burnt. Not only was it dangerous to show an interest in the Song of Songs and in Luis de León's translation; it was also considered scandalous that a woman should have the audacity to expound the Scriptures at all, for women in Teresa's culture were allowed no theological learning and hence effectively excluded from preaching or writing on matters considered the exclusive province of scholars. A woman who already had a somewhat controversial reputation would be exposing herself to certain trouble with the Inquisition if it became widely known that she had dared to write about this book, which was not only a favourite text of the Kabbalists, but which also made use of erotic imagery which no respectable woman of the time – let alone a nun! – should contemplate. The original manuscript, then, of *Conceptions of the Love of God* was burnt – but copies had been made, and some of these (possibly without Teresa's knowledge) were saved.

Concerning the romantic and sexual images in which the Song of Songs abounds, Teresa goes to some length to explain that we do not need to have any misgivings about this, for God 'did not adopt this method of communication without good reason'.[87] Teresa picks out for extended commentary the following verses from the first two chapters of the Song of Songs, which she interprets as representing the love between the Bride (the soul) and the Divine Bridegroom. Here the Bride speaks:

> Let Him kiss me with the kisses of his mouth: for thy love is better than wine.
> Because of the savour of thy good ointments thy name is as ointment poured forth, therefore do the virgins love thee.
> Draw me, we will run after thee: the King hath brought me into his chambers. . . .
> As the apple tree among the trees of the wood, so is my beloved among the sons. I sat down under his shadow with great delight, and his fruit was sweet to my taste.
> He brought me to the banqueting-house, and his banner over me was love.
> Stay me with flagons, comfort me with apples: for I am sick of love.[88]

Teresa's commentary on these lines is little short of a Christianised Rabbinic-Kabbalistic exegesis. It should be noted that the line 'Let Him kiss me with the kisses of his mouth' – which Teresa, in common with many Jewish Kabbalists, considers worthy of especially lengthy analytical treatment – was used as a mystical prayer by Kabbalists. It was sometimes seen as referring to the 'kiss of love' that unites God and the soul in the seventh palace described in the *Zohar*. A distinguishing feature of the esoteric scriptural interpretations of the Jewish Kabbalists consisted in drawing complex symbolic meanings out of every single image, word, and even every letter of a given text: the very letters of the Hebrew alphabet were believed to possess a magical and mystical potency which could be deciphered by those skilled in Kabbalistic lore. The *Zohar* insists that each single word of the Song of Songs is to be held as sacred. It is significant, then, that Teresa insists that there is 'not a superfluous letter' in the text of the Song of Songs, and that even one word of this sacred book may contain 'a thousand mysteries', 'tremendous secrets'; a sense of awe and magic too is conveyed in her feeling that 'it causes one fear even to hear them [the words of the Song of Songs], so great is the majesty which they enshrine.'[89] There is no lack either of specific esoteric interpretations of the lines of scripture in question. For example, the 'shadow' under which the Bride is described as sitting is seen by Teresa as a 'cloud of the Godhead'; it is identified with the 'power of the Most High' that 'overshadowed' the Virgin Mary at the annunciation.[90] In this shadow dwells the resplendent Sun who is the Divine King and who is also likened to an 'apple tree among the trees of the wood'. When the Bride is sitting in the shadow of the Godhead she does not need to practise meditation, for her Beloved is giving her the fruit from his apple tree without any effort on her part. The apple tree is further identified with the tree of the cross, and we are told that Christ watered the apple tree with his blood. Then Teresa takes off on a different tack and identifies the apple tree with the 'tree of fervent love' of God, from which spring flowers (good deeds) which produce good fruit.[91] (Elsewhere she uses the image of a tree that produces good fruit to signify the state of the soul in grace.) So from this one verse of the Song of Songs ('As the apple tree among the trees of the wood, so is my beloved among the sons. I sat under his shadow with great delight, and his fruit was sweet to my taste') Teresa draws out multiple threads of meaning; threads which do not always connect with each other with rigorous logical precision, but which make perfect sense in the context of the freer, more creative associations of meditative reflections on a scriptural text.

The style, the way of interpretative procedure, which she adopts is almost identical to that used by the Kabbalists in their esoteric scriptural exegesis. The images merge into each other with a fluidity of meaning, and each image has many meanings on different levels. Each symbol is as multifaceted as the diamond or crystal jewel of Teresa's castle. Each line of scripture is shown to have some hidden significance within this symbolic world of endless interrelationships and associations. Compare the first passage quoted below, a Kabbalistic discourse on a verse from the Song of Songs, taken from the *Zohar*, with the second passage which comments on a different verse from the same scripture, taken from *Conceptions of the Love of God*:

> Discoursing on the verse: 'I am a rose of Sharon, a lily of the valleys' [Cant. 2:1], Rabbi Simeon said: The Holy One, be blessed, bears great love to the Community of Israel, wherefore he constantly praises her, and she, from the store of chants and hymns she keeps for the King, constantly sings his praises.
>
> Because she flowers splendidly in the Garden of Eden, the Community of Israel is called rose of Sharon; because her desire is to be watered from the deep stream which is the source of all spiritual rivers, she is called lily of the valleys. . . . She is named 'rose' when she is about to join with the King, and after she has come together with him in her kisses, she is named 'lily'.[92]

> Let us now question the Bride. Let us learn from this blessed soul, which has drawn near to this Divine mouth and been nourished from these heavenly breasts. . . . Her words are: 'I sat down under the shadow of Him Whom I had desired, and His fruit is sweet to my palate. The King brought me into the cellar of wine and set in order charity in me.' . . . Dear God, how this soul is drawn into the very Sun and enkindled by Him! She says that she sat down under the shadow of Him Whom she had desired. Here she likens Him to nothing less than an apple-tree and says that His fruit is sweet to her palate. O souls that practise prayer, savour all these words! In how many different ways can we think of our God! To how many different kinds of food can we compare Him! For He is manna, the taste of which is to each of us as we wish it to be. Oh, what heavenly shadow is this! Oh, that one could express all that the Lord signifies by it! . . . While the soul is enjoying the delight which has been described, it seems to be wholly engulfed and protected by a shadow, and, as it were, a cloud of the Godhead, whence come to it certain influences and a dew so delectable as to free it immediately, and with good reason, from the weariness caused it by the things of the world. . . . the Lord is giving her the fruit from the apple-tree with which she compares her Beloved: He picks it and cooks it and almost eats it for her. And so she says: 'His fruit is sweet to my palate.' For here all is enjoyment, without any labour of the faculties, and in this shadow of the Godhead . . . dwells that resplendent Sun, who sends out to the soul a message of love, communicating His Majesty's nearness to

it – a nearness which is ineffable. I am sure that anyone who has experienced it will know how applicable this meaning is to these words spoken here by the Bride.[93]

Notwithstanding the more intimate devotional tone of Teresa's passage, its more colloquial form of expression, and, obviously, the Christian interpretations put upon it, the method of procedure adopted in drawing meanings out of the text is almost identical to that used by the Rabbis.

That the sensuality of the images of the Song of Songs was not lost on Teresa is obvious; she does not shrink from elaborating in her own words.

> . . . when this most wealthy Spouse desires to enrich and comfort the Bride still more, He draws her so closely to Him that she is like one who swoons from excess of pleasure and joy and seems to be suspended in those Divine arms and drawn near to that sacred side and to those Divine breasts.[94]

Such symbolically sensual expressions of mysticism, in which mystical union is seen as a sacred marriage (*hieros gamos*), had been a part of Jewish mystical tradition since at least the time of the *Zohar*, though most often describing not the relationship between God and the individual soul, but, as already indicated, that between the masculine and feminine aspects of the Godhead itself as conceived in Kabbalistic philosophy, or alternatively between God and the children of Israel. We have already mentioned in Chapter 1 the sensual vision of Gracián of which Teresa tells us, in which she saw Gracián enter a beautiful garden and heard the words from the Song of Songs 5:1, 'Let my beloved come into his garden'. It cannot be denied that there was a tendency in Teresa to confuse the divine Bridegroom with earthly 'beloveds', to see particular men as in some way standing for or symbolising divine love, to project, perhaps, her mystical ardour onto these rather more concrete and identifiable figures. We will recall her musing over the nature of spiritual love on the one hand and sensual love on the other. Perhaps this trait in her character needs to be seen in the context of the ambivalence of sensual-mystical imagery in Jewish tradition.

In this chapter we have shown that Teresa's Christian faith, like that of many *conversos*, is a Christianity replete with Jewish influences in its symbolism and religious presuppositions. As a *conversa*,

Teresa absorbed into her writings elements of the religious heritage of Jewish mysticism, taken perhaps in some cases from the Christian Kabbalah then popular in Spain, but at the very least in the case of the seven-mansioned castle, it seems, from the Hekhalot/Zoharic tradition itself as it was perpetuated orally among Jewish converts to Christianity. Teresa found the language and symbolism of Jewish mysticism an appropriate descriptive tool for the expression of her experiences. The question to what extent she was aware of the Judaic origins of some of her descriptive terminology remains: in some cases she may have used Jewish images in a semi-conscious, unreflective manner, for many of these images, as we have said, had passed into the *converso* 'folk' culture of Spain and were common intellectual property, while others had been adopted by Christian Kabbalists. I have argued, however, that it seems likely that Teresa was aware of the significance of her symbol of the castle and used it in full consciousness of its origins. In any case, it is certain that, if Teresa *was* aware of the origin of those elements of Jewish mystical tradition found in her writings, she would certainly have kept this knowledge to herself, for fear of more serious persecution from the Inquisition and the terrors that might entail.

Orthodoxy and Heresy: the Inquisition and Contemporary Mystical Movements

God leads souls along many roads and paths, as he has led mine. . . . there is no reason why we should expect everyone else to travel by our own road, and we should not attempt to point them to the spiritual path when perhaps we do not know what it is.[1]

So far we have looked largely at Teresa's life and work, at her teachings and her accounts of her experiences, with attention being given, too, to the social and cultural background in which she lived, the history of the Jews and the *conversos* in Spain, and relevant historical details regarding Jewish mysticism. In order to obtain a more far-reaching and balanced perspective we have also looked briefly at Teresa in a broader, more comparative context.

In the present chapter we look at aspects of the contemporary mystical tradition. We shall begin with a brief overview of aspects of the Spanish Christian Kabbalah of Teresa's own lifetime. This stream of Christian Kabbalah in Spain affords a close affinity with Teresa's writings (notwithstanding the fact that, as I have argued, much of Teresa's mystical symbolism can be shown to be drawn from Jewish Kabbalistic tradition whose origins are many centuries earlier). The question of Teresa's orthodoxy or heterodoxy will then be examined, with particular attention being paid to the interventions of the Spanish Inquisition in Teresa's life. As a result of these investigations we hope to gain a clearer perspective on the contemporary mystical and esoteric tradition and on Teresa's place within that tradition.

We have already seen that Kabbalah was perpetuated in Spain during Teresa's lifetime both by Christian apologists who adopted Kabbalistic themes for their own purposes, and by the *conversos*, among whom the more popular elements of Kabbalistic belief were transmitted as part of a continuing oral 'folk' tradition. The growth of the former Christian Kabbalistic thought in the Spain of Teresa's time can be linked to the attempts of Renaissance thinkers in Italy and elsewhere to synthesise Kabbalah, Neoplatonism and Hermetic thought with Christianity. During the Renaissance it was believed that Kabbalah was an ancient and sacred heritage revealed by God to Moses (or, some argued, to Adam) and later handed down in oral tradition among select groups of initiates. Modern historical criticism has exploded this myth of Kabbalah's great antiquity, but that does not make Kabbalah any less profound as a mystical system or any less important as a cultural phenomenon. Renaissance Christian Kabbalah, as we have said, was used in the service of Christian apologetics – the aim of the authors being to persuade the Jews that Christianity was the true fulfilment of Mosaic Law and that the Christian Kabbalah was the valid continuation of God's secret revelation to Moses referred to above. Christian Kabbalah in Spain may also, however, have fused with the surviving oral Jewish Kabbalah of the *conversos*, and the case of Teresa seems to be one of special interest here, for as we have suggested, it is likely that she absorbed her Kabbalah from both Jewish and Christian sources.

Christian Kabbalah in the Renaissance was part of a general preoccupation with and enthusiasm for ancient philosophies, which intellectuals of the day tried to weld into an all-embracing whole:

Neoplatonism, Hermetic-thought, alchemy, Gnosticism, elements of Pythagorean teaching, astrology, the occult arts. Among the more important exponents of the Renaissance synthesis may be mentioned the Italians Giovanni Pico della Mirandola (1463–1494) and Francesco Giorgi (1466–1540), the Germans Johannes Reuchlin (1455–1522), Heinrich Cornelius Agrippa von Nettesheim (1486–1535), Heinrich Khunrath, and Christian Knorr von Rosenroth, and in England, John Dee (1527–1608) and Robert Fludd (1574–1637).

In sixteenth-century Spain, Christian Kabbalah and Renaissance occult thought was subjected by the Inquisition and Catholic dogma to greater restraints than elsewhere in Europe. While Renaissance ideology was having a marked effect on art, architecture and the sciences in sixteenth-century Avila, its influence was more restricted so far as religion was concerned. Spanish writers used Kabbalistic ideas more cautiously and in a more veiled manner than was the case in Italy, Germany or Britain, and avoided the more magical or occult aspects of Kabbalah which were a part, for example, of the studies of Pico della Mirandola or Agrippa. Nevertheless, books and treatises on such matters were available to those who were sufficiently interested to go to some effort to obtain them. Many intellectuals and members of the Spanish nobility and royal family cultivated such pursuits. In fact Philip II, who was a supporter of Teresa's Reform and who helped her during her time of persecution from the Calced Carmelites, has been seen as the greatest patron of Renaissance occultism in the Spanish royal house. In spite of his support of the Inquisition and the effort he expended in stamping out heretical thought, it seems that he himself nurtured such ideas in the creation of San Lorenzo del Escorial, his royal palace some 35 miles south-east of Avila. The palace was intended as a re-creation of the Temple of Solomon: geomancers were consulted to select the proper site, astrologers to pick the date for laying the foundation stone, and Hermetic philosophers, in consultation with the architects, designed every proportion of the building in accordance with numerological principles that had long played a part in Kabbalah. The reasons for the dedication to St Lawrence (San Lorenzo) are unclear. Philip won a victory on the saint's day (in Flanders, 1557) and it is said that he vowed to build something in return; this is unlikely, as the dedication was not made until ten years after the Escorial was completed. There is, however, an obscure legend that

St Lawrence brought the Holy Grail to Spain, and there may be some connection here with the web of eclectic esotericism behind the creation of the palace. The 'Western esoteric tradition' (as it has become known) today continues to show similar syncretistic tendencies. A statue of St Lawrence guards the west entrance of the 'Temple', as the complex's church is called; six Kings of Israel adorn its façade with two statues in the centre representing David and Solomon.

Of even greater interest is Philip's library, one of the largest collections of Greek and Hebrew mystical and philosophical works in Europe, containing many of the major Renaissance Kabbalistic, Neoplatonic and Hermetic works of the time. Philip's agents apparently watched over the burning of prohibited books that the Inquisition undertook from 1559 (described in more detail shortly) and saved from the flames anything that looked especially interesting! The ceiling of the library is painted in a fashion highly popular among Renaissance Hermeticists, with representations of the great philosophers, the Greek gods, the seven liberal arts (personified as female figures), and numerous scholars with astrolabes and compasses taking measurements in pursuit of the all-important ideal Hermetic proportions. After Teresa's death, Philip requested for his library the manuscript copy of her *Life*, and it can still be seen there today, along with early copies of others of her works. He evidently admired Teresa greatly, and they corresponded regularly.

Numerous other instances could be cited of the interest in Renaissance occultism and Kabbalah in the Spain of Teresa's time. But Spain had in addition a history of Christian Kabbalistic thought of its own that predated the influx of Renaissance philosophies, intimately associated with *converso* culture. The first known instance of the influence of Jewish mystical tradition on Christianity in Spain is found in the works of the *converso* previously known as Moshe Sefardi, baptised as Pedro Alfonso in 1106. We might also mention here Ramón Martín, who wrote in the thirteenth century an influential work of Christian Kabbalah. Other such early Christian Kabbalist writers included Abner de Burgos (1270–1348) and Solomon Halevi, also known as Pablo de Santa María (c. 1351–1435). Possibly the most important early author so far as our study of Teresa is concerned, however, was Ramón Lull (1232–1316), whose writings, again showing Kabbalistic leanings, continued to have an influence in Spain several centuries later; it is quite possible that Luis de León and John of the Cross had read Lull's writings, and that Teresa became familiar with his work through conversations with St John or others of her associates.

Luis de León (1527–1591), the first editor of Teresa's works after her death, has much in common with the concerns of the Renaissance Kabbalists. He apparently never met Teresa, but was evidently a great admirer of her work, while her *Conceptions of the Love of God*, as we have said, was inspired by his translation of the Song of Songs. A *converso*, humanist in the Renaissance mould, Hebrew scholar, and Professor of Theology, scholars have found in his work traces of Neoplatonic, Pythagorean and other Greek philosophies, while the influence of Kabbalah and of Hebrew tradition on his thought is now undoubted. Fray Luis counted among his friends and acquaintances many of those intellectuals who were foremost in the advancement of Renaissance Kabbalah. For example, Benito Arias Montano, whom Phillip II appointed as Librarian at San Lorenzo del Escorial, was a friend of Fray Luis' who shared his interest in the Song of Songs, in Christian Kabbalah and in mysticism. Montano supplied Luis with books from the Netherlands and in one letter warns Luis not to mention the Inquisition in their correspondence, since most of the letters they exchange are intercepted and read. (Presumably he was hoping that *this* letter was to be an exception!) As we have commented earlier, Kottman has argued that Fray Luis' commentary on the Song of Songs is based on the portion of the *Zohar* known as the *Greater Holy Assembly*. Kottman also argues that Luis de León's moral and social theory is influenced by Kabbalah.[2] Swietlicki has examined the influence of Christian Kabbalah in Fray Luis' work *De los Nombres de Cristo* ('Concerning the Names of Christ') and in his poetry. The magical powers and symbolic meanings of sacred names played a major role in Jewish Kabbalah. In his *De los Nombres de Cristo*, 'Fray Luis recognizes the secret essence of words, and, similar to a Cabalist concentrating and meditating on the qualities of the Hebrew words, he tries to explore all their qualities.'[3] He shows himself to be familiar with Kabbalistic techniques of manipulating and combining the letters of the Hebrew alphabet (*gimatriyya, notarikon, temurah*), and with the various permutations of the Tetragrammaton (YHVH) which had important mystical significance for the Kabbalists. Swietlicki documents examples of Luis de León's use of particular divine names, showing their correspondences with

Kabbalistic sources, and argues that his techniques of contemplation of the names of Christ recall Kabbalistic methods of meditation on sacred god-names. A study of Fray Luis' poetry, too, Swietlicki argues, shows that he uses the poetic medium as a subtle means of communicating Kabbalistic and Neoplatonic ideas.

Still more important with regard to the influence of Jewish mysticism on Teresa's thought, is John of the Cross, who (as we have remarked) shared a close spiritual friendship with Teresa. It is certain that mutual influence can be detected in the writings of the two mystics, though the exact details as to who influenced whom in respect of specific aspects of teaching is still debated. John of the Cross was a *converso*; his family, like that of Teresa, originated in Toledo, where they followed typically Jewish trades and callings, again like Teresa's family; it is likely that the two families were acquainted. John spent most of his youth living in or near Arévalo, the village near Avila which had previously been a centre for Zoharic tradition among *conversos* since its association with Moses de León and the *Zohar*, described in the last chapter. As is the case with Teresa's family history, the same probable 'Judaising' by some of John's family members is evident, and the same reticence on the part of St John to talk about his lineage. Gómez-Menor Fuentes has argued that John's grandfather may have been burnt at the stake for 'Judaising'. There is also the fact that John's father was disinherited by the family for reasons not as yet fully understood, but thought to be related to the issue of Jewish-Christian relationships.[4]

John was a Latin scholar, and so unlike Teresa he would have had direct access to Christian Kabbalistic literature. He could not, however, read Hebrew (so far as we know), and so (unlike Luis de León) he could not have read Jewish Kabbalistic works in the original. Nevertheless, like Teresa, John would have absorbed aspects of Jewish Kabbalistic teaching and imagery from the *converso* culture in which he grew up.

John of the Cross, like Teresa, makes liberal use of quotations from the Old Testament, and it has been remarked that he frequently dwells on the relationship between the prophetic experiences described in the Old Testament, and his own Christian mystical experience. The tradition of the Hebrew prophets seems for him to be continued in Christian mysticism, and he uses ideas and images drawn from Christian (and possibly Jewish) Kabbalah to bridge the two traditions, and to attempt to show that Christianity is the true inheritor of the old Mosaic Law – an interpretation of the relationship between Judaism and Christianity which would appeal to *conversos* whose Christian faith was sincere.[5] In this respect, John's attitude is not unlike that of Teresa, and we may remind ourselves here of the importance that the prophet Elijah, in particular, held for members of the Carmelite Order. There are also numerous other examples of probable Kabbalistic influence in John's writings. Like Teresa, he is very fond of the Song of Songs and makes liberal use of the warmly sensual and even erotic imagery of Bride and Bridegroom which his meditations on this scripture occasion. A prime example is St John's poem 'Songs between the Soul and the Bridegroom' and his own commentary thereon, 'The Spiritual Canticle', in which the language, imagery and mood of the Song of Songs are used without reservation to recount the quest of the Bride (the soul) for her Divine Bridegroom, and her eventual Spiritual Marriage to him. Swietlicki has also argued that Kabbalistic elements can be detected in several other aspects of John's teachings, literary style, and uses of symbolism. Especially worthy of note, perhaps, is that, reminiscent of the seven mansions of Teresa's castle, John of the Cross uses the imagery of seven 'wine-cellars' representing seven stages of mystical progress or seven 'chambers of love': in the seventh and innermost cellar, hidden and secret, the mystic may drink of the Beloved in the final and intimate union. Links with Teresa's sevenfold castle and with Jewish mystical tradition can be postulated. It should be added, however, that the use of this imagery in St John's writings is neither as fully developed nor as central to his scheme of mystical progress as is the sevenfold castle of Teresa. In fact, the overriding scheme used by John is fivefold, consisting of the classic three stages of Catholic mysticism – Purgation, Contemplation, Union – interspersed with his own Dark Night of Sense and Dark Night of Spirit. But it seems likely that Teresa and John had discussed together the Zoharic imagery of the seven mansions, known from one or both of their family backgrounds.

We have explained how the Spanish Inquisition in Teresa's lifetime was on the alert for any actual or potential forms of heresy. The efforts of the Inquisition were directed towards various classes of people who might be brought to trial: those of Jewish descent who showed signs of lapsing back into the practice of their ancestral religion; those of Islamic sympathies (*moriscos* or 'Moors'); Protestants; mystics of all types, including *alumbrados, beatas, dejados* (explained below) and monks or nuns who claimed special revelatory experiences or visions; witches, astrologers, fortune-tellers; and those given to pre-Christian or 'pagan' practices which the Church branded as demonic. In the case of Teresa, the potential points of concern for the Inquisition were clearly her mysticism along with her visions and ecstasies, and, if they had come to light, her Jewish ancestry and the Jewish influence in her writings.

The *alumbrados* or 'Illumined Ones' have already been mentioned. Believing themselves to be illuminated by an inward divine light, they were contemptuous of ecclesiastical authority and priestly hierarchy, and repudiated the use of images in worship. They also believed that when a person reached an exalted stage of union with God, nothing he or she did was sinful; this had led to a licentious sexuality at which the Church was horrified. They spoke of raptures, ecstasies and visions of the Divine which, as we shall see, Teresa's opponents claimed were the same as her own descriptions of these experiences.

Related to some degree to the *alumbrados* were the *dejados* ('abandoned ones') who advocated total abandonment of the will and personality to the Divine. They also believed that they could reach perfection without fighting against temptations. By means of their 'abandonment' they induced meditative trances in which ideas or impulses might come to them; the *dejados* apparently believed in allowing free rein to these impulses. The most famous *dejado* was perhaps Miguel de Molinos, author of an influential guide on the spiritual life, who was tried by the Inquisition and died in prison in 1696.

Many of the *alumbrados* and *dejados* are thought to have been *conversos*. We have already remarked that Teresa was accused on several occasions of being an *alumbrada*. Francisco de Osuna, author of the *Third Spiritual Alphabet* which made such an impact on Teresa, is thought to have been a *converso* and is known to have been an early associate of the *alumbrados*. Osuna was a Franciscan, and the *dejados* considered themselves followers of the Franciscans. Osuna tried to distance himself from the *dejados* in his *Third Spiritual Alphabet*, in which he contrasted their path with the way of 'recollection' (*recogimiento*). Recollection was allied to the way of the *dejados* inasmuch as both implied a withdrawal from the objects of the senses, from everyday preoccupations and from rational and intellectual thinking processes; by means of this withdrawal one would be caught up to God. Teresa's own teachings regarding Recollection were profoundly influenced by Osuna here. But 'recollection' differed from the 'abandon' of the *dejados* in that Osuna believed that it was not enough simply to abandon oneself to the Divine; human effort was also necessary, in particular moral effort, the fight against temptations and other aspects of our natures that hold us back from perfection. In addition, one must attempt to rise above all particular images and ideas (including those that would have come to the *dejados* in meditative trance) all of which were seen as fallible and incomplete human attempts to represent the transcendent. (In this respect, Osuna followed the *Via Negativa* of Scholastic teaching.) The *dejados*, who came to be regarded as heretical, accepted '. . . all behaviour, however immoral . . . as God's working, and the result was an excessive, sometimes scandalous, quietism.'[6] The *recogidos* or 'recollects' remained orthodox, and played a key role in the revival of the religious Orders.

Although the *alumbrados* taught substantially different doctrines to Teresa in some respects, and although she denied any association with them, this did not prevent the Inquisition from seeing all mystics as birds of a feather. Indeed, as Williams has remarked, differences notwithstanding, Teresa and her like, the *alumbrados*, and the rise of Protestant 'heresies' (as they were seen by the Inquisition), '. . . had a common source, and are not to be considered as entirely diverse or antagonistic to each other'. A new and rising awareness of the worth of the individual in spiritual matters meant that many people were no longer content simply to accept the Church's received traditional teaching. There was a new conviction that the individual must reflect on and assimilate Christian teaching for himself or herself. Hence there was a 'new outburst of "ways" to union with God',[7] a popularisation of mysticism and contemplative spirituality, a sense of searching for deeper and more individually meaningful spiritual experience, resulting in the growth of numerous spiritual movements which in spite of their differences shared at least this common basic orientation.

The popularisation of mysticism had its negative results, most notably perhaps in the increased numbers of impostors claiming to be 'mystics', who produced fake 'miracles' or 'wonders', or who claimed spiritual gifts that they did not possess, in order to make money from the credulous. The Inquisition also sought to bring such 'fake mystics' to trial: those found guilty could expect the harshest penalties. But, as we have said, the Inquisition did not draw fine distinctions between types of mysticism; its officials tended to see all mystics as possible *alumbrados* and to be suspicious of any form of 'mental prayer' (contemplative as opposed to vocal prayer). In such an atmosphere, people leading the spiritual life naturally became afraid and insecure, regardless of the degree of their sincerity and good intentions. There was a universal belief in the power of the devil, who was said to be capable of transforming himself into an angel of light, thus deceiving even the devout and pious. Even those who led a blameless life could easily have become preoccupied with their fear of being deceived in such a way. Heretics (so the Inquisition saw them) propagated false doctrines under the guise of piety; and in the eyes of the Inquisition, all mysticism meant potential heresy. Anyone who claimed to receive visions, revelations, ecstasies, or other supernormal experiences, was closely watched, for in the eyes of the Inquisition these phenomena were synonymous with diabolical influence.[8]

It is, furthermore, significant that *conversos* were believed to be more prone to mysticism than others. This may, ironically, have been true, for their forced conversions and the discrimination which they suffered could well have induced a sense of spiritual emptiness in some, which might lead them to seek for a deeper and more immediately felt religious life, and indeed there had been a number of mystical and messianic movements among the *converso* communities in Castile in the early sixteenth century. More controversial, however, are the Inquisition's further racist and sexist assumptions that *conversos* were more prone than others to *false* mystical illuminations or to demonic possession, that women were more prone to such symptoms than men, and that sexual licentiousness often went hand in hand with such diabolical phenomena. Clearly any woman who was also a *conversa* and a mystic would have had a hard time persuading those around her that her illuminations were genuine. Teresa's struggle, then, it has been remarked, was partially a struggle for the recognition of a woman's right to the inner prayer of recollection.[9] Teresa's visionary experiences could not have been more dangerously timed, with *autos de fé* being held in Castile and many people being burnt at the stake for supposed heresy. Bernardino Carleval was one such unfortunate *converso*, a visionary who went to the stake at the hands of the Inquisition. Carleval, Rector of the University of Baeza, had been appointed Confessor to the nuns at Teresa's Malagón convent, and was apparently on good terms with Teresa. Between 1572 and 1574 he came under the attack of the Inquisition, who accused him of being an *alumbrado* and of other heresies. In the records of his trial the chief influences cited on Carleval's beliefs were 'the false prophetess, María Mejías' and 'the nun, Teresa de Jesús' whose *Life* Carleval had read, probably in 1568. María Mejías also went to the stake. One of the enigmas that we must try to unravel in this chapter is why Teresa did not. Luis de León, as we have said, was arrested by the Inquisition in 1576 and remained in their dungeons for five years. John of the Cross came under suspicion, being denounced as an *alumbrado* three times, to the tribunals of the Inquisition at Valladolid, Toledo and Seville. Rank or status did not preclude the attentions of the Inquisition: some of the most eminent and distinguished scholars and Churchmen of the day came under trial. In 1576, for example, Bartolomé de Carranza, Archbishop of Toledo, died after seventeen years of imprisonment. The Inquisition, as we shall see, was always there in the background of Teresa's life (when it was not indeed in the foreground) and always to be reckoned with. In the latter years of her life in particular, she seems to have lived in more or less constant dread of the Inquisition – not only on her own behalf, but also for the sake of John of the Cross, Gracián and others of her co-workers.

A brief explanation regarding the *beatas* may be appended here, which will bring our account of the types of persons whom the Inquisition found worthy of suspicion to a close. We will remember Teresa's dealings with the *beata* María de Jesús mentioned in Chapter 1. The word *beata* is often used rather loosely; in the sixteenth century it frequently denoted simply a woman who had taken a private vow of chastity, who wore a religious habit and observed a religious rule, whether cloistered or not, whether alone or in the company of others. Many *beatas* were simply devout single or widowed women who continued to live in their own houses. In other cases they lived in their own communities (known as *beaterías*). The Convent of the Incarnation where Teresa spent twenty-seven years of her life had previously been a *beatería*, and before this the site of a Jewish cemetery and synagogue. The *alumbrados* emphasised direct communion with God without the organised discipline of monasticism – a personal consecration to God through a simple vow and through self-imposed religious practice – and the *beatas* can be seen as carrying on this tradition. The Church saw these women who were trying to be religiously independent as a threat, and tried to regularise and control *beatas*, encouraging them to become cloistered nuns. The pressure became more intense as *beaterías* were found to be common breeding-grounds of heresy. Furthermore it became common for *beatas*, and also for nuns and friars, to be taken before the Inquisition on charges of false or diabolical visions. Diego Pérez de Valdiva, who had himself been tried by the Inquisition at Córdoba as a confessor of *beatas*, warned *beatas* and nuns in a subsequent work to pray that they should not receive visions, for fear of the danger that might result.[10] Teresa herself, writing of visions, reflects this necessary caution in her warning to her nuns: 'We must all take great care that things like these, even if they are clearly of God, or favours recognized as being miraculous, are not discussed with people outside the convent, or with confessors who are not prudent enough to keep silent about them; this is a more important point than may be realized.'[11]

The attitude of the Inquisition to Christianised Kabbalah was ambiguous. If a particular use of Christian Kabbalah could be shown to be in accord with the already existing tradition within Spanish Christianity of adopting Kabbalistic ideas and images to Christian purposes, with the aim of proving that Christianity was the one true religion, it might perhaps be found acceptable. But if it could not be shown to fit squarely within this orthodox framework – and in particular, if it showed any hint of Jewish sympathies or interest in the occult; if it seemed to suggest moral attitudes deemed ungodly by the Church; or if it was thought that it might lead to 'free thinking' or to a rejection of the Church's hierarchical structure and claims to divine authority – then it would be condemned.

It was during Teresa's lifetime, in 1559, that the Inquisition attempted to prohibit the reading of books that were considered heterodox, by drawing up the 'Spanish Index' of forbidden books. Many books deemed dangerous were destroyed; convents and monasteries were searched and all such books, which included many which Teresa had liked to read, were burned. It is of this event that Teresa tells us that Jesus gave her the consolation of himself as a 'living book':

When a number of books in Spanish were taken away from us, and we were told not to read them, I felt it deeply because some of them gave me recreation and I could not go on reading them, since now I only had them in Latin. Then the Lord said to me: 'Do not be distressed, for I will give you a living book.' I could not understand why this had been said to me, for I had not yet had visions. But a very few days afterwards I understood perfectly. What I saw before me gave me so much to think about and so many subjects for recollection, and the Lord showed me such love and taught me in so many ways, that I have had very little or no need of books since. His Majesty has been a veritable book in which I have read the truth.[12]

The books condemned by the Inquisition included almost all books in the vernacular with mystical overtones; many of these same works were in fact prohibited in the Latin as well, but, as we know, Teresa could not, in any case, have read any Latin works that remained accessible. Any books imported from abroad were subject to very severe restrictions, and this in itself must have curtailed the spread into Spain of the Christian Kabbalah of Renaissance Italy and Germany. The Bible in the vernacular was prohibited (until the end of the eighteenth century) for fear of the effects of 'free enquiry'. It was largely because of this that Luis de León suffered such severe punishment for translating the Song of Songs into Castilian. But since women in sixteenth-century Spain were not given a Latin education, these new regulations and restrictions meant that there were – in theory at least – practically no religious or spiritual works available to them. Indeed, the Inquisition condemned the very practice of reading on the part of so-called 'idiots' (i.e. those who did not understand Latin) and 'little women' (a literal translation of *mujercillas*, the expression used in the Inquisitorial records to denote all those of female gender). The fact that so many books were lost to Teresa no doubt meant that she had to fashion her teachings all the more out of her own spiritual experiences and her conversations with her associates.

Those books deemed suspicious, but not dangerous enough to be burnt outright, were 'corrected' by the Spanish censors: one still comes across such books in libraries, with passages scratched out. Other books were reserved in a special section of the libraries, or were only allowed to be read by those who held a special licence to do so. But despite all these precautions, a number of prohibited works continued to circulate secretly and were kept in private collections.[13]

Teresa did not escape investigation from the Inquisition any more than she escaped opposition and persecution from her contemporaries. As her visions and ecstasies attracted more attention, the intervention of the Inquisition became more likely. But it was not until she had committed herself in writing – namely, in her *Life* – that any real concern was shown. Once Teresa had a book in circulation describing her own experiences and her ideas on the spiritual life, once she was recognised as a woman of authority and influence, any accusations made against her had to be taken seriously.

In 1574–75 Teresa was travelling around Castile (visiting Valladolid, Medina del Campo, Avila, Toledo); the Inquisition was apparently watching her movements and gathering data on her life and conduct. After the trial of Bernardino Carleval, mentioned earlier, the Tribunal of the Inquisition at Córdoba gave an account to the main office of the Inquisition at Madrid consisting of information received about Teresa and accusations raised against her. By this time, Teresa's *Life* – which Carleval had cited as having influenced him – had become very popular, with many copies in circulation.

The Princess of Eboli seems to have been a major cause of trouble to Teresa at this time. She had entered Teresa's Pastrana convent, of which she was patroness, on the death of her husband, but was totally unsuited to the monastic life and greatly disturbed the community. Quite soon she left again, and henceforth did her best to put obstacles in Teresa's way. She ridiculed Teresa's *Life* at court, and it was the Princess too who lodged complaints with the Inquisition at this time. She alleged that the *Life* contained dangerous teachings. She claimed that its accounts of visions and revelations were similar to those of Magdalena de la Cruz, an infamous visionary and prophetess who, although at first highly esteemed, had recently been burnt at the stake for her confession that her ecstasies were feigned, and her wonder-working the result of a pact with the devil.

The main office of the Inquisition in Madrid, then, took over the case from Córdoba, and was also in communication with the tribunal at Valladolid, where other accusations had been raised. Teresa was accused of being an *alumbrada*, and of practising a dangerous form of mental prayer which went against the Church's teachings; her visions, it was claimed, were either illusory fancies or the result of demonic possession. At this time, the Inquisition had discovered hitherto unknown groups of *alumbrados* in some of the more isolated regions of Spain, particularly Extremadura and

Andalusia. These *alumbrados* spoke of raptures of the faculties which immobilised their physical bodies as if they were dead; these phenomena could be identified, by those who were unconcerned over finer details, with Teresa's 'suspension of faculties'. They believed too that they received visions and inner voices from God, and spoke of an intimate union with him. Still more unfortunately for Teresa, many *alumbrados* emphasised, like her, intense devotion to the humanity of Jesus. It must have appeared that the teachings outlined in Teresa's *Life* supported the ideas of the *alumbrados*, and her name became associated with them.

Domingo Báñez, then Teresa's Confessor, was alert to the danger. In 1575 he decided that the wisest course of action was to hand the original manuscript of the *Life* over to the central office in Madrid – after, we may note, he had made a few emendations. Báñez himself was convinced of Teresa's genuine piety and true spiritual insight, but he also understood the social climate of the time, and was against the book being freely circulated. Luckily, it was Inquisitor Soto y Salazar who was put in charge of the case; Teresa had previously met him and had made quite a good impression. Soto y Salazar asked Báñez to draw up a report on the book. In Báñez's report, no reason for censure was found; Teresa's intensions were clearly good, said Báñez, but he recommended that the book should not be published during Teresa's lifetime, and that the Inquisition should retain it, for some caution was necessary when it came to accounts of visions and personal revelations, and it was not appropriate that the book should be read by all and sundry.[14] Báñez's report put paid to the opposition for a little while; but after Soto y Salazar left his post as Inquisitorial officer (later in 1575) the Inquisition decided to renew investigations. Since Báñez was Teresa's Confessor, his view might be biased; another theologian should be asked for his opinion of the *Life*. This task was given to Hernando de Castillo, adviser of Philip II and a man of great authority and prestige; luckily his verdict was also favourable. (We will recall that Teresa had already found favour with Philip II.)

The Inquisition, then, retained the *Life* for ten years, until after Teresa's death, finally releasing it in 1586; copies of the original manuscript were, however, retained in secret all along, but were not openly circulated. Gradually more copies were made so that eventually quite a number were kept in the various Discalced convents. Nothing serious came of the Inquisition's investigation of the *Life* within Teresa's lifetime, although to have the book confiscated, and to be investigated by the Inquisition at all, meant further scandal, slander, and adverse publicity for Teresa and her Reform. Nor were Teresa's dealings with the Inquisition yet over; between 1575 and 1579 she was to endure further persecution sparked off by the foundation of her Seville convent. This, as touched upon in Chapter 1, was a very trying foundation for Teresa, with many difficulties to overcome. One reason for the problems was that the Bishop of Seville turned out to be opposed to the foundation, perhaps because he had had previous dealings with *alumbrados* and had heard of Teresa's recent investigation by the Inquisition.

After the convent had been founded, a number of women found their way into the community who in one way or another brought it into disrepute. One novice in particular, María del Corro, was apparently not up to the rigours of monastic discipline and left after about four months. To absolve herself of charges of spiritual weakness and to buttress her own self-righteousness (or so the picture is painted) she denounced the Discalced nuns to the Inquisition, accusing them of laxity, immorality, and of being guided by the same spirit as the *alumbrados*. It was claimed that Teresa lashed her nuns with a whip as penance, while they were suspended, dangling, by hands and feet; that the nuns did not veil themselves to go to Mass; that they held strange and suspicious ceremonies which might be of Jewish origin; that they confessed to each other or to a Prioress (that is, not to a male Confessor as prescribed). Most of these accusations turned out to be groundless, but Teresa had to endure tremendous worry and stress during the investigations. The tribunal at Seville could not verify the accusations or find a solution to Teresa's case, so asked for advice from Madrid as to how to proceed, sending a record of accusations received. The request was also made that Madrid should send to Seville the manuscript of the *Life* for investigation, for further allegations had been made about its content. The Seville Tribunal at this time seems almost to have decided that Teresa was, indeed, an *alumbrada* and a heretic. The Madrid Central Office, however, replied that the matter was already under consideration; the *Life* was not to be sent to Seville since it had already been examined by the Madrid Committee. Madrid recommended simply that the Seville Office investigate the matter more closely and questioned the nuns, in particular Isabel de San Jerónimo, whose name was at this time often linked with that of Teresa as possible *alumbradas*.

The Inquisitors, then, cross-examined the nuns at Seville ruthlessly, sometimes arriving unannounced so as to try to catch the 'culprits' unawares. Several Discalced convents were searched, and Teresa had to write for the Inquisition a defence of her religious life (the document known as *Spiritual Testimonies*). Gracián was very much afraid, believing that Teresa was about to be imprisoned by the Inquisition, and the whole community was living under the shadow of fear. Teresa, however, seemed not to lose her composure or inner peace. The Seville Tribunal did not have authority to make a final judgement on the case, but merely sent the results of these examinations to Madrid. We do not have the exact text of the final decision of the Madrid Committee, but we must assume that in 1576 a verdict was passed in Teresa's favour. In any case, victory was short-lived; rumours were soon circulating again in Seville and a new wave of persecution was initiated by the Calced Carmelites (as mentioned in Chapter 1), who sent accusations regarding the Discalced to the Inquisition.

This time allegations centred on the nature of Teresa's relationship with Gracián. It was claimed that she was notorious for her sexual excesses and that she had a string of lovers of whom Gracián was the most recent, and that Gracián also behaved in too intimate a fashion with some of the other nuns. One ludicrous accusation creates a rather amusing picture: that Gracián used to strip and dance naked before the nuns before retiring to Teresa's cell for the night! Teresa managed to persuade the Inquisition that these sexual accusations were ridiculous. By this time she was 61 years old; one wonders if she would have been so readily believed when she was younger, and, as all accounts make her out to have been, very beautiful. We need to note in this context that in sixteenth-century Spain insinuations were often made about the nature of relationships between confessors or spiritual directors and those women in their charge. The Inquisition had intervened in such cases several times and sometimes found the suspicions justified. Perhaps they thought they had uncovered another similar case. Teresa certainly made no secret of her friendship with Gracián, and the admiration and love which she held for him could easily be misconstrued.

The battle lasted until well into 1579, and all the members of the Seville convent had to endure great stress and suffering. Many old allegations against Teresa were repeated, including the claim that her visions were the work of the devil. Certain calumnies against Teresa were even perpetrated by some of her own nuns at Seville, under pressure of persecution and interrogation. Unfortunately, there were, too, in the Seville convent some nuns who had fallen into excesses which gave some weight to the accusations of illuminism. What Teresa judged to be the fruits of imagination and psychological disequilibrium, were believed by these nuns to be genuine God-sent visions. In spite of the fact that Teresa had tried to intervene and rectify the situation, she was held responsible for these anomalies as founder of the Discalced.

Teresa had written the *Interior Castle* in 1577, but the Inquisition had not investigated this work. Her meditations on the Song of Songs, *Conceptions of the Love of God*, had also been written some years previously. As we have shown, these two works contained strong Jewish mystical influences. It will now be seen that it was not surprising that Teresa's Confessor ordered her to destroy the manuscript of the *Conceptions*. It is my opinion that if the Inquisition had been aware of the full extent of Jewish influence in Teresa's writings – if, for example, they had investigated the *Interior Castle* or the *Conceptions* and had known enough about Jewish mysticism to recognise their debt to Judaism – their author might have ended her life at the stake.

In spite of the fact that Teresa's case was won, much damage had been done by this time to her reputation and that of her Reform. Rumours that she was an *alumbrada* and led an immoral life continued to plague her until her death in 1582. Occasional complaints continued to be made to the Inquisition, but these came to nothing.

A few years after Teresa's death, Luis de León prepared an edition of her works which was first published in Salamanca in 1588. Empress Doña María, sister of Philip II, helped smooth out some difficulties standing in the way of publication. (The *Book of the Foundations* was excluded from this edition, as it referred to many people who were still alive; but the *Life, Interior Castle, Way of Perfection*, and other works were included. The *Conceptions of the Love of God* was omitted; no doubt Luis de León was mindful of the trouble that his own translation of the Song of Songs had caused him with the Inquisition, and shrank from publishing any commentary on the scripture.) The books were at first received extremely favourably. But in 1589 a group of Scholastic Dominicans, led by Alonso de la Fuente, an active anti-illuminist who had worked to stamp out the *alumbrados* over more than seventeen years, delated the collected works to the Inquisition. Alonso de la Fuente was, no doubt, rigidly dogmatic, over-critical, even fanatical, seeing heresy in almost every form of spirituality. Nevertheless, it is interesting that this man, who had investigated the *alumbrados* closely over many years, believed that Teresa's doctrines and those of the *alumbrados* showed sufficient parallels as to be more or less identical. La Fuente had reduced the teachings of the *alumbrados* to a series of propositions; he believed that Teresa's books illustrated these propositions and that they contained a kind of secret, veiled heresy perpetrated within the Church, rather than outside it as in the case of the *alumbrados*.

Although 'heresy' is not part of my own conceptual vocabulary, I suspect that la Fuente was right in at least one sense. The *Interior Castle*, for example, as we have shown, refers in a secret or veiled way to Jewish mystical teachings. This is not, of course, to imply my approval of la Fuente's *censure* of Teresa's teachings on the basis of the fact that they were different from those of Catholic orthodoxy. La Fuente, and Teresa's other accusers, did not understand the nature of mystical experience or of *converso* culture; in this sense they condemned Teresa unjustly, seeking to understand phenomena of which they themselves had no experience by means of a narrow logic and a rigidly defined orthodoxy.

La Fuente asked that Teresa's works should be revised by competent and orthodox theologians. Ordinary women, la Fuente maintained, would read Teresa's writings and be unable to detect the potentially heretical errors in them because of their lack of training in theology. This man (who, it might be added, was no more sexist than many of his time and culture) furthermore held that it was by definition impossible for Teresa to receive genuine divine revelations on grounds of gender:

> The author of the said book passes it off and recommends it as doctrine revealed by God and inspired by the Holy Spirit; but if in fact the author was that nun whose name is on the title-page, it is a matter *praeter naturam* [outside the course of nature] for her to have written something taught by an angel, because it exceeds a woman's capacity.

And just in case this argument does not hit home, he weakly adds

In any case it could not have been a good angel, but a bad one, the same one that deceived Mohammed and Luther and the other leaders of heretics.[15]

Not very long had elapsed since the *Life* had been released from the offices of the Inquisition. In many cases, the same men were still in power in those offices; the nature of Teresa's teachings and their verdict on them had not changed since they last examined them, and understandably they responded less than enthusiastically to la Fuente's demand for an investigation. Nevertheless, the issue now concerned not just a manuscript copy of the *Life*, but the collected works, printed books which were being made widely available. Furthermore, the collected works included some writings – such as the *Interior Castle* – that the Inquisition had not yet examined.

The Inquisition therefore asked la Fuente for more specific charges. He drew up twelve articles covering, in summary, the following points. Teresa's apparent humility was in reality a 'false humility'. She was not a good woman, but possessed by a dangerous spirit, and her experiences were the work of the devil. Her teachings on rapture and ecstasy were the same as those of the *alumbrados*. She claimed, also like the *alumbrados*, that spiritual perfection could be gained in a very short time – as little as a few days. (In this, la Fuente was certainly misinterpreting Teresa's teachings.) La Fuente also found it objectionable that a woman should consider herself able to act as a spiritual teacher and to teach men. (As we shall see, sexist or misogynist attitudes coloured this phase of attack on Teresa's works.) He denounced her teaching that God dwelt in the centre of the soul, and her image of the soul as a castle with many mansions. The connections of Teresa's sevenfold castle with Jewish mysticism were not noticed. La Fuente's objection to the inner castle was that it was reminiscent of the writings of Tauler, a fourteenth-century German mystic who was a pupil of Eckhart, inasmuch as both Tauler and Teresa appeared to teach that the soul could be divided up into separate 'compartments' and that God was to be found most fully in the innermost of these, where that intimate union which is the culmination of the mystical life could be attained. La Fuente further argued against Teresa's teaching that it was necessary to 'recollect' the senses in order to enter the inner castle, and he objected too to her statements that we do not need to seek for God outside of ourselves, that mental prayer is sufficient to communicate with the divine and that we can hear God within. Teresa, he held, did not pay sufficient attention to vocal prayer and external rites, again like the *alumbrados*.

An anonymous defence of Teresa's books, and censure of la Fuente's criticisms, was sent to the offices of the Inquisition. Luis de León also wrote a further defence. During 1589–90 la Fuente sent three further letters to the Inquisition, reiterating his denunciations. In the second of these, he compared Teresa's teachings on mental prayer to those of the *alumbrados* in quite some detail, attempting to show their identity, misrepresenting Teresa's doctrines to some extent in the process. The Inquisitorial Office apparently gave no response, perhaps considering la Fuente's criticisms exaggerated, for over the next year or so it certainly seems that la Fuente fell out of favour with the Inquisition; he was suspected of making accusations without good foundation. Quiroga, the Inquisitor General, was favourably disposed towards Teresa; and furthermore, during 1590–91 the Inquisition was occupied with many newly discovered cases of illuminism and these, no doubt, had to take priority over la Fuente's concerns. La Fuente nevertheless persisted in his complaints against Teresa right up to his death in 1591. In this year the Teresian case was reopened and Juan de Orellana, who had known Teresa in her lifetime, was asked to examine her works. His verdict was that he considered Teresa to be a good Christian woman; her *intentions* were clearly good, but the books which she had written did contain heresies and should be banned. Orellana concentrated in particular on Teresa's assertions regarding the nature of union with God, which he claimed led to pantheism – a classic point of conflict between many mystics and orthodoxy, but not, in fact, a very convincing point on which to attack Teresa. Another theologian, Antonio de Quevedo, was also asked to report on Teresa's books at around the same time: he supported both Teresa's character and her teachings.

The Inquisitors now held all the relevant papers and judgements on Teresa and her writings, and could have made a decision either to condemn or to absolve Teresa. Strangely, they did neither. Another Dominican, Juan de Lorenzana, previously a supporter of Teresa, changed his mind, apparently due to Orellana's influence. He sent a report to the Inquisition in which he said that Teresa was a virtuous woman, but her teachings, due to her ignorance and lack of theo-logical education, were heretical. Her visions and personal revelations had been the result of deception by an evil spirit. Lorenzana also objected to the fact that a woman should presume to teach learned men regarding prayer and the spiritual life. Related to this point, which today we can see in terms of sexism and the battle for recognition of 'women's spirituality', is the interesting fact that Lorenzana also took objection to Teresa's claim that love and contemplation were more important than the discursive knowledge given by a theological training, which could sometimes be an impediment in the life of the spirit. As we shall argue in the next chapter, the need for recognition of women's spirituality is bound up with the need to overcome a rationalistic rejection of or fear of mysticism. We need a theology that will take into account women's religious experiences, and indeed those religious experiences of male mystics too, which fall outside the narrowly defined boundaries of theological orthodoxy and rationalist religious thinking.

Teresa's case was therefore reactivated in 1593. The Inquisition wrote to Toledo asking Orellana again for his opinion. Not surprisingly, his verdict was the same as before: he censured Teresa's teachings, accused Luis de León of sharing her ideas, and recommended that her books should be prohibited. In his new report, Orellana too drew attention to the fact that Teresa held that *experience* was the most important thing in understanding the life of the spirit, and that she gave greater weight to her own experiences than to the advice of learned men, scripture and Church authority. Teresa was a *mujercilla*, a 'little woman' with no education or theological training; if she ventured to sail on the ocean of spiritual knowledge it was inevitable that she would ground upon a rock, Orellana proffered condescendingly.

But, strangely, the Inquisition did not act on this advice, and withheld a decision. Before the eyes of its officers were many accusations and relatively few defences. Why did the Inquisition maintain silence on the issue? Williams writes:

> It was uncharacteristic of the Inquisition to neglect such reports. Its examiners were men of high standing, there was no question about their sincerity, they were courageous and were never afraid of bringing down the strong and successful. . . . Teresa was an important figure and there was still concern about illuminism. Yet it seemed almost as if by its refusal to act, the Inquisition was giving approval to the silent majority who supported Teresa and her writings.[16]

Perhaps this was the case, for Teresa's popular following had grown; the supposed incorruptibility of her body had been taken as a proof of her sanctity by many, and it was claimed that miracles had been worked through her supernatural intervention. But this strange refusal of the Inquisition to pass judgement could perhaps equally well be explained by the presence of Teresa's 'friends in high places' who included Philip II himself, Inquisitor Francisco de Soto y Salazar (mentioned earlier), and various influential theologians. Furthermore, Doña Luisa de la Cerda, a good friend of Teresa, was in the confidence both of Philip II and of Inquisitor General Quiroga (who was in any case, as we have said, inclined to view Teresa favourably). Doña Luisa had certainly used her influence to help Teresa earlier, when the Princess of Eboli condemned Teresa's *Life*; she had persuaded Quiroga that the Princess's accusations were unjust. She could have exercised her influence again in this new round of accusations. (It should not escape our notice, too, that the Inquisition was not above bribery; it was not unknown for its officers to be induced to remit sentences.)

When a further accusation was lodged by Francisco de Pisa in 1598, repeating many of the old charges, it was simply filed away in the Inquisition's archives and nothing more was heard of it.

In many ways, it seems to me, Alonso de la Fuente may have been right: Teresa may have been closer to the *alumbrados* than her orthodox apologists have led us to believe. Her accounts of visions, raptures and other mystical experiences are certainly similar (though in some respects not identical). Not only she, but many of her closest associates, were perceived as being sufficiently comparable to the *alumbrados* to occasion frequent accusations to that effect. Clearly, Teresa led a more virtuous life than many *alumbrados*; many would agree that she was a greater mystic and a more remarkable woman than most if not all of them. But she was also fortunate – fortunate enough not to be denounced as a heretic by the Inquisition. She managed to stay 'within the system' and to be accepted within it. From this vantage point she was able to offer much good counsel on subjects of tremendous contemporary importance – such as how to distinguish true visions from false ones, or why vocal prayer should not be abandoned altogether but practised alongside mental prayer.

But how many visionaries and mystics might there have been who were equally genuine, yet who were placed outside orthodoxy, persecuted and ultimately condemned by the Inquisition, their own search for truth brought to an end at some *auto de fé* because they chose to pursue the religious life in a way that orthodoxy deemed unacceptable? We do not need to labour the point regarding how perilously close Teresa came to the same fate.

One may even suggest that there are more similarities than are immediately evident between Teresa and the *alumbrados* regarding that most emotive of subjects in sixteenth-century Spain, sexuality. I do not wish to imply that Teresa broke her vow of celibacy, that she was involved in sexual practices like those of the *alumbrados*, or that her emotional dependence on Gracián and other men (commented on in Chapter 1) was any more than emotional. Nevertheless, one may perhaps suggest that Teresa's expression of mystical union in terms of the Marriage with the Divine King, her use of sensual imagery drawn from the Song of Songs, and even those aspects of her psychological and emotional nature that caused her strong attachments to her confessors – that these symbolic and emotional factors might spring from the same basic *impulse* as that which motivated the *alumbrados* in their sexual practices, that is, an intuition that divine love and human love are in some respects similar, and that one can serve as an apt symbol for the other. This is not to reduce divine love to the level of sublimated sexual frustration on the part of celibate ascetics, as some psychologists would have us believe; rather it is to acknowledge that human love has something of the divine in it and can be a genuinely spiritual experience. The sexual practices of the *alumbrados* were, of course, denounced without question by the Catholic Church in the sixteenth century. Today, however, in the light of the comparative study of religion and also of more broad-minded social attitudes, we may wonder whether the *alumbrados* might not have suffered from biased evaluation. Sexuality is, after all, used in a ritual context in Tantra (an esoteric teaching found in both Hindu and Buddhist forms) and has similarly been used by some modern esoteric groups.

The fact that Teresa escaped the Inquisition's clutches is on the face of it surprising. Certainly, she had a degree of popular opinion in her favour, and she had friends in high places, as we have said; but this in itself may not be sufficient to explain her escape.

We have seen that as a *conversa*, as a woman, as a mystic and visionary, and as a reformer, Teresa was very vulnerable. She had to protect herself from accusations of heresy by frequent statements of her submission to the authority of the Church, and she had constantly to convince the theologians of her milieu that her visions and voices were not demonic. She submits her writings to her confessors and spiritual directors with an apology for her lack of learning, asking them to correct anything that they find amiss. If she has written anything that is not in conformity with the teachings of the Church, she says, it will be through ignorance. Until recently, such statements – found in Teresa's prefaces and prologues, and in her letters to her confessors – have been read at face value. But the matter is more subtle than it may appear. Teresa was a very shrewd woman, and she had a carefully nuanced way of submitting herself to the authority of the Church while at the same time never abandoning her belief in the veracity of her own direct, personal experience of God. It is obvious that there are many facets of the Church of Teresa's day with which she is less than satisfied; yet her devotion to the Church as an *ideal* does not falter, and more importantly for our present discussion, she is willing to open and close her works with formal statements of submission to the Church, statements, that is, which are formal inasmuch as they sound much like the confessions that were soon to preface the works of all Roman Catholics. Some examples from the prologues, forewords and epilogues of Teresa's works include the following:

> In all that I shall say in this Book, I submit to what is taught by Our Mother, the Holy Roman Church; if there is anything in it contrary to this, it will be without my knowledge. Therefore, for the love of Our Lord, I beg the learned men who are to revise it to look at it very carefully and to amend any faults of this nature which there may be in it. . . .

> If I should say anything that is not in conformity with what is held by the Holy Roman Catholic Church, it will be through ignorance and not through malice.

> If there is any error in it [the *Interior Castle*], that is due to my lack of understanding, for in all things I submit to what is held by the Holy Roman Catholic Church.[17]

Egan, commenting on the formal tone of these submissions, feels that Teresa is willing to comply with what she must feel to be a requirement of the contemporary ecclesiastical atmosphere in Spain, in order to achieve her goals. In this respect she is a pragmatist, recognising that to achieve things 'within the system' she must yield on non-essentials.[18]

We need to distinguish here, no doubt, between Teresa's submission to the Church and her attitude to the Inquisition; the Inquisition 'may be an arm of ecclesiastical polity, but for Teresa it is obviously not at the heart of what it means to be Church'.[19] Her submission to the Church – especially when she has in mind her own ideal view of the Church, what it spiritually ought to be, what it could become if her Reform and others like it take effect – is perhaps more genuine than her shows of humility before the Inquisition. Nevertheless, she only submits to the Church on the implicit understanding that she will continue to adhere to her own unique interpretation of Christianity which she finds compatible with the 'ideal Church'. Never does she allow her individual vision to be obscured by the weight of tradition and ecclesiastical hierarchy. She does not always accept the dictum of the Catholicism of her time that priests and confessors speak with the authority of God and therefore must know better than she. As for the Inquisition, her submission to this body is probably little more than politic. Those who have wished to uphold Teresa's orthodoxy have often cited her expressions of submission to the Inquisition and to the authority of the Church, taking them, as I have said, at face value. But this ignores the fact that a woman in Teresa's already dangerous position would have been in effect committing suicide if she had said anything other than what she did say. Anyone whose life and writings were being investigated by the Inquisition, if they valued their personal safety and set a high premium on the continuation of their work, would be bound to make numerous humble submissions of faith and orthodoxy. The question is to what extent these submissions were a 'front'. To suggest that this may have been the case is not to accuse Teresa of dishonesty, still less of any lack of genuine Christian faith: she was working within an oppressive, racist, sexist, and fanatically dogmatic system, and anyone who has ever tried to change such a system from within will understand the compromises that she would sometimes have had to make.

Against Teresa's formal statements of submission, we need to set some of her more revolutionary pronouncements. For example, during the course of the problems in Seville, Gracián expressed his alarm and fear at the turn which the Inquisition's investigations were taking. Teresa, however, declared to him that she was not afraid, for even if she should go to the stake, she would be willing to die a thousand deaths as a martyr for Christ's sake.[20] Here she sets her own judgement above that of the Inquisition, for according to the latter, anyone who went to the stake could not be a martyr for Christ. A further example concerns the teaching of the Church in Teresa's day that women should not teach or expound the Scriptures, but be silent and submissive: a dogma derived from an injunction attributed to St Paul, the implications of which we shall have occasion to look at in the next chapter. Although Teresa was happy to make formal statements of submission to the Church, when her visions or revelations dictated a different course she would obey the latter. Musing over these oppressive regulations regarding the role of women in the Church, Teresa experienced a locution in which Jesus said to her: 'Tell them [the men of the Church] that they shouldn't follow just one part of Scripture but that they should look at other parts, and ask them if they can by chance tie my hands.' Morón-Arroyo points out the explosive potential of this text, in which the theological basis for the silent position of women in the Church is seen in Teresa's vision as being challenged by Jesus Christ himself.[21] Teresa, in other words, sets her own understanding of Jesus' revelation to her, over and above the interpretation of Christian tradition advanced by the Church authorities. On other occasions, she receives divine permission to refuse obedience to her superiors, and is 'forever receiving special commands straight from the top to get out there and be herself'.[22]

Teresa was, then, treading a thin line between orthodoxy and heresy in the eyes of the authorities. In spite of the revolutionary potential of aspects of her teachings, and in spite of her vulnerability as a woman, *conversa* and visionary, she managed to escape serious condemnation because of her political shrewdness and her willingness to clothe her writings in expressions of humility. (We might add, too, that the bureaucratic inefficiency of the Inquisition seems to have worked in her favour!) Thus while she did in fact set her own spiritual experiences above the Church's received tradition on certain specific occasions, she nevertheless is willing to make a 'blanket' statement to the effect that her spiritual favours are as nothing compared to obedience to the Church. Aware of the virtues of flattering the enemy, she speaks of herself as an ignorant woman always ready to submit to the judgement of learned men. 'In short, she disarms the Inquisition, as she did all who would lord it over others, with a gentle, ironic show of submission.'[23]

Were Teresa's teachings an example of what have been called esoteric teachings? What has come to be known as the Western esoteric tradition (though the 'tradition' may have been discontinuous) developed largely out of the synthesis of Kabbalah, Hermeticism, Platonism and Rosicrucianism in the Renaissance. Its best-known revival in recent times was initiated by the Hermetic Order of the Golden Dawn in the late nineteenth century, and the 'tradition' has been continued to the present day by a variety of related esoteric schools. We have seen that Teresa's work is deeply influenced by Kabbalah and that it bears some relation to the broader stream of Christian Kabbalah that became popular in the Renaissance. At the same time, it could not be said to be central to this upsurge of Renaissance thought in the same way as, say, the writings of Pico della Mirandola, Agrippa, Reuchlin, or the other major European exponents of the esoteric synthesis. It was once alleged, during the course of the Inquisition's investigation of Teresa and her works, that she held doctrines similar to those espoused by Pico della Mirandola, but in reality the comparison is not very convincing, except inasmuch as both were influenced by Kabbalah in different ways. Many of Teresa's Kabbalistic images, as we have seen, derive from an earlier stratum of Spanish Kabbalah which had been perpetuated by *converso* families, rather than rediscovered by Christian Renaissance scholars. Her central symbol of the sevenfold castle, we have argued, is derived from Jewish Kabbalah. Unlike the writings of the Renaissance Christian Kabbalists, her works do not show evidence of the influence of Neoplatonic and Hermetic thought. Overall, her writings may be said to show more Jewish than Christian Kabbalistic influence.

Nevertheless, this earlier Kabbalistic stratum could itself be described as esoteric. By an esoteric teaching is usually meant a 'secret' body of knowledge of a spiritual or salvific kind, transmitted, often though not always, orally, to a relatively small group of select disciples – a transmission which will often, though not inevitably, involve initiation of some kind. In addition, it is often the case that teachings described as esoteric offer a hierarchical map of reality which must be followed closely if true knowledge is to be attained.[24] That is to say, the cosmology of esotericism is highly structured; the vision is of a universe consisting of many interrelated layers of being or reality, which are reflected in a similarly 'layered' psychology, for the human being is the microcosm that reflects the wider macrocosm, or the universe seen as a spiritual whole. Through initiation and/or transmission of the secret teachings, the esoteric seeker gains access to the different levels of the multi-layered universe. A further claim often made regarding esoteric teachings by their exponents is that they offer a 'short cut' to divine reality: a swift method, but one that has its risks, and is full of danger for the unprepared or unworthy.

The early Hekhalot/Merkavah tradition of Judaism and the Spanish Kabbalah of the *Zohar* could easily be described as esoteric traditions according to these criteria. So too, perhaps, could the oral Kabbalistic teachings perpetuated by the *conversos*. Many of the essential characteristics of esotericism could also be said to apply to certain aspects of Teresa's teachings. The notion of a many-layered spiritual universe, and of ourselves as a microcosm mirroring this macrocosmic pattern, is seen in Teresa's sevenfold castle: the castle is simultaneously both God and the self, both the soul and the terrain through which it must travel, and the septenary division of the castle into mansions reflects a layered hierarchy of distinct yet interrelated inner experiences, corresponding to seven levels of being or spiritual reality. Teresa reminds us that we are each of us a microcosm reflecting the macrocosm: we are each 'an interior world, wherein are the many and beauteous Mansions'.[25] She also appears to credit the possibility of a 'short cut' to the King in the seventh mansion of the castle[26] and she certainly speaks of dangers and sufferings involved in attempting this journey, as we have seen, warning us that if we meet with any resistance we must not try to force an entry into any of the mansions, and that if our level of spiritual development renders us unworthy of approaching the King, we will not progress far.

Can her teachings be said to be secret, available only to a select few? Certainly during her own lifetime this was the case, though by accident rather than design, because of the fact that she wrote primarily for the nuns of her own Reform and because of the restrictions placed on the circulation of her writings. But here we need further to draw a distinction between the potential and the actual. In most esoteric bodies of knowledge it is in fact held that all human beings have the *potential*, innate within themselves, which would allow them to attain the culminative heights of esoteric experience, but that few are aware of, or make use of, this potential in *practice*.

Writers have often denounced esoteric systems for their supposed 'élitism' without appreciating this point. Now as far as Teresa is concerned, the experience of the inner castle is in theory available to us all – we are *each one of us* an 'interior world'. Nevertheless, few of us realise this divine heritage within, or bring it to fruition: most of us are content to stay in the environs of the outer court of the castle; we are not interested in entering it and do not know how many rooms it has;[27] or if we do get into the castle, we do not often progress beyond the first or second mansions. The heights of mystical attainment, then, are reserved *in practice*, though not *in theory*, for a minority. The castle itself is indeed an apt symbol of an experience reserved for relatively few, walled, defended, and protected from the outside world as it is, with its inner rooms difficult to penetrate.

We have already noted Teresa's frequent references to the 'secrets' (*secretos*) and 'mysteries' (*misterios*) revealed in the Spiritual Marriage and contained, she says, in the very words of the Song of Songs. The *Zohar* speaks of the seventh palace, the Palace of Love in which the mystic is united to the King, as 'a secret entrusted to the wise alone'.[28] Teresa also sees the seventh mansion of her castle as a place where secret knowledge is revealed:

> In the centre and midst of them all [i.e all the mansions] is the chiefest mansion where the most secret things pass between God and the soul.
> . . . this secret union takes place in the deepest centre of the soul, which must be where God Himself dwells. . . . This instantaneous communication of God to the soul is so great a secret and so sublime a favour . . . that I do not know with what to compare it.[29]

The question must be raised why the Kabbalistic elements in Teresa's works – and in the *Interior Castle* in particular – did not attract more attention; why were they not denounced by the Inquisition? Swietlicki has, implausibly to my mind, suggested that this might be because Kabbalistic symbolism was regarded as acceptably 'orthodox' by the Inquisition, because of its having been used in Christian Kabbalistic apologetics for several centuries. But, as has been said, the Hekhalot/Zoharic symbolism of the seven-roomed palace had not been employed by Christian Kabbalists in this way, and I have argued that this aspect, at least, of Teresa's

Kabbalistic symbolism is likely to be derived from *converso* tradition. It seems to me that the Inquisition was simply not aware of the origins of Teresa's castle image. If this is so, and if Teresa herself *was* consciously aware of its origins in Jewish tradition, then it follows that her teachings were 'secret' or 'esoteric' in this respect too, that is to say, nuances of her meaning were concealed under a veil of symbolism.

It is not necessary to postulate here some clandestine esoteric Jewish society to which Teresa belonged. The 'esoteric' works more subtly than some popular writers on the subject would have us believe, and more often than one might suppose, it is found within the 'system' or established religious authority, its 'secrecy' being maintained by pulling the wool over the authorities' eyes, so to speak, as Teresa did *vis-à-vis* the Inquisition. Teresa's beliefs and experiences placed her on the borderline of orthodoxy as it was then understood. She chose to 'fight the system from within', and by means of the creative tension thus produced, to revitalise and reform established structures. Her understanding of religion had been transformed by the living reality of personal experience, yet she chose to accept the Church's structures and forms of interpretation as parameters within which she could work, and which she could enhance through her unique vision. Others whose beliefs were not so different from hers placed themselves (or were placed) outside the fold, as the trials of the *alumbrados* and others indicate.[30] With the Inquisition always at hand, contemplatives like Teresa whose religious life was founded on personal spiritual experience found themselves always on the verge of being branded as heretics. There was an ongoing tension between contemplatives, and the orthodox Scholastic theologians (*letrados*), whom Teresa spent so much time trying to convince that her experiences were not of the devil. Egido sees Teresa's apparent congeniality towards and friendship with some of these theologians as a 'tactical maneuver adopted to allay suspicions'.[31] Whether this was so or not, in sixteenth-century Spain there was certainly a rift between theologians, and *espirituales* – those who lived and wrote about the spiritual or contemplative life through their own direct experience. Thus one of the major theological issues of the day was the question of the relationship between 'subjective' personal religious experience (represented by the 'spirituals') and religious truth as defined by the theology of the time, believed to be 'objective'. The rift between the two is clearly relevant to the question of Teresa's orthodoxy, and to her need to defend the value of her own experiences. 'Teresa had to present her experience in a way which would clearly distinguish it from Illuminism and Lutheranism, so that it would not be considered suspect or condemned by the Inquisition, hence her constant preoccupation with orthodoxy and her frequent recourse to her spiritual directors and confessors.'[32]

I must emphasise that in suggesting that Teresa was not fully orthodox, I do not mean to discredit her. Her hidden heterodoxy does not make her any less saintly, for the Inquisition was founded on premises that we today would not accept. Teresa's life was guided by the highest standards and in my view she had genuine spiritual insight: but spiritual insight is not coextensive with narrowly defined orthodoxy or dogmatism (indeed one might well suggest that it is rare for the two to coexist). This then raises the question: how many of those who were denounced by the Inquisition and went to the stake, also had genuine insight? Their unfortunate end came about because the Inquisition chose to find them unorthodox and Teresa acceptable: but 'orthodoxy' is simply that which is given sanction or made 'official' by a particular culture. There are many reasons why Teresa was found acceptable; some have been given in this chapter, and to them one must add her genuine integrity, love of truth and of virtue. But this should not lead us to suppose that it is an easy matter to divide mystics into the 'good' and the 'bad', their doctrines into the 'true' and the 'false'. In the light of cultural pluralism and the comparative study of religions, we must admit that it is probable that many who went to the stake had genuine spiritual experiences and ought not to have been denounced. It was purely the narrow dogmatism of the Inquisition and of the Church in sixteenth-century Spain that determined their tragic fate. As O'Donoghue says,

> There is a kind of massive assumption . . . in the writings of Catholic historians and commentators that these other visionaries who were condemned and destroyed were deluded or depraved. This assumption, it seems to me, is wide open to challenge. . . . It may be well to add that the assumption of some non-Catholic authors that all these visionaries were neurotic is an equally massive and obtuse assumption.[33]

Many previous studies of mysticism have been based on the intellectual prejudices or religious leanings of the author, who holds that one characteristic type of experience expresses the 'essence' of mysticism. Any example of religious experience that does not exhibit this characteristic is regarded as not being an instance of 'true' mysticism – it is seen as being inferior or even entirely delusive.[34] It is, however, becoming increasingly clear in the light of the comparative study of religions, that it is not possible to uphold such assumptions, which are usually based either on religious dogmatism, or on ethnocentric attitudes which fail to allow us to appreciate the mystical experiences of other cultures on their own terms. Today, we need to begin to evaluate with a more open mind certain forms of spiritual experience previously denounced as not being instances of 'true' mysticism – such as the experiences of those condemned by the Inquisition. We are beginning to appreciate that different types of spiritual experience must be understood on their own terms rather than from the standpoint of the orthodox establishment.

'Orthodoxy' is that which is sanctioned by a given religious and cultural tradition: and in any given culture it is the norms of the ruling sex, class and race that are sanctioned in this way, as Rosemary Radford Ruether has argued. In any particular culture, the experiences of those of other sexes, classes or races are not given official recognition; they are often seen as unorthodox, subversive, heretical. Ruether has shown that witches, Jews and heretics alike were seen in late medieval Christian imagination as agents of the devil plotting to subvert the true faith, and, interestingly, suggests that many of the same stereotypes came to be projected onto both witches and Jews: both groups were seen as devil worshippers who stole the Eucharist, performed blasphemous caricatures of Catholic rituals, practised child immolation and so on; both were held to be impious and insatiably lustful for sex.[35] (One might suggest that official Christian thought has projected onto witches, Jews, heretics and other similarly oppressed groups images corresponding to all those aspects of its own imagination which it wished to repress or deny. It need not surprise us, then, that Teresa was accused of sexual promiscuity.) In the next chapter, we see how the norms of the ruling sex, in particular, affected evaluations of Teresa's experiences, her quest for reform, and the issue of her orthodoxy.

CHAPTER 5

Teresa and the Issue of Women's Spirituality

A restless, disobedient, stubborn, gad-about female
who, under the guise of piety, has invented false doctrines, left the enclosure of her convent against the
orders of the Council of Trent and her own superiors,
and has gone around teaching like a Professor, contrary
to the exhortations of St Paul who said that women were
not to teach.[1]

This was how one of the most powerful Churchmen of Teresa's
time – Felipe Sega, the Papal Nuncio – described her. The
denunciation was uttered during the course of Teresa's troubles with
the Inquisition over the events at her Seville convent, and it should
not escape our notice that in referring to Teresa as a *fémina
inquieta* – which I have translated as a 'restless female' – Sega may
have had more than just this simple statement in mind. The term
inquietos, 'restless ones', was also used by the Inquisitors to refer to
the disciples of Juan de Avila, a *converso* prophet and mystic who
had attracted a large popular following in Avila a little earlier in
Teresa's lifetime. The *inquietos*, many of whom were *conversos*,

experimented with the spiritual exercises of Ignatius Loyola – that is, the Jesuit spiritual methods – and practised prohecy. We have seen that Teresa was greatly influenced by Jesuit forms of spiritual training and meditation. Did Felipe Sega suspect her of being a sympathiser of Juan de Avila?

Whatever the answer to this may be, we must read Sega's denunciation of Teresa in the light of the Inquisition's investigations of her and also of the sexist – even misogynist – attitudes prevalent in sixteenth-century Spain. Teresa was vulnerable, and at risk from the Inquisition and the ecclesiastical authorities, for three inter-related reasons: because she was a visionary and mystic; because she was of Jewish ancestry; and because she was a woman. Her difficulties in justifying her own religious experiences to theologians and confessors, and in implementing her work of reform, were very much bound up with these three factors. We have looked at the first two points in previous chapters. In this chapter we shall take up the final point, and we shall be concentrating on how Teresa's female gender affected her religious experience, her expressions of religious belief, and her attempts to bring about religious reform, in sixteenth-century Spain. In the process we hope to point to some common areas of concern for feminism and mysticism, and to indicate the importance of looking at female mystics for both women's studies and the study of religions.

There is, at present at least, no conclusive evidence to suggest that men and women mystics have substantially different *experiences*. As Ursula King notes, religious experience has so far been described largely without attention being paid to gender differences: scholars have examined different variables which might affect the content of religious experience, but sexual differentiation has not been one of them.[2] Much research, then, still needs to be done in this area; but for the present we can say that as far as we can tell, there do not seem to be distinctively 'female' and distinctively 'male' forms of mystical *consciousness*. Indeed, one of the things that strikes many people about the writings of different mystics is the similarity, independent of gender, of the experiences described.

It is worth a brief diversion here to mention that many forms of mysticism in fact advocate the attainment of a state of consciousness that is, psychologically speaking, *beyond* sexual differentiation. These forms of mysticism describe their goal as the attainment of a psychologically androgynous state, that is to say a state in which qualities traditionally seen as 'feminine' (such as receptivity, intuition, compassion) are held in perfect balance and synthesis with qualities traditionally seen as 'masculine' (such as outward-going activity, strength, logic). Now this very polarity of so-called 'masculine' and so-called 'feminine' traits may itself be defined by an androcentric (male-centred) way of viewing the world – a point to which we shall return. If this is so, then the usefulness of the polarity itself in any attempts to formulate a spirituality for women is limited, although certainly the androgynous ideal of uniting the opposites and rising above sexual dualism is one that holds much promise for contemporary spirituality. But whatever we make of this, Teresa herself is certainly a good example of one who combined in her person both types of characteristics (whether we see them as 'masculine' and 'feminine' or not): she was both contemplative and highly practical, both strong and deeply caring.

Mystical traditions that espouse such a notion of androgyny tend also to see the Deity or the spiritual Absolute as having both masculine and feminine aspects; or the Deity may be seen as being beyond all opposites, with the explicit implication that this includes being beyond the polarity of masculine and feminine. Examples include, in the East, Taoism, Tantra, and Śaivism; in the West, spiritual alchemy, Gnosticism, and the Kabbalah, which were all elements of the Renaissance Hermeticism current in Spain and Europe in Teresa's time. But in spite of the fact that Kabbalah taught that the Godhead was composed of both male and female qualities, Teresa, notwithstanding the Kabbalistic influence elsewhere in her works, always speaks of God as male. It is possible that her devotion to the Virgin Mary might have answered on the psychological level to some inner need for balance between male and female images of Deity, but it cannot be said that, for a Catholic, her devotion to the Virgin is especially marked. What is perhaps a more tantalising speculation in this context is that the union of Teresa, as a woman, with the male God, Jesus – with the King in the seventh mansion – may approximate on a psychological level to the notion of the union of feminine and masculine found in the figure of the androgyne. (If Teresa is made one with Jesus, then she presumably experiences herself as both female and male.)

Even supposing, however, that the mystical *experiences* of women and men are fundamentally similar, and that they may each often tend towards an 'androgynous' goal, there may well be gender-related differences in modes of expression of these experiences. Aspects of Teresa's *self-expression* are related to her gender, as is the fact that her religious life as a woman was constrained in various ways by the society in which she lived.

As we have seen, women in Teresa's culture had only two lifestyle options open to them: marriage, which meant constant pregnancy and childbirth, having to surrender one's autonomy and submit to the will of one's husband in everything; or secondly the religious life. It is well known that some women who chose the latter did so, not so much from a genuine sense of religious calling, as because they failed to marry; but it is only recently that we have come to appreciate that others who became nuns did not *wish* to marry. The monastic life, for these women, was a way of gaining a measure of personal autonomy and of accomplishing something outside the restricted sphere of the home. Many of these women found in the cloister greater freedom than they would have found in the home, ironic as that seems to most of us today. The institution of celibate monasticism allowed them to create what women today might call their own 'space'.³

In Teresa's case, her religious experiences from her forties onwards, and the strength and confidence that she eventually found through these, enabled her to affirm that her true vocation did, indeed, lie in the monastic life; but she entered the Convent of the Incarnation some twenty years before this, when she was only 21, and at this stage in her life she was certainly not motivated by any great feelings of pious devotion. In fact her perception of the role of women in sixteenth-century Castile played an important part in her decision to become a nun. As we have seen in Chapter 1, her own mother had died, unhappy, unfulfilled, her health eroded through increasingly difficult pregnancies, in her thirties, when Teresa was only 13; '. . . a traumatic loss to Teresa in those early years when she herself was entering adolescence and the ambiguity that accompanies adolescence for girls in a patriarchal culture'.⁴ Significantly, then, Teresa later reminds her nuns how thankful they should be to Jesus, the Heavenly Bridegroom to whom nuns are bound in spiritual union, for having released them from (in her own words) 'being subject to some man, who so often brings a woman's life to an end – and God grant he may not also ruin her soul'.⁵

She was, she says, 'afraid of marriage'⁶ which she saw as little more than being a slave to one's husband. A wife, she says, must follow her husband's every whim, appearing happy if her husband is happy and sad if he is sad, regardless of how she may actually feel. 'See what slavery you have escaped from, sisters!'[7] A natural 'leader', courageous, adventurous, intelligent, a little headstrong, Teresa could not bring herself to take on a role of total submission. It seems that her feeling that marriage and family life were not right for her has been shared by many nuns, female mystics, and women religious leaders in diverse cultures.

Within the religious life, on the other hand, women had greater opportunities for self-expression, for taking on leadership roles, and for autonomy, although even here their activities were curtailed in many ways. McLaughlin, in an article on women in medieval theology (which still dominated Spanish Catholicism in Teresa's time, in spite of the influx of Renaissance philosophies), shows how, despite general medieval suppositions of woman's inferiority and subordination to man, there could be found in the religious life a theoretical equality between the sexes; nevertheless, this theoretical equality was 'from the first undercut by fundamentally androcentric conceptions'.[8] But Teresa could at least have found a more positive role for herself within Christian monasticism than she could have expected in the even more male-dominated ambience of orthodox Judaism, had her family left Spain in 1492 along with those other Jews who refused even to give lip-service to Christianity. Within the context of Christian monastic celibacy, women could claim virtual equality with men on a spiritual level by renouncing their worldly sexual role and function. They could transcend what was seen as their natural subordination to men by living at a more transcendent level at which sexual hierarchy no longer applied.[9] Furthermore, it is, I think, true that many women of centuries past who have been called to the spiritual life – and this is so within many religious traditions – have managed to attain a freedom from the usual social and cultural roles which bound the great majority of their contemporaries. The pursuit of and fruition of their spirituality gave them, it seems, a certain power, authority and personal integration, making them stand out in the history of religion as strong women who have been prepared to take a courageous and dynamic stand against many odds on the basis of their own experiences. They stand out as women who have found themselves, who have truly realised themselves; and this in itself makes them not only mystics but also feminists of a type, for one of the most pervasive strands of feminism has been its insistence on the necessity for women to find and express their real selves, rather than being made to feel that they must conform to culturally imposed stereotypes of femininity which do not provide fulfilment for all women. Other Christian women mystics who offer parallels with Teresa in this respect include Hildegard of Bingen and Catherine of Siena. McLaughlin shows how similar patterns can also be observed in the lives of the Anglo-Saxon nuns Lioba (eighth century) and Christina (twelfth century).[10] In the East, we could cite several female mystics who were adherents of the *bhakti* devotional movements mentioned in Chapter 2, such as Mīrā Bāī, Mahādēvī, and Lalleśwarī. Ramanujan has shown how many female *bhakti* mystics defy traditional social norms, particularly those relating to accepted stereotypes of womanhood, marriage and the family.[11]

A short discussion of Hildegard of Bingen's life will illustrate this point. Hildegard, who lived from 1098 to 1179, was a Benedictine nun, mystic, visionary, and religious reformer. Like Teresa, she founded several monastic houses, travelling widely until her mid-seventies. She taught on spiritual matters and wrote many books, not only on mysticism and theology but also on medicine, in which she was a recognised authority of her time. She was obviously very talented in many different ways, for she also composed highly acclaimed music. In some ways she was more lucky than Teresa: she was not deprived of the opportunity of education. She studied the sciences of her day avidly, and probably wrote in Latin (although some believe that her Confessor translated her dictation from Middle High German into Latin). Furthermore, although Hildegard encountered some opposition to her teaching, preaching, and reforming activities, this was not as severe as the persecution which Teresa suffered. We have to remember, of course, that Hildegard was not living under the shadow of the Inquisition. The Church ruled in Hildegard's own lifetime that her visions were divinely inspired, and this seems to have caused relatively little controversy. Her visions, recorded in several of her works, are complex, emotionally powerful, and replete with vivid imagery: Hildegard had miniatures drawn to illustrate them and a study of the text of her visions together with the illustrations is fascinating.

Nevertheless, Hildegard's quest for self-realisation was not devoid of the problems encountered by women in male-dominated societies. As Fox has said, 'She is a woman in a patriarchal culture and a male-run church who strove to be heard, who struggled to offer her own wisdom and gifts borne of the experience and suffering of women of the past. In a letter to St Bernard of Clairvaux she complains of the burden she carries as a woman in a patriarchal culture.'[12] She has been called the first medieval woman to reflect and write at length on women, and was actively involved in the social and political life of her time, corresponding with popes, bishops and monarchs:

> She castigated a pope for his timidity and an emperor for moral blindness. She taught scholars and preached to clergy and laity as no woman before her had ever done. . . . She claimed that now woman rather than man – obviously Hildegard herself – was to do God's work. It is difficult not to see in her visionary experience and activism, as well as her claim for the mission of women in a male-dominated age, a gesture of protest, the reaction of an intelligent and energetic woman who chafed under the restraints imposed on women by the culture in which she lived.[13]

Like Teresa, Hildegard had to break away from her original Order, founding her own Abbey, becoming a determined and strong religious leader in her own right. She freed her community from the control of her former abbot, and secured the protection of the Emperor in a way perhaps similar to Teresa's finding of favour with Philip II. It is interesting to note, too, that like Teresa, Hildegard had a spiritual awakening in her forties – at age 42, one or two years older than Teresa – as a result of which she 'took command of her vocation and creative life'.[14] She had apparently had visions from an early age, and so the disjuncture with her earlier life is perhaps not so great as it was for Teresa. Nevertheless, just as Teresa's health, previously extremely poor, improved somewhat after she had taken her life and her vocation into her own hands and acknowledged her unique calling and vision, so Hildegard was cured of sickness when she allowed her creative and mystical powers to come to fruition. Even though she had experienced wonderful visions and insights previously, she had repressed them, partly, it seems, because of social pressures, refusing to write them down or communicate them to others. But once she decided to write, it literally got her out of bed. Both Teresa and Hildegard, then, experienced in their early forties a breakthrough in which, as a result of religious and visionary experience, they refused to be constrained by the limitations

placed upon them as women in male-dominated cultures, limitations which told them it was not their place to write or preach or
found convents or abbeys. Both insisted on following their own
forms of self-expression and reforming action, on expressing themselves as individuals and following what was right for them,
refusing to be stereotyped on grounds of their gender. And in each
case this finding of themselves, this acknowledging of their true
paths in life, had a healing effect on body and psyche.

In centuries past, then, it has sometimes been possible for determined women to accomplish, within the religious life, more than
they might have done if they had opted for the alternative role of
submissive wife and mother. Nevertheless, this should not blind us
to the fact that the restrictions that women have had to face in their
pursuit of spirituality have often created ambiguities which have
made it impossible for them to participate in the religious life on
equal terms with men. For example, in Teresa's culture, it was generally believed that both sexes were created in the image of God, and
that both could therefore be called to know their Creator by following the spiritual life; but the image of the male was believed to be the
more perfect or to possess God's image more fully! Men were identified with the rational mind and with spirit, women with the 'sins of
the flesh' and the downward drag of corporeality which held one
back (so it was believed) from knowing God. Much could be said by
way of challenge to this very dualism, which still persists today in
popular assumptions that women are more passive, emotional, sup-
posedly embodying the 'Mother Earth' archetype, and that men are
more rational and active. Paradoxically, in some contemporary
religious groups the identification of women with the earth, nature,
the emotions, intuition, etc., is uncritically accepted, though an
entirely new and more positive evaluation is put upon these aspects
of existence.[15] In my opinion, we need to ask, on the contrary,
whether this supposed polarity of women/body/emotion/earth
and men/mind/logic/spirit is itself androcentric. It could even be
said to be, in origin, misogynist, since the body is seen as subordinate to the spirit, emotions inferior to reason, and hence women as
inferior to and dependent on men, in all examples of this polarity
before the modern period. As McLaughlin argues,

> The misogynist elements of the medieval Christian tradition had their
> theological basis in the dualist and spiritualist anthropology inherited

from New Testament and patristic sources, reinforcing the patriarchal character of the religion of the Old Testament. This dualism
between flesh and spirit, body and intellect, was clearly androcentric
in its identification of the male with the element of spirit or mind, the
female with flesh and sexuality.

Arguing that it is necessary to make explicit the assumptions that
still permeate many people's thoughts today, and which derive from
this tradition about male/female difference and hierarchy,
McLaughlin points out that the insights of the social sciences have

> . . . called into question the implicitly rationalist definition of human
> nature by which the feeling and responding side of our being is deni-
> grated and perceived as specifically feminine.[16]

Rosemary Radford Ruether likewise tries to expose the misogynistic
nature of these forms of dualism:

> Sexism is based symbolically on misappropriated dualisms. The dia-
> lectics of human existence: mind/body, spirituality/carnality,
> being/becoming, truth/appearance, life/death – these dualisms are
> identified as male and female and are socially projected upon men
> and women as their 'natures'. The meaning of the feminine thus
> becomes modeled in classical spirituality on the images of the lower
> self and world. Autonomous spiritual selfhood is imaged (by males,
> the cultural creators of this view) as intrinsically masculine, while the
> feminine becomes the symbol of the repressed, subjugated and
> dreaded 'abysmal' side of 'man'. . . . The woman, the body, and the
> world were the lower half of a dualism that must be declared pos-
> terior to, created by, subject to, and ultimately alien to the nature of
> (male) consciousness, in whose image man made his God.[17]

It is true that the identification of women with the earth, which
may have its origin ultimately in agrarian fertility symbolism, is
found in many societies, and cannot be ascribed in all these cases to
the influence of medieval dualism in Christian culture. It is found,
for example, in India and in some African societies. But this does not
exclude the possibility that the woman/body/emotion/earth,
men/mind/logic/spirit polarity might be identifiable with androcentric ways of thought, that is to say with patriarchal cultures. In
this case we may suggest that it does not promote equality but
represents men's views of women rather than women's views of

themselves. A perspective that is really in women's interests must allow women's experiences, ideas and ways of being to be evaluated on their own terms, rather than from within the framework of a preconceived androcentrism. A great deal more research needs to be undertaken on this topic, on which we can say no more at present; the importance of further investigation in this field is illustrated by Rita Gross' statement that 'the fundamental challenge and potential of women's studies in religion . . . is its delineation and critique of androcentrism.'[18]

For our present purposes, we may return to the fact that in Teresa's time and culture males were identified with the rational mind; therefore intellectual knowledge was considered fitting only for men, and women were denied an education. Teresa was lucky inasmuch as her wealthy background ensured that she had at least had the opportunity to learn to read and write; but she frequently laments the fact that she is at a great disadvantage because she has not had the opportunity to study. The limitations that her initial lack of education imposed on her were made still worse when in 1559, as we have described in Chapter 4, the Inquisition condemned and burned books that were considered unorthodox, thus in effect leaving next to no religious or spiritual works available in the vernacular which women could read; and since they were not granted a Latin education, they could not read any works that remained available in Latin. But further, Teresa's lack of training in theology made it extremely difficult for her to justify her spiritual experiences to learned men (*letrados*), who could present counter-arguments to challenge her intuitive promptings, debate fine points of doctrine, and cite scriptural passages in support of their own convictions. Teresa had great respect for learning and intelligence, and, not unnaturally, she was sometimes intimidated by the interrogations of the theologians who were asked to investigate the nature of her religious experiences. As we have seen, Teresa had to defend the value of her own experiences before confessors, theologians, and Inquisitors, and had to convince these men – and herself – that she was not another of those women visionaries whom the Inquisition had recently been declared to be heretics deceived by the devil. It was widely believed that such deceptive, demonic experiences occurred principally to women and seldom to men, for women were believed to be inherently defective creatures, morally, intellectually and physically. (It is worth remembering that in the vast majority of witchcraft accusations in the Middle Ages – surely the prime example of misogyny in Christian history – the victims were women, believed to be in league with the devil.) It must have taken a great deal of courage for Teresa to stand up for herself, to trust her own heart and conscience, and to insist on the validity of her own experiences, particularly in such a dangerous political climate. One theologian who had been very supportive of Teresa, Pedro Ibáñez, in a written statement composed between 1562 and 1564, inadvertently gives us information about Teresa which in retrospect we can see to reflect a typical experience of a woman lacking self-confidence in a patriarchal culture. 'Whenever these visions and raptures came to her', he writes, 'she felt perfectly certain that they came, not from the devil, but from God; but, once they had gone, as she feared God and was mistrustful of herself, she believed what these people said to her and accepted the reasons which they gave her for thinking her to be deceived.'[19] Teresa bears this out herself:

> . . . when I am in prayer, and on days when I am enjoying quiet and my thoughts are fixed on God, all the learned men and saints in the world might unite in tormenting me with all imaginable tortures, and, even if I wanted to believe them, they could not make me believe that this is the devil's work, because I cannot. When they did try to make me believe this, I was afraid, seeing who they were that spoke to me in that way, for I thought that they must be speaking the truth, and that I, being who I was, must be mistaken.[20]

When she trusts her own experience, Teresa is convinced of its divine origin. As we have seen, she refers on a number of occasions to the problems that can occur if one's spiritual director does not understand the nature of personal religious experience or of one's particular spiritual path. One passage in her writings also suggests that she had to combat the attitude of some of her opponents that the mystical life was not suited to women at all: '. . . again and again people will say to us: "It is dangerous", "So-and-so was lost through doing this" . . . "It is not meant for women; it may lead them into delusions", "They would do better to stick to their spinning", "These subtleties are of no use to them".'[21]

Teresa, then, as we have already discussed in previous chapters, had to take a stand on the authority of her own experiences. This point has wider implications. Recent studies in the area of women and religion have suggested that women's own religious experiences have not been taken into account in the articulation of doctrine and religious teaching. Women's experience has not, with very few exceptions, been reflected upon or creatively drawn upon; rather, it has been excluded, even, at times, ridiculed. In our time, feminist thought generally has emphasised the primacy of women's experience as authoritative; experience itself is seen as having a normative function, that is to say, it is women's own experiences and their reflections on them, rather than preconceived imposed cultural stereotypes, that should establish standards against which women and their ideas or actions may be assessed. Feminist religious writers have thus tried to put forward new evaluations of women's religious experiences, but these, of course, are still a long way from winning general acceptance. For Teresa, in her culture, the definition of 'truth' put forward by the Church authorities often defined women's religious experiences as 'heresy' or excluded them from consideration altogether. Indeed, as we have seen, Alonso de la Fuente, one of the theologians who denounced Teresa's works to the Inquisition after her death, held that it was by definition impossible for a woman to receive genuine divine revelations, simply on grounds of gender! A more satisfactory theology, which we still stand in need of today, would have to entail acceptance of a wider variety of types of religious experience, as experienced by both women and men. Religion must take into account the experiences of human beings of both sexes; a male-centred spirituality written by men, from the perspective of men, and primarily for men, cannot do this.

We have referred to the traditional polarity whereby men are identified with logic and learning, and women with intuition, emotion and the body. The mistrust shown by many traditional forms of theology towards intuition, lived experience, and ·other non-rational dimensions of awareness, is inextricably related to rejection of the feminine. Women have, as a matter of historical fact, been identified, by male theologians and philosophers, with the body, emotions, experiential knowledge, etc.; and both women, and the body/emotion/intuition complex, have then been simultaneously repressed, seen as the 'lower' of the two categories of reality, the inferior pole of the dichotomy.

This is not to say that the polarity is itself *correct*; I have already suggested that the view of reality which sees it as dichotomised into these two opposing poles, represented by the male and the female respectively, is itself androcentric. Social pressures in the past (and even, to some extent, in the present) have banned women from the pursuit of intellectual knowledge, and have likewise discouraged men from acknowledging and expressing their emotions. It may well be true that women in the past have embodied a more affective mode of spirituality and men a more intellectual mode. (Teresa, as we have seen, valued love of the divine more highly than rational knowledge.) But this, in my view, is due not to innate predispositions of the sexes themselves, but to the social pressures that have encouraged different norms for men and women, considering different forms of behaviour as socially acceptable for each gender. That this is so is illustrated by the fact that some male mystics do adopt an emotional, affective mode of expression. An example is Richard Rolle, discussed in Chapter 2; significantly, Rolle 'dropped out' of the traditional intellectual education prescribed for males in his culture, rejecting this analytical form of knowledge for a more emotional approach to the love of God.

In my view, we need to envision a more holistic view of human nature in which we acknowledge that *both* reason and logic, *and* intuition and experiential understanding, are equally important to us as human beings, whether we are male or female; that these are complementary and equally valid aspects of our living, each necessary for our wholeness and personal integration. Those writers who, in the cause of women, uncritically accept the male/spirit, female/earth dichotomy and all that it implies, thereby attempting to argue for a re-evaluation of the female/earth, are in my view perpetuating a polarised view of reality which itself needs to be challenged. Nevertheless, this does not negate the fact that the mistrust of non-rational dimensions of awareness has been historically and socially connected with rejection of the feminine. But the repression of experiential awareness and intuition has also gone hand in hand with suspicious attitudes towards mysticism, religious experience, and claims to personal revelations or visions, because, of course, mysticism is so deeply rooted in personal experience and is less rationalistic than formal theology. This suspicion of mysticism is buttressed by the political and social control exercised by a Church hierarchy for which any claim to direct knowledge of God is a threat to established order. Now since many women in centuries past were excluded from the study of theology, they naturally had only their own experience to fall back upon in their quest for religious meaning. Hence, as King notes, women have made a considerable contribution to the mystical traditions of all religions. (In more recent years, as women have been allowed access to education, they have also been prominent as scholars of mysticism.) In the mystical aspects of religion, 'spiritual authority and experience come into their own. . . . we deal with a creative area of religion with more flexibility and less rigidity and institutionalisation.' Thus King suggests that 'the interrelationship between feminism and mysticism deserves particularly close study.'[22]

A more satisfactory theology, then, must emphasise personal experience and must be based on our reflections on our experiences and their relevance to our lives, rather than on ratiocination unrelated to living experience. It must seek to include different types of experience rather than automatically rejecting certain types as deluded. It must recognise that reality is something greater than any one person's experience of it, and that what may appear to us to be a misapprehension may in fact be an insight into an aspect of reality which we ourselves do not see.

This is not to say that experience itself is the be-all and end-all of spirituality. Teresa, like many other mystics, warns us against seeking after spiritual experiences – such as visions and raptures – for their own sake. She teaches that the important thing is the effect these experiences have on the way we live (a true vision is known as such by its 'fruits'). The value of spiritual experiences lies in their ability to transform the self and bring it into closer relationship with a reality broader and more comprehensive than our previous limited understanding could show to us.

Nor is it to say that *all* experiences must necessarily reflect spiritual truth (though they are certainly all valid as *experiences*, that is to say, we can learn something even from a delusive experience). Teresa puts forward numerous criteria, as we have seen, for distinguishing true visions, auditions, and raptures, from false ones (though today we would wish to modify some of her criteria in certain respects, in the light of inter-religious dialogue and our awareness of the value of the different faiths of the world). But it seems to me that the criteria advanced by many traditional Christian theologies exclude and repress many forms of spiritual experience which should be regarded as valid and valuable. If experiences are to be measured against external standards, these standards must be far broader and more all-encompassing than has so far been the case. Teresa says that God leads souls by many paths and that there is no reason why we should expect everyone else to travel by our own road.[23] She certainly suffered a great deal at the hands of those who believed that her own path led in the direction of hell and that her experiences had no part to play in a correct view of reality. It would be wrong to see her as a model of modern ecumenism – she is as prejudiced against the growing wave of Protestantism as most Catholics of her time. Nevertheless, it is clear that her experiences opened her to a realisation that reality was broader or more multi-faceted than she had previously supposed, and that there might therefore be more than one path to God.

Teresa's religious options were restricted still further by the strict rules of enclosure with which nuns were supposed to comply, and by related limitations placed on women in her culture. Needless to say, women were excluded from the sacramental function of the priest-hood: they could not be ordained. Nor were they supposed to undertake any form of religious teaching, missionary activity, or expounding of the Scriptures. They should not preach or write on matters considered the exclusive province of scholars. It was dan-gerous to presume to advise learned men on the spiritual life, as Teresa did; as we have said, Alonso de la Fuente and Juan de Lorenzana, in their denunciations of Teresa's writings to the Inquisi-tion, both took objection to the fact that Teresa, as a woman, should consider herself able to act as a spiritual teacher to men. Finally women should not travel about but should be gathered protectively behind cloistered walls. Although Teresa had to make formal state-ments of her submission to such rules, she was far from happy with them, as her less formal statements show. The Church's dogma that women should not teach or expound the Scriptures was based on injunctions attributed to St Paul: 'Let a woman learn in silence, with all submissiveness. I permit no woman to teach or to have authority over men; she is to keep silent.' 'The women should keep silence in the churches. For they are not permitted to speak, but should be subordinate. . . . it is shameful for a woman to speak in church.'[24]

As mentioned in Chapter 4, when Teresa was once musing over these oppressive regulations regarding the role of women, she experienced a locution in which Jesus himself challenged the Church's position. In other words, she gives greater weight to her own understanding of what she believes to be Jesus' revelation to her, than to the Church's traditional teachings regarding the appro-priate place of women.

Teresa envied those men who were able to travel abroad as missionaries, to preach, and to spread their beliefs through their theological training and knowledge. She complains at the fact that her sex bars her from these activities. The soul advanced to the state of the sixth mansion of Teresa's sevenfold castle 'would like to plunge right into the heart of the world, to see if by doing this it could help one soul to praise God more; a woman in this state will be distressed at being prevented from doing this by the obstacle of sex and very envious of those who are free to cry aloud and proclaim abroad Who is this great God of Hosts.'[25] Part of her remedy was to proclaim the efficacy of prayer, and the important, though silent, role played by women following the spiritual life in her convents. In her small communities of nuns, the perfection of the spiritual life would be adhered to as closely as possible, and the nuns would carry out an apostolate of prayer for those who were involved in the Church's affairs on a more worldly and practical level. But in addition, Teresa herself refused to be constrained by the restrictive roles prescribed for women. In spite of active disapproval, she did travel around founding monasteries all over Spain, undergoing, as we have seen, tremendous physical hardship in the process. She did teach. She did not always accept that her confessors and superiors must know best. She did carry on spiritual friendships with men, in spite of the malicious gossip this caused at a time when nuns were subjected to as strict a separation as possible from men, even those who administered the sacraments to them. She even dares to expound the Scriptures, writing, incredibly, her own commentary on the Song of Songs, as we have seen. It is in the light of these facts that we must understand Felipe Sega's denunciation of Teresa given at the beginning of this chapter.

Yet cultural biases which perpetuate sexual stereotyping have coloured the view of Teresa advanced not only by her contemporaries, but also by many writers much nearer to our own time. Baker, in 1919, reflects biases almost as powerful as Sega's in his one-sided evaluation of Teresa:

> It is difficult to dispute the fact that women, even the greatest of them, fail in invention. With all her gifts Teresa could not rise above restoration of a religious order to its original purity, a work parallel to restorations accomplished by others, already perhaps a little out of date. She was surpassed by Ignatius Loyola, whose masculine genius

perceived . . . that, if headway was to be made against Protestantism, it must be by the foundation of something new.[26]

Even as recently as 1972, Llamas Martínez holds that Gracián,
being a man, was by virtue of this fact more 'objective' and less
governed by emotion than Teresa.[27] Yet when Teresa shows characteristics or personality traits of which critics of this type approve,
they do not hesitate to label them as 'masculine'! Mary Giles notes
the unfortunate tendency, among Spanish writers in particular, to
refer to the prose of their women writers as 'masculine' if it is terse,
strong, incisive, direct.[28] Likewise an English scholar writes in 1957
that Teresa's mind 'often showed a masculine turn in its readiness to
take the lead'.[29] Why does he not simply take Teresa's case as
evidence that women *can* be good leaders? Teresa is seen as
truly feminine on account of certain aspects of her personality
which such critics find wanting, while they claim as typical characteristics of their own sex, those features of her character which they
admire! Anne Borrowdale illustrates how difficult it is for women
to escape such forms of stereotyping, which confirm and perpetuate
prejudice:

> People notice when women behave in an expected way, and this
> behaviour confirms and strengthens the stereotype. Thus a woman
> who preaches a bad sermon proves the generalisation that 'women
> can't preach', although men have preached bad sermons for centuries
> without this reflecting on men as a whole. But if women behave in an
> unexpected way, it either goes unnoticed, or the woman is seen as an
> exception who does not prove that other women can be able. Either
> way, the stereotype can continue.[30]

As King has noted, women mystics of the past who achieved spiritual authority became recognised as persons in their own right (as
we would put it today); but the dominant androcentric perspective,
and the enormous limitations inherent in the traditional understanding of women's roles and abilities, meant that women of such
strength of spirit were seen as being 'men', meaning that they had
transcended what were believed to be the innate limitations of
womanhood. (Another way of looking at this would be to say that,
in effect, only men were seen as capable of being persons in their
own right. Comparable attitudes are still encountered today, and
have led to the possibly cynical observation that women who

achieve public or professional recognition are seen as 'honorary men'!) King highlights the inherent sexist presuppositions in such attitudes, which attribute certain desirable roles or qualities to one sex only: why did Teresa have to exhort her nuns to be courageous as strong men? Why can women not be seen as being courageous and strong in their own right?[31] This point is graphically and ironically illustrated, as it happens, by an incident in Teresa's own life. The Dominican Provincial, Juan de Salinas, was suspicious of Teresa before he met her; but when Domingo Báñez, then Teresa's Confessor, persuaded him to see her, he became convinced of her great virtues and abilities. But since women could not possibly be credited with such admirable qualities as strength and wisdom, de Salinas forthwith declared to Báñez: 'You informed me wrongly when you told me that Mother Teresa was a woman; i'faith she's a man and one of those most worthy to wear a beard.'[32]

A related point concerns the assumption, referred to in Chapter 2, of male commentators that Teresa's account of the 'Transverberation' (her vision in which her heart was pierced with a flaming spear) is self-evidently erotic. In interpretation, commentators must avoid both stereotyping on grounds of gender, and projection of their own perceptions of sexuality and sexual symbolism onto subjects of the opposite sex.

I do not mean to imply that it is only men who are guilty of sexist attitudes: some women writers also perpetuate the process of sexual stereotyping. For example, Quitslund, in an otherwise helpful article on feminist spirituality and Teresa, makes considerable assumptions as to what may be said about women in general, ignoring the fact that women are individuals and may differ from each other as much as individual men do. In particular, she identifies the 'feminine' with the 'maternal', arguing for example that Teresa's love of children showed that she had not denied her femininity.[33] The danger with such an attitude is that it appears to suggest that women's spirituality is essentially linked to motherhood, or else to some other form of expression of 'maternal' feelings. Not only does this view become almost self-contradictory in its exclusion of most nuns; it also perpetuates sexual stereotyping of the kind that we need to transcend (in this case, the stereotyping that defines women primarily in terms of their biological role as bearers of children). While it should not, of course, be denied that motherhood is a genuinely spiritual experience for *some women* (as, one hopes, fatherhood is for some men) a comprehensive view of women's spirituality must explore the many different spheres of women's experience, including, for example, work, creativity, and so on, and must allow too for a full expression of spirituality on the part of women who do not have children and who may not be 'maternal'.[34]

Was Teresa what we would now call a feminist? While, as King notes, it would be falsifying historical evidence to present all women mystics of the past as espousing all our modern feminist ideals, it remains true that the liberating qualities inherent in mysticism allowed female mystics to exemplify women's struggle for autonomy and self-affirmation.[35] There are many different kinds of feminism, many different possible feminist stances; but a feminist might be defined as one who supports the right of women to define their own path in life, to express themselves and realise themselves, without being stereotyped, discriminated against, or forced into particular roles, on grounds of gender. (In this sense, as others have pointed out, not all feminists are women – men who are supportive of the feminist cause can also be called feminists. The right of men to a similar freedom from stereotyping also needs to be supported, although this lies outside the scope of our present discussion.)

Some writers have seen Teresa as an entirely inappropriate spokesperson for the self-realisation and autonomy of women, but I believe that this is due to a failure to see some of her statements in their social context. It is true that she sometimes refers to women as weak, lacking courage, easily taken in, and slow in understanding (though always allowing that there are exceptions to these rules, among which she often includes herself!).[36] She makes occasional disparaging remarks about being a woman which, as she puts it, is enough to make your wings droop.[37] But these remarks must be seen in the context of the limitations, repressions and prejudices that the culture of sixteenth-century Spain placed upon women. As Hellwig says, Teresa's apparently negative and self-deprecatory allusions to being a woman often turn out to be simply a ruthlessly realistic acknowledgement of the limitations under which women in sixteenth-century Spain were forced to operate.[38] Thus when Teresa refers to her female body as an added trial from God, she is making a realistic statement of fact about limitations caused by sexually determined role-definitions in her culture: she is not condoning these role-definitions, and it seems to me that it is incorrect to see her as 'anti-feminist' on this account, as does the writer of one recent review.[39] It is hardly surprising, either, that Teresa thought of her body as something vile and dirty: this was a general feature of medieval thought, and was held to apply to men's bodies as well as those of women (although, since women were identified with the body and men with the mind, this belief does seem to have affected women disproportionately). But the fact that Teresa refers to her body in disparaging terms must be seen in the light of her social context; it is inappropriate to criticise her for not espousing late twentieth-century ideals.[40] (One might also add that even today, many women, including those who consider themselves feminists, continue to wrestle with deep-seated problems concerning their perceptions of their bodies, problems which have their roots at least partially in this same medieval identification of woman with 'sinful' sexuality/body/earth.)

Similarly, when Teresa refers, as she frequently does, to her sin and unworthiness, her self-reproach and sometimes excessive humility reflect the accepted religious thinking of her time; some feminist writers are apt to forget such contextual issues when looking at women of other times and cultures. But more than this, it was advisable, even necessary, for Teresa to make such statements under the watchful eye of the Inquisition. As we have seen, Teresa had to protect herself from accusations of heresy by frequent statements of her submission to the authority of the Church, and she had constantly to convince the theologians of her milieu that her visions and voices were not demonic. So too, she had to make numerous submissions of faith and orthodoxy, emphasising her humility and imperfection, to the Inquisition. And it was advisable that she sometimes gave lip-service, in these submissions, to the accepted role of women.

It is not an exaggeration to refer to such statements as 'lip-service', I believe, for Teresa's apparently negative statements about women are usually very brief, even passing remarks; but when we look at those longer passages where she seems to be expressing her own viewpoint rather more forcefully, we find that such negative remarks can sometimes be little more than a shrewd use of politics on her part. In the following passage, for example, in which Teresa is giving advice on prayer and the spiritual life, she begins by referring to herself as a weak, irresolute woman; she goes on to flatter the egos of the learned men whom she is addressing; and she ends by giving them a piece of her mind and calling *them* weak!:

As for a poor woman like myself, a weak and irresolute creature, it seems right that the Lord should lead me on with favours [i.e. visions and related spiritual phenomena]. . . . But when I hear servants of God, men of weight, learning and understanding, worrying so much because He is not giving them devotion, it makes me sick to listen to them. . . . They should realize that since the Lord does not give it to them they do not need it. They should exercise control over themselves and go right ahead. Let them take it from me that all this fuss is a mistake, as I have myself seen and proved. It is an imperfection in them; they are not advancing in freedom of spirit but hanging back through weakness.[41]

In another passage, quoted below, Teresa begins by giving brief voice to the generally accepted view of her time that women are weak; goes on to advise women to keep their spiritual experiences to themselves in view of the indiscretions of certain men; and ends by saying that women should be encouraged in their pursuit of spirituality. The context of this passage shows that the 'certain persons' with whom Teresa says she discussed her prayers, were the theologians who declared her visions and voices to be demonic, and the 'great trial' that she refers to at the beginning is the trial of having one's inner life investigated in this way.

This is certainly a great trial to undergo, and requires cautious treatment, especially from those in charge of women. For we are very weak and could come to great harm if we were told outright that the devil was deluding us. These cases should be very carefully considered, and women should be removed from all possible dangers. They should be advised to keep their experiences to themselves, and their advisers should keep them secret too. I speak as one who has suffered grave trials from the indiscretions of certain persons with whom I have discussed my prayers . . . . For they have divulged things which should rightly have been kept private, since they are not for everyone. . . . I think they should have kept completely silent. . . . I think then that women should be directed with great discretion, and should receive encouragement.[42]

Against Teresa's occasional negative statements about women we need to set those passages where she defends women loudly and clearly, affirming their worth, seeing beyond the narrow outlook of her own era. As a Prioress, she was naturally well aware of the problems that could be experienced among a community of nuns

living together, and she admits candidly to many of the imperfections of these women. But she did believe that it was possible for her
nuns to rise above those faults that were in her day considered
characteristic of women – such as petty rivalries, and lack of courage – and to be as strong and courageous as men, so that men
themselves would be amazed.[43] There are many passages in her
writings that suggest deep dissatisfaction with the role of women in
her culture. We have already mentioned the locution in which Jesus
himself is portrayed as challenging, through a vision he grants to
Teresa, the position of women advanced by the ecclesiastical authorities. It is interesting to note that the emphasis Teresa places in this
former passage on the attitude to women held by Jesus – as opposed
to the attitude sanctioned by Church tradition – is echoed by much
modern feminist Christian theology. The same emphasis can be seen
in the following passage in which Teresa contrasts Jesus' view of
women with that of the men she has to deal with, and complains at
the limitations caused by enclosure of nuns:

> Nor did you, Lord, when you walked in the world, despise women;
> rather, you always, with great compassion, helped them. And you
> found as much love and more faith in them than you did in men.
> Among them was your most blessed mother. . . . Is it not enough,
> Lord, that the world has intimidated us . . . so that we may not do
> anything worthwhile for you in public or dare speak some truths that
> we lament over in secret, without your also failing to hear so just a
> petition? I do not believe, Lord, that this could be true of your good-
> ness and justice, for you are a just judge and not like those of the
> world. Since the world's judges are sons of Adam and all of them are
> men, there is no virtue in women that they do not hold suspect. Yes,
> indeed, the day will come, my king, when everyone will be known for
> what he is . . . these are times in which it would be wrong to under-
> value virtuous and strong souls, even though they are women.[44]

This entire passage, with the exception of the first sentence, was
omitted from the second redaction of the *Way of Perfection*, at the
insistence of a certain theologian who thought Teresa's statements
too bold! It is still frequently omitted from Spanish editions of
Teresa's works. This is a clear illustration of the way in which
women's writings have often been 'edited' to make them accord with
official and less challenging views of women.
    Equally telling is Teresa's account of her sufferings when she

began to experience visions and other mystical phenomena. She was very much afraid, as we have seen, since there had recently been several cases of women who had reported such phenomena and who had been judged to be deceived by the devil, and burnt at the fires of the Inquisition. As we know, some of the men who investigated Teresa's case did indeed consider that she was being deluded by the devil, a phenomenon which in fact is not confined to Christianity or to the period of the Inquisition, for it seems that controversial female religious leaders will very often be judged by men in institutionalised positions of religious authority to be possessed by evil spirits.[45] Teresa was so intimidated by her own lack of learning in the presence of theologians that she could not find words with which to dispute the verdict of these men regarding her experiences. She says that she did not dare to contradict them for fear that they would accuse her, a 'mere woman', of trying to instruct them. She felt that they were mocking her, as if her experiences were just feminine fancies. She does not mince words in her insistence on the value of rapture and the way in which, she feels, women who claim such experiences are oppressed:

> What power the soul has when the Lord raises it to a height from which it looks down on everything and is not enmeshed in it! . . . it feels pity for those who are still blind, especially if they are men of prayer to whom God is granting consolations. It longs to cry aloud and call their attention to their delusions; and sometimes it actually does so, only to bring down a storm of persecutions on its head. Particularly if the person in question is a woman, it is accused of lacking humility, and of wishing to teach those from whom it should learn. So they condemn it . . . for they know nothing of the force that impels it.[46]

Luckily, as we have seen, Teresa did begin to meet people who understood her. She went to stay with her friend Doña Guiomar de Ulloa and in fact stayed with her, away from the Incarnation, for a full three years, a fact which is not often mentioned in accounts of Teresa's life. Doña Guiomar had supported Teresa all along. She too had had spiritual experiences of her own, and it seems that the two women understood each other, for Teresa says that Doña Guiomar was enlightened where learned men remained in the dark, and describes their friendship as closer than that between sisters.[47] Doña Guiomar's manifestations of religious enthusiasm were apparently considered rather dubious in Avila. Some thought her foolish but harmless, while others considered that she too was being deceived by the devil. Doña Guiomar had been widowed for three years and, given the social and moral norms of sixteenth-century Castile, no doubt her reputation was not enhanced by the fact that she, as a widow, had been fond of wearing brightly coloured clothes and heavy make-up, although she may have become rather more restrained at the time of her friendship with Teresa. It seems likely too that she associated with certain heretical figures, some of whom Teresa might have met. It is hard to tell whether Doña Guiomar was the victim of the same sort of sex-based discrimination as Teresa, or whether her religious enthusiasm really was of a much lower order than Teresa's, and possibly due to psychological or emotional imbalance, as previous writers have unanimously declared. Yet if Teresa's judgement of character is to be credited here, it would seem that we have to accept the authenticity of Doña Guiomar's spirituality.

As mentioned in Chapter 1, it was Doña Guiomar who arranged for Teresa to meet Peter of Alcántara, and we have seen what respect and admiration Teresa had for this remarkable man. She tells how much encouragement he gave her just when she needed it; how he understood her because of his own spiritual experience; how he explained to her the nature of her visions. And, she adds, 'He used to say that women made much more progress on this path than men, and he gave excellent reasons for it . . . all in women's favour.'[48]

The view that 'women made much more progress on this path than men' may be borne out by Teresa in certain respects. Although she appears to concur with the generally accepted view of her time that women are more easily deceived than men by the devil, she seems to suggest in one place that this is due to women's lack of education in the psychology of the inner life rather than to any innate intellectual defect.[49] In this connection Quitslund believes that 'While Teresa certainly recognized a difference between men and women in terms of academic accomplishment and psychological maturity, she did not accept this as a permanent ontological reality' so much as a result of women's lack of education and training.[50] But furthermore, it seems that Teresa may have believed that the very openness and receptivity that made women more easily led by the devil's wiles, also made them more open to God's grace, and hence, perhaps, more likely than men to receive genuine divinely sent mystical experiences, or at least more likely to experience visions and other phenomena. 'The Lord grants these favours to many more women than men, as I have heard from the saintly friar Peter of Alcántara, and have also observed for myself' she confirms.[51] In spite of her respect for scholarship and her regret at not having been granted an education, she certainly believes, too, that unlettered women have a certain quality of intuitive or experiential insight into the ways of the spirit, to which the majority of theologians of her time were blinded by their exclusive concentration on discursive knowledge.

It is worth saying a little more on this latter issue. On the one hand, Teresa certainly valued book-learning. She was distraught when the Inquisition prohibited the reading of so many books on the spiritual life. She lists among the duties of a Prioress that of providing books for the community of nuns, and of teaching novices to read where they were illiterate. She regretted that she herself did not have more time for reading. She expresses a preference for 'women of intelligence' in the choice of nuns for her communities. When one of the Prioresses at a convent Teresa had founded complained that a particular nun was too fond of reading, Teresa retorted, 'Better a bookworm than a fool!'[52] Thus although Teresa takes a stand on the importance of personal experience as a way to knowing the divine, she respects the different type of knowledge of the scholar. Given the prevailing attitudes of her culture, her approach to the education of women was forward-looking.

On the other hand, Teresa often found herself caught in a dilemma over the relative values of these two modes of knowledge or perception – rational learning and intellectual knowledge on the one hand, and experiential perception and intuitive awareness on the other. Her dilemma was due to the fact that she was aware that she was poorly educated by comparison with the theologians under whose guidance she pursued her life of contemplative prayer; rarely did she dare to contradict them. Yet she realised too that men who had had no personal spiritual experience of their own could not fully understand her, however learned they might be. Mary Giles suggests that Teresa's ambiguity here 'is reflected in her contradictory advice to her nuns – that they should seek spiritual counsel because they were, after all, ignorant and weak women, but at the same time they were to remain silent about their experiences lest they be misunderstood and ill advised'.[53]

As Teresa became older and gained in self-confidence it seems that she grew to trust her own conscience in her evaluation of her experiences. Thus in a document written near the end of her life she asserts that 'I no longer need to consult theologians . . . I only want to satisfy myself as to whether I am on the right road and can do some work.'[54] In her *Conceptions of the Love of God* she speaks disparagingly of certain learned men (*letrados*) who do not even have the beginnings of spirituality and who try 'to reduce everything to reason and to measure everything by their own understanding'.[55] According to Pedro Ibáñez's statement · in support of Teresa (referred to earlier), she once received a locution in which Jesus revealed to her that he chose to communicate with women because learned men would not or could not commune with him:

> Once, in particular, when speaking to Him, she said: 'Lord, are there no other people, especially men and persons of learning, who, if Thou didst speak to them, would do this that Thou commandest me, far better than I, who am so evil?' But His Majesty answered her, as one sad at heart: 'Nay, the men and the persons of learning will not fit themselves to commune with Me, and so I come, in need, yet rejected by them, to seek feeble women to whom I can speak freely and with whom I can discuss My business.'[56]

The implications of such statements are revolutionary. But this should not lead us to suppose that Teresa did not have good relationships with a number of theologians and male scholars. As we have seen, she had a number of close spiritual friendships with men, and even many of those theologians who were initially sceptical of her experiences came eventually to respect her. We can imagine, however, that the types of men with whom Teresa got on best were those like Peter of Alcántara, who had a regard for women unusual in his time and was prepared to encourage and support their spiritual quest; or like John of the Cross, who was so ethereal and otherworldly a character that it is easy to believe that he 'saw only souls'[57] and treated everyone alike regardless of their sex. By contrast, Gracián once rebuked Teresa for daring to criticise her betters when she tried to give him some unwelcome advice. Although some thirty years her junior, he was to be regarded as her 'Father' and superior by virtue of his sex.

Related to Teresa's emphasis on personal experience as a means of religious knowledge, is her use of forms of religious expression which it has been suggested are typical of women mystics generally before the modern period. Since Teresa was excluded from studying theology, she could not express her religious experiences in abstract, metaphysical language, and indeed, on the occasions when she tries to use the language of medieval psychology – the language of the 'faculties' – she is often imprecise. Instead, she turned primarily to two alternative and more concrete forms of expression: the mystical autobiography, and the use of allegory and symbolism.

The autobiographical literary form permeates not only Teresa's *Life*, of course, but also her *Interior Castle*, *Book of the Foundations*, and other works. The use of this literary form enables Teresa to take her own personal experience as her starting-point, and enables her to formulate broader statements about the spiritual life in general through her reflection on her own experiences. Although it is easy to see that she might have been accused of subjectivism here, it has been argued that Teresa managed to overcome the tension between 'subjective' religious experience, and what was believed to be 'objective' religious truth as represented by theology (a tension that was at the forefront of religious thought in her day, as discussed in Chapter 4). Teresa does this, Chorpenning argues, by relating her accounts of her own experiences to accepted hagiographies: that is, she uses the life stories of the saints as 'role-models'. Hagiography, as an established part of Church teaching and tradition, offered a

> . . . formal model for assimilating personal experience into that teaching and tradition . . . it provided a method of relating the experience of a particular individual to the ways of divine Providence and to an objective pattern of spiritual growth. . . . St Teresa consciously or unconsciously found in hagiography not only an interpretive aid for understanding but also a method for presenting her life and experience in an objective way. Consequently, hagiography provides Teresa [with] a way of resolving the medieval dilemma of the tension between subjective religious experience and objective truth, without resorting to the abstract concepts and theorems of Scholasticism.[58]

Secondly, Teresa makes use of numerous allegories and forms of symbolism, which play a crucial role in her attempts to communicate her mystical experiences, ideas and teachings. (This may well be due to her Jewish background as well as to her lack of training in abstract modes of theological thought, for, as we have shown, Jewish mystical tradition uses allegory and symbol in a very similar manner to Teresa.) In one famous allegory, Teresa sees the soul as a garden, the plants in the garden representing the qualities cultivated by the self. This garden can be watered in four ways: by taking the water from a well by hand, which is laborious; by means of a water-wheel and buckets drawn by a windlass; from a stream or brook; and by means of rain, direct from the heavens. In each of these methods there is progressively less need for heavy labour on the part of the gardener (the mystic); Teresa uses this simile to illustrate a fourfold division of prayer which she puts forward in her *Life*, the soul receiving greater grace as it progresses along the way. Elizabeth Jennings' poem 'Teresa of Avila' is based on this allegory.[59] It is significant that Teresa introduces this allegory with a comment to the effect that women such as herself, who have no learning, cannot use the usual forms of religious expression: therefore she must find some other means.

Likewise, when Teresa introduces the image of an inner palace within which God dwells, in the *Way of Perfection* (prior to her more systematic development of the image in the *Interior Castle*), she remarks that the use of a symbol such as the palace to explain her point may prove very useful to women, who are not learned and who may therefore grasp the point of her teaching more easily when it is expressed in such a manner.[60] The symbol of the castle or palace as fully developed in the *Interior Castle* is, of course, one of Teresa's most celebrated and effective allegories. We may look briefly at some other examples of Teresa's use of symbolism here: all such uses of symbol might serve as means of expressing spiritual experience by and for women who had been denied a theological education (although I draw the line at Quitslund's suggestion that the castle is a form of 'womb symbolism' and therefore an essentially 'feminine' form of imagery). It should not escape our notice, in this connection, that Teresa wrote specifically for women, that is, for the nuns of her Reform. She was asked to write a number of her books specifically as guides to prayer and the religious life for these Carmelite women. The *Interior Castle*, for example, was written at Gracián's request because 'the nuns of these convents of Our Lady of Carmel need someone to solve their difficulties concerning prayer'; Gracián felt that anything Teresa could say on the subject would be particularly helpful because 'women best understand each other's language'.[61] Symbols, for Teresa as for many other mystics, are a means of communicating experiences and realisations in relatively concrete form, and hence of making the more paradoxical and inward aspects of mysticism more readily understandable. In addition, symbols may be used as part of meditative techniques: they are powerful tools that can be used in meditation to evoke experience, by us today equally as well as by Teresa's nuns.

Teresa finds the symbolism of water very apt for illustrating spiritual experience: 'I am so fond of this element, I have observed it more attentively than anything else,' she informs us.[62] In the *Way of Perfection* almost one whole chapter is devoted to extolling the virtues of water and showing how each of its natural properties is symbolic of some aspect of the spiritual life. Water extinguishes fire, where fire represents the sufferings of the soul wounded by the fiery arrow (on other occasions, fire symbolises the love of God which will never be extinguished once it is firmly established). It cleanses the soul, dissolving and washing away impurities. It refreshes and revivifies; the living water of life, representing contemplation granted by the grace of God, quenches our spiritual thirst. The source of this living water is seen as a fountain or spring which represents sometimes the Deity, sometimes the centre of the soul.[63] Varying the metaphor, Teresa uses elsewhere the image of two fountains, the basins of which can be filled with water, to explain the nature of the Prayer of Quiet. To one of the fountains the water comes by means of numerous conduits and through human skill: this represents the spiritual experiences produced through meditation. To the other fountain the water comes direct from its source, representing contemplation.[64] In another metaphor, one which I have suggested is derived from the Jewish mystical tradition by which Teresa was so deeply influenced, she sees the soul as a 'tree of life, planted in the living waters of life'.[65] The living waters sustain the tree and cause it to produce good fruit; if on the other hand the soul leaves the clear spring and roots itself in a pool of black, evil-smelling water, it will produce nothing but misery and filth. We have already seen that Teresa also uses another form of water symbolism to illustrate the Spiritual Marriage: rain falling into a river, or a river flowing to the sea. She also refers occasionally to the soul's journey as a sea-voyage and to God as an ocean – images which find counterparts in the mystical teachings of other cultures, for to cross a wide expanse of water is very often symbolic of a transition from one level of consciousness to another.[66] A more unusual illustration of the soul's journey is shown in Teresa's analogy of a game of chess. In the 'game of love' (*ludus amoris*) played between God and the soul, we have to checkmate the Divine King. More generally, Teresa's use of the imagery of the love relationship (where Jesus is seen as the Beloved or the Bridegroom) is an affective form of expression which, while it might naturally suggest itself to a nun who saw herself as the 'Bride of Christ', contrasts with the abstract metaphysical expressions of theology. Teresa also sees God as the sun, illuminating the centre of the soul, while the soul itself is seen as a temple into which we can withdraw for tranquillity and contemplation; this latter image is more or less synonymous, in practice, with that of the interior castle.

Symbols of the transformative process of inner 'death' and 'rebirth' undergone by the mystic include the phoenix, rising from its own ashes, and the silkworm in its metamorphosis emerging as a butterfly. The soul's purification and transformation in the burning inner fire of love is also seen as analogous to the refinement of gold in the crucible, the image which has determined this book's title, for Teresa's life was like gold in the crucible of the divine fire in more ways than one. This was so inwardly, as her soul was refined and purged again and again, ever deeper, both by her worldly trials and by her spiritual conflicts. It was so outwardly, as the Inquisition, in its attempts to purge Spain of what its authorities considered heresy, created a crucible of religious turmoil in which Teresa became caught up. And this woman's whole life was lived in the transforming divine fire, in the ardour of love of God, out of which she persevered to the bitter end to justify her experiences, to guide other souls, to draw her work of reform to a successful conclusion, to accomplish what she felt she was called to do.[67]

A study of Teresa raises a final question with regard to the nature of women's spirituality: this is whether there might be a cross-cultural form of religious experience to which women are especially given, and which is characterised by ecstatic trance and visions. It is very often women who are ecstatics and mediums, from the Spiritualist Church in Britain to the Muslim Somali of North-East Africa and the spirit cults of Thailand, Burma and Sri Lanka that have blended with Buddhism over the centuries; many other examples of this phenomenon could also be cited from other cultures. Is this because women are often excluded from full participation in 'official' or institutionalised forms of religion, so that they cannot exercise priestly authority or become religious leaders, and therefore satisfy their religious longings through the less orthodox forms of religion available, which often include these kinds of religious movements and groups? Or, on the other hand, is there something in the nature of woman, and of ecstatic trance, that go together? I. M. Lewis, an anthropologist studying ecstatic forms of religion, came to the former conclusion. He argues that certain types of ecstatic cult have always attracted followers from among the weak and oppressed, particularly women in male-dominated societies who are not able to participate on equal terms with men in the more established or institutionalised forms of religion dominant in their own society. Such women's cults, Lewis argues, are a form of protest against men in male-dominated societies where women lack more direct means for achieving their aims. But membership of these cults is not absolutely restricted to women; men of low social position who are also subject to discrimination in the society in question do sometimes join these cults. Thus the phenomenon cannot be explained in terms of any innate tendency on the part of women, as such, to ecstatic religious experience.[68] It is interesting to speculate whether there may have been a connection between Teresa's ecstatic experiences and her feelings of subordination as a woman. Lucy Bregman comes to a similar conclusion to Lewis after providing a brief survey of some of the questions involved, suggesting that ecstatic experience, by acting as a channel for religious pronouncements in ways that bypass more structured forms of authority, can serve as a means of liberation from the coercions of an oppressive society: '. . . through ecstatic experiences and their use in ritual life, women in other societies gained chances to exist more effectively and humanly in a total context which we would find unbearably restricting.'[69]

We may now suggest some common areas of concern for mysticism and feminism which, it is hoped, have been highlighted by this chapter. Firstly, both mysticism and feminism declare the primacy of personal experience as the most important guide in understanding reality: this has already been explored. Secondly, both entail a search for one's true self or identity, and for self-fulfilment through what one knows, deep within, to be right for oneself, irrespective of the stereotypical patterns imposed by social pres-

sures. Third, both mysticism and feminism point to a transformation in consciousness. The mystic searches for spiritual transformation validated in personal experience, often finding this awareness
outside the domain of established religion, or at its fringes. Feminism points to a transformation in our consciousness of women's
roles and abilities. Although these are two different forms of
transformation, I would argue that they are not unrelated, for both
mysticism and feminism offer a new, liberating vision of the order of
things that challenges established views, 'an increasing sharpening
of perspective which everywhere explores new areas of experience
and yields new kinds of awareness'.[70] Fourth, both mysticism and
feminism have tended on the whole to espouse a holistic world-view
entailing an awareness of the interconnectedness of all things, looking beyond the strictures of dualistic models of reality and dicho-
tomous modes of thought. This is not particularly marked, as it
happens, in Teresa's writings, but is very noticeable in many
instances of both Jewish and Christian mysticism (and not least, in
fact, in the *Zohar*), not to mention the mystical traditions of other
religions. King succinctly outlines the role of holistic consciousness in
feminism:

> Feminist consciousness-raising aims to uncover and overcome all the
> dualistic notions on which patriarchal thinking is based – the opposi-
> tions between mind and body, culture and nature, conscious and
> unconscious, intellectual and emotional, good and evil, spiritual and
> material, man and woman. Patriarchal structures are shaped by the
> politics of separation, not by wholeness and integration. By contrast,
> women do not believe in the validity of an exclusive 'either/or'; they
> desire to make connections, to relate and integrate and thereby over-
> come all separations based on sex, race, class, age, nationality, reli-
> gion or politics. Such a vision of wholeness is central to feminism.[71]

Fifth, both mysticism and feminism deny that reason and logic
alone, as defined by (largely male) rationalist philosophers and
theologians, can tell us all there is to know about reality, and insist
that feeling and intuition too have their own contribution to make to
our understanding of life.

Identification with spiritual ideals, and the sense of self-transcen-
dence that may arise from this, can generate dynamic strength and
energy; Teresa, and many other mystics, are living proof of this. If
this dynamic strength can be put to use to fight for social justice and

religious equality for women – as Teresa tried to do herself, within the confines of her own culture – we have an active feminist mysticism.

In conclusion, Teresa was a woman who was true to herself: she found her vocation and direction in life and resolutely accomplished all that it entailed, in spite of the most difficult social pressures. In a culture where women were not encouraged to realise themselves, she persisted in discovering and living out her own model for being.[72] She took her life into her own hands, refusing to be constrained by the social norms of her time. She needed tremendous faith to do this: faith in her own heart and conscience, faith in what she believed to be right; faith in her God, of whom she said that if he had not bestowed on her such spiritual favours, she would not have had the courage or strength to carry her work through to the end in the face of such opposition and criticism.[73] She needed, too, great persistence, practical ability, and wisdom: Luis de León, shortly after Teresa's death, wrote that ' . . . it is a miracle in itself that one woman alone should have restored perfection to a whole Order, both of men and of women . . . it is a fresh miracle to find a weak woman with courage enough for beginning so great a work and with wisdom and efficiency enough for succeeding in it.'[74] But above all, Teresa needed to have found that inner freedom and integrity that comes from truly knowing oneself. She supported women's autonomy and spoke out for women so far as that was possible within the confines of her culture. She was a woman who found herself: in that sense she was a feminist. And through finding herself she found God: it is this that makes her a mystic.

Afterword

We have seen in this book how Teresa, through the rooting of her inner life in the divine, and the strength and wisdom that she drew from this, triumphed against three major factors that discriminated against her: her *converso* ancestry, the fact that she was a woman in a strongly male-dominated society, and the fact that her visions, ecstasies and revelations occasioned suspicion. In spite of strong social and ecclesiastical pressures, she not only succeeded in reforming the Carmelite Order, but also left us a priceless legacy in her mystical writings, which continue to inspire and guide many today. Contemplating Teresa's life, we see a clear illustration in action of how love of God is a transforming vision that gives to those who centre themselves in it boundless inspiration, creative energy, and power to accomplish objectives.

When we consider Teresa's battle to establish the validity of her own experiences; her search to 'work out her own path' with very little effective guidance; the intense physical hardships to which she was exposed on her long journeys to establish her convents and priories; the years of persecution and condemnation that she suffered; then we see in her life, too, how those who are caught up, enraptured, by this love of God are refined like gold in the crucible, ground to powder, reduced to nothing. Again and again their lives, their presuppositions, their attachments, are turned upside down, until in the end there is a strange comfort in insecurity, a security in the feeling of being lost to the world. Yet paradoxically, out of this harrowing experience, and out of the plumbing of the depths of oneself that accompanies it, comes a determination, a one-pointedness of direction: strength out of suffering. Through this one-pointedness the spiritual power received by or generated by the mystic can become a purity of impulse which can be directed with unwavering zeal: in Teresa's case, towards her work of reform.

It is sometimes almost painful to read Teresa's reflections because of the absolute honesty and lack of pretension in her self-criticism. She does not try to gloss over her failings, nor does she omit what some might consider trivial details: she exposes her whole self to us. Her symbol of the soul as a clear diamond or crystal is apt: we can see right into her in all her humanity. In doing so, we are often brought up against the pain of seeing ourselves, too, as we really are, and the pain of knowing that that which we call God sees us in this same nakedness.

But I have endeavoured to represent Teresa in this study as honestly as she would, I believe, have wished. I have tried to look at her afresh, as she has not been seen before: to see the living woman rather than the immobile statue of the saint obscured by hagiography and legend. Over the centuries, the facts of Teresa's life have sometimes been reinterpreted, misrepresented, misunderstood, hidden, or suppressed, whether by anti-Semitism, misogyny, theological dogmatism, or pious hagiography. I have attempted to uncover the facts of Teresa's life, experience and reflections *as lived by her*: to see what was there rather than what we had been told was there. This has meant looking at Teresa's mystical experiences, visions and so on, in terms of what she herself says about them, seeing them in their own light rather than filtering that light through a dark glass of dogmatic interpretation. It has meant looking at her actual religious experiences and feelings as a woman in a male-dominated society, rather than at men's perceptions of the woman. It has meant a candid investigation of the facts of her Jewish background and the influence this had on her mystical writings, and of the realities of her encounters with the Inquisition. To look at Teresa straightforwardly in this way does not detract from her greatness: if anything, it makes us wonder at it all the more as we reflect on this complex, fascinating and remarkable woman who accomplished so much within a system whose many inbuilt prejudices could so easily have led to her downfall.

Notes and References

The following abbreviations are used in the Notes and References in referring to works by St Teresa:

CW – *Complete Works of Saint Teresa of Jesus*, trans. & ed. E. Allison Peers (3 vols.) (London: Sheed & Ward, 1946)

OC – *Santa Teresa de Jesús: Obras Completas*, eds. Enrique Llamas, Teófanes Egido, *et al.* (Madrid: Editorial de Espiritualidad, 1984)

L – *Life*, in CW

L (C) – *The Life of Saint Teresa*, trans. J. M. Cohen (Harmondsworth: Penguin, 1957)

IC – *Interior Castle*; independent edn, Sheed & Ward, 1974; first published in CW, 1946. (Page references are to the 1974 edition; page numbers for CW edition can be found by adding 200 to the page numbers given.)

F – *Book of the Foundations*, in CW

SR – *Spiritual Relations*, in CW

WP – *Book called Way of Perfection*, in CW

ESG – *Exclamations of the Soul to God*, in CW

CLG – *Conceptions of the Love of God*, in CW

Lt. – *The Letters of Saint Teresa of Jesus*, trans. & ed. E. Allison Peers (2 vols.) (London: Burns Oates & Washbourne Ltd, 1951)

Frontispiece

The quotation from the *Life* is taken from L (C) 142. The Spanish text reads: '. . . en esta pena se purificaba el alma, y se labra o purifica, como el oro en el crisol, para poder mejor poner los esmaltes de sus dones.' (OC, 126). The quotation from the *Zohar* is taken from Bension, *The Zohar in Moslem and Christian Spain*, 182.

Chapter 1

1 L (C) 314
2 For those with an interest in astrology, she was born, according to her father's testimony, at about 5.30 a.m., and has Sun in Aries, Moon in Virgo, Pisces Ascendant with Venus rising.
3 L (C) 24
4 L, CW (I), 13
5 L (C) 27
6 L, CW (I), 15
7 Sackville-West, *The Eagle and the Dove*, 21
8 Hamilton, *The Great Teresa*, 20
9 L (C) 28–9
10 L (C) 29
11 L (C) 31; L, CW (I), 19
12 Auclair, *Saint Teresa of Avila*, 69
13 L (C) 61
14 L (C) 40–2
15 I do not mean to imply that I necessarily condone the moral judgements implicit in the account of this episode. Inevitably, we have no information about the priest's lover, and the passing reference to her does not paint her in a favourable light; no doubt only one side of the story is presented.
16 SR, CW (I), 357–8
17 L (C) 278–9
18 Lincoln, *Teresa: A Woman*, 383.
19 WP, CW (II) 30
20 L (C) 278
21 WP, CW (II), 29
22 WP, CW (II), 19–22, 27
23 L (C) 57, 61

24 L (C) 64
25 L (C) 58–60
26 L (C) 167
27 L (C) 254
28 L (C) 85, 75, 93, 109
29 SR, CW (I), 333
30 L (C) 180, 203
31 L (C) 169
32 L (C) 193, 213, 309
33 'Virtues of our Mother Saint Teresa according to a Report made by her own Cousin the Venerable Mother María de San Jerónimo', Appendix to CW (III), 351.
34 L (C) 238
35 L (C) 241. 'An absurd feminine whimsy': *disparate de mujeres*, 'women's foolishness' (OC, 227)
36 L (C) 246
37 L (C) 259
38 L (C) 271
39 Hamilton, *The Great Teresa*, 94
40 F, CW (III) 145–6
41 F, CW (III) 11–12
42 F, CW (III) 62–3
43 F, CW (III) 123–4
44 Auclair, *Saint Teresa of Avila*, 260
45 Allison Peers, *Mother of Carmel*, 102
46 Ibid., 138
47 'The Last Acts of the Life of Saint Teresa. By the Venerable Ana de San Bartolomé', Appendix to CW (III), 361
48 Auclair, *Saint Teresa of Avila*, 429
49 Psalm 50.19; A. V. 51.17
50 IC, 21, 20
51 Hamilton, *The Great Teresa*, 29–30
52 L, CW (I), 140
53 Allison Peers, *Mother of Carmel*, 153
54 Ibid., 159
55 Lt., 354
56 SR, CW (I), 318: *Así que veo claro que de estas revelaciones y arrobamientos – que yo ninguna parte soy, ni hago para ellos más que una tabla – me vienen estas ganancias.* (OC, 1010)
57 SR, CW (I), 351

Chapter 2

1 L Chap. 10, as cited in Introduction, *Carmelite Studies*, 3, vii
2 I have discussed these and other issues related to the methodology of the study of mysticism in greater depth in my *A Study of Mysticism and its Forms of Expression*.
3 IC 38
4 WP, CW (II), 115: *Recoge el alma todas las potencias y se entra dentro de sí con su Dios* (OC, 714)
5 WP, CW (II), 115
6 Trueman Dicken, *The Crucible of Love*, 181–2.
7 WP, CW (II) 129
8 CLG, CW (II) 383–4
9 L, CW (I) 110. 'Meditating': *pensando*, 'thinking about' (OC, 110).
10 IC, 51
11 L, CW (I), 96; IC 48; WP, CW (II), 104
12 IC, 51, 87–8
13 IC, 57
14 L, CW (I) 192–3
15 For example, Leuba explains the experience as being 'the participation of sex organs tormented by an insufficient stimulation'! Leuba, *The Psychology of Religious Mysticism*, 145
16 IC, 69, 76
17 Fr. Ermanno, 'The Degrees of Teresian Prayer'
18 IC, 124
19 IC, 125. 'Suspended aloft': *colgada*, 'hanged, hanging' (OC, 970)
20 IC, 55
21 IC, 104
22 IC, 143
23 IC, 135. A typical example from Vedāntic tradition is found in Chāndogya Upaniṣad, 6.6.10.
24 'Judgement given by Saint Teresa upon Various Writings on the Words: "Seek Thyself in Me" ', CW (III) 267
25 CLG, CW (II) 396
26 IC, 150
27 SR, CW (I) 320; L (C) 197
28 L, CW (I) 192. 'In bodily form': *en forma corporal* (OC, 195)
29 L (C) 53, 197
30 L (C) 296
31 L (C) 278; SR, CW (I) 308
32 F, CW (III) 40–1
33 IC, 115
34 L, CW (I) 292. 'Became recollected': *se recogió*. 'It was explained to me': *dióseme a entender*, 'it was given to me to understand' (OC, 296).

35 In Zen Buddhism, it is said that the mind must be like a clear mirror, faithfully reflecting reality as it is and yet retaining no mark from any of the images reflected (i.e. maintaining its purity and detachment). We must not let dust collect on the mirror.

36 L (C) 247

37 L (C) 174; IC 81

38 L (C) 187–190. 'Speaks to it without words': *la habla sin hablar*, literally 'speaks to it without speaking', a good example of mystical paradox. 'The innermost parts of the soul': *lo muy interior del alma*, 'the very centre of the soul' (OC, 174).

39 IC 79–86, L (C) 174–9

40 Underhill, *Mysticism*, 276

41 L, CW (I) 184–5

42 IC, 117

43 SR, CW (I) 313

44 L, CW (I) 207

45 Hamilton, *The Great Teresa*, 83

46 L (C) 125. See also IC, 125, 127, 91

47 L, CW (I), 125–6

48 L, CW (I) 119. 'Raises it up till it is right out of itself': *levántala toda ella* (OC, 120)

49 L (C) 136

50 L, CW (I) 120, 128

51 IC, 95

52 IC, 91

53 L, CW (I) 288

54 Laski, *Ecstasy*, 369–71

55 F, CW (III) 26–35. See also IC 45–6

56 Morón-Arroyo, ' "I Will Give You a Living Book". . .', 103

57 L (C) 154

58 L, CW (I) 140

59 L, CW (I) 140

60 IC, 107

61 O'Donoghue, 'The Human Form Divine'

62 IC, 134

63 Carroll, 'The Saving Role of the Human Christ for St Teresa', 134

64 The writings of this anonymous mystic include *The Mystical Theology, The Celestial Hierarchies, The Divine Names*. They have had a great influence on Christian mysticism in spite of the fact that modern scholarship has determined that the author was not after all a disciple of St Paul (which supposition had previously lent his writings the aura of orthodoxy).

65 Further on this point, see my 'St John of the Cross and Mystical "Unknowing" '.

66 I have discussed Eckhart's mystical thought in greater depth in my *A Study of Mysticism and its Forms of Expression*.

67 Rolle's mysticism is also discussed in my *A Study of Mysticism and its Forms of Expression*.

68 I have discussed the bearing that philosophical discussions on the context-dependence of meaning have on the study of mysticism, and the problems that arise in connection with previous and existing typologies of mysticism, with reference to the writings of Katz, Stace, Zaehner, Smart and others, in my 'Unity in Diversity'. These and related matters such as mysticism and epistemology, mysticism and metaphysics, and the relationship between experience and interpretation, are also discussed in greater detail in my *A Study of Mysticism and its Forms of Expression*.

69 Śankara's mystical system is discussed more fully in my *A Study of Mysticism and its Forms of Expression*.

70 See my 'Living Between the Worlds: Bhakti Poetry and the Carmelite Mystics'; also my *A Study of Mysticism and its Forms of Expression*.

71 Mīrā Bāī, in Alston, *The Devotional Poems of Mīrābāī*, 49, 97. Similar imagery of the heart being pierced with the arrow of divine love is found in the accounts of the experiences of St Gertrude of Helfta, a thirteenth-century Cistercian abbess.

Chapter 3

1 Egido, 'The Historical Setting of St Teresa's Life'.

2 Davies, 'Saint Teresa and the Jewish Question'.

3 Ibid., 54

4 Egido, 'The Historical Setting of St Teresa's Life', 139–40

5 Davies, 'Saint Teresa and the Jewish Question', 55, 51

6 Beinart, 'The *Converso* Community in Sixteenth and Seventeenth Century Spain', 473

7 Egido, 'The Historical Setting . . .', 149

8 Ibid., 150f.

9 Ibid., 133

10 Davies, 'Saint Teresa and the Jewish Question', 55; Auclair, *Saint Teresa of Avila*, 198

11 Davies, 'Saint Teresa and the Jewish Question', 66

12 Beinart, 'The *Converso* Community in Sixteenth and Seventeenth Century Spain', 466

13 Egido, 'The Historical Setting . . .', 135

14 Davies, 'Saint Teresa and the Jewish Question', 57

15 Ibid., 58

16 Ibid., 61–2

194   *Gold in the Crucible*

17 Cf. Edwards, 'Religious Belief and Social Conformity: The "Converso" Problem in Late-Medieval Córdoba'.

18 Cf. Beinart, 'The *Converso* Community in Sixteenth and Seventeenth Century Spain'.

19 Davies, 'Saint Teresa and the Jewish Question', 63. Davies' argument does not exclude the possibility that the Spanish concept of 'purity' (*limpieza*) might have an equally important role to play in Teresa's conception of the 'clean' and 'unclean'.

20 Davies, 'Saint Teresa and the Jewish Question', 65

21 Ibid., 68

22 Ibid., 70

23 Deirdre Green, 'St Teresa of Avila and Hekhalot Mysticism'. After publishing this article I discovered that Cuevas García had mentioned, in passing, the *Hekhalot Rabbati* and the *Zohar* in connection with the symbolism of the *Interior Castle*: Cuevas García, 'El significante alegórico en el "Castillo" teresiano', 89–90. The theme was not, however, developed in Cuevas García's article.

24 Letter from Diego de Yepes to Luis de León, cited in Introduction, IC.

25 WP, CW (II), 117. Teresa also makes a few other very minor allusions, in passing, to the symbol of the castle or palace representing the soul, elsewhere in her works.

26 IC, viii.

27 See Isaiah 6; Ezekiel 1, 8 and 10; II Kings 2:11. In fact, there are certain differences between the Jewish Tanach and what Christians call the Old Testament, but these need not detain us here.

28 Contrary to my usual practice, I have not referred to 'his or her inner strivings' since no female Merkavah mystics are known. Jewish mysticism, until very recently, has been sadly exclusivist where women are concerned, in spite of the wide use of feminine symbols of the divine in Kabbalah.

29 Hai Gaon (938–1038), in Kaplan, *Meditation and Kabbalah*, 26

30 *Hekhalot Rabbati*, 17, in Alexander, *Textual Sources for the Study of Judaism*, 122. TVTRVSY'Y is an esoteric God-name.

31 For example, in Enoch's ascension, he sees two crystal houses one within the other, surrounded by a further wall of crystal, with the whole surrounded by flames. See Gruenwald, *Apocalyptic and Merkavah Mysticism*. Cf. also examples of visions of crystal firmaments in Jewish tradition, such as Ezekiel 1:22.

32 Exodus 33:20

33 Further on Merkavah/Hekhalot mysticism, see Scholem, *Jewish Gnosticism, Merkabah Mysticism, and Talmudic Tradition*; Smith, 'Observations on Hekhalot Rabbati'; Dan, 'The Religious Experience of the Merkavah'; Green, Deirdre, 'The Seven Palaces in Early Jewish Mysticism'. For comparative studies of the types of experience

described in Merkavah/Kabbalistic forms of meditation and in the Hindu systems of *kuṇḍalinī yoga* and Tantra, see Green, Deirdre, 'Kuṇḍalinī Yoga and Kabbalistic Meditation'; for a briefer exposition, see also my 'Mysticism and the Sevenfold Castle'.

34 Bension, *The Zohar in Moslem and Christian Spain*, 202
35 *Zohar*, trans. de Manhar, 123. This is unfortunately the only English translation of the Hekhalot portions of the *Zohar*. See also Bension, *The Zohar in Moslem and Christian Spain*, 193ff.
36 *Zohar*, 2:97a, 1:168a, in Ginsburg, *The Kabbalah: its Doctrines, Development and Literature*
37 Bension, *The Zohar in Moslem and Christian Spain*, 207
38 *Zohar*, trans. de Manhar, 196–7
39 See Davies, 'Saint Teresa and the Jewish Question', 71
40 Cf. Apocalypse 4:6–8
41 L, CW (I), 288. Teresa nowhere tells us of any other visions entailing a door into the heavens. The Spanish text gives simply *entrada*, an 'entrance' into the heavens (OC, 292). The Evangelists: Christian Kabbalah reinterpreted the Holy Living Creatures who support the throne as symbolic of the four evangelists. Gruenwald, *Apocalyptic and Merkavah Mysticism*, argues for the Merkavah origins of the Apocalypse.
42 Egido, 'The Historical Setting of St Teresa's Life', 165–6
43 Scholem, 'Zohar', *Encyclopedia Judaica*, XVI, 1211–12
44 Kottman, *Law and Apocalypse: the Moral Thought of Luis de León*
45 Swietlicki, *Spanish Christian Cabala*
46 Introduction to IC, CW (II) 193
47 IC, 2
48 Bension, *The Zohar in Moslem and Christian Spain*, 198, 201, 205
49 Gruenwald, *Apocalyptic and Merkavah Mysticism*, 152, 209–10
50 IC, 3
51 Underhill, *The House of the Soul*, 22
52 IC, 3
53 IC, 7–8. The *palmito* is a shrub common in Spain which has thick layers of leaves enclosing an edible kernel.
54 Underhill, *The House of the Soul*, 21
55 Teresa sometimes refers to the 'first mansion', 'second mansion', etc., and sometimes to the 'first mansions', 'second mansions', and so on, presumably bearing in mind that each mansion has many chambers (*aposentos*); cf. IC 151, 'Although I have spoken here only of seven Mansions, yet in each there are comprised many more, both above and below and around.' IC 4, Teresa refers to the 'first rooms on the *lowest floor*'. Possibly her interior castle reflects the design of some actual physical castles in which each ward or tower is built higher than the last and also closer to the centre. Cf. also IC 2, 10.

56 IC, 9–10
57 IC, 10
58 IC, 10–11
59 IC, 30
60 IC, 34
61 IC, 47
62 IC, 48
63 IC, 115
64 *Hekhalot Rabbati*, 24, in Kaplan, *Meditation and Kabbalah*
65 IC, 87
66 IC, 132–3. 'the interior of her heart': *lo interior de su alma*, 'the interior of her soul' (OC, 976)
67 IC, 143
68 IC, 138
69 IC, 134–5; see also IC 52
70 IC, 150; see also IC 16, 17
71 Underhill, *The House of the Soul*, 22
72 IC, 131; OC 975
73 IC, 150–1. 'Not to make any effort to get in': the word translated 'effort' is *fuerza*, 'force' or 'violence' (OC, 996)
74 See Chorpenning, 'The Literary and Theological Method of the *Castillo Interior*'; Trueman Dicken, 'The Imagery of the Interior Castle and its Implications'; Cuevas García, 'El significante alegórico en el "Castillo" teresiano'; López-Baralt, 'Santa Teresa y el Islam'; López-Baralt, 'Simbología mística musulmana en San Juan de la Cruz y en Santa Teresa de Jesús'; Asín Palacios, 'El símil de los castillos y moradas del alma en la mística islámica y en Santa Teresa'.
75 IC, 88, 98
76 IC, 36–7, 93–4; cf. *Zohar* II.42b–43a; this passage may be found in Scholem's brief selection, *Zohar*, 79–80, and also in Alexander, *Textual Sources for the Study of Judaism*, 126.
77 See Deirdre Green, 'The Seven Palaces in Early Jewish Mysticism', 11–12, where I have already discussed mirror symbolism. To explain the full significance of the 'Tree of the Sefirot' would take us too far outside our theme, but for those who are already familiar with it we may add that the luminous mirror was identified with Tiferet and the dull mirror with Malkhut. Swietlicki, *Spanish Christian Cabala*, 67–8, discusses mirror symbolism, but is incorrect in stating that this image is used in the *Interior Castle*; Teresa's image here is of a crystal (*cristal*). Swietlicki's arguments that the images of the silkworm and the nut are also common both to the *Interior Castle* and to Kabbalistic tradition are not entirely convincing. On the one hand she presents Kabbalah as having been more standardised than it probably was by the time of the *Zohar*. On the other hand she does not allow for the fact that certain

symbols in Teresa's writings which she traces to Zoharic origins can equally be found in the writings of mystics of other traditions and cultures, and Teresa's use of the images in question is not sufficiently detailed to provide a full comparison with Jewish tradition. (In some cases it is not even similar enough to bear any degree of meaningful comparison.) What we may have here, then, is simply an example of how mystics from widely different cultures come up with similar symbols spontaneously and independently of each other. Swietlicki, for example, tries to compare the image of the nut in the *Zohar* with that of the *palmito* shrub in the *Interior Castle*. Teresa does not actually use the image of the nut at all, while on the other hand, a closer parallel to the Zoharic symbolism of kernel and shell is found in the writings of Meister Eckhart.

78 IC, 16, 96, 142, 52. See Song of Songs 2:4; the 'wine-cellar' is more often rendered 'banqueting-house'.
79 L (C) 145; SR, CW (I) 353
80 Davies, 'Saint Teresa and the Jewish Question', 68–9
81 L (C) 182; WP, CW (II) 78
82 Alexander, *Textual Sources for the Study of Judaism*, 27
83 L (C) 74–5
84 IC, vi
85 Arthur Green, 'The Song of Songs in Early Jewish Mysticism', 59
86 Ibid., 57–9
87 CLG, CW (II) 360
88 Song of Songs 1:2–4, 2:3–5
89 CLG, CW (II) 371, 359, 383, 364
90 CLG, CW (II) 388–9; see Luke 1:35
91 CLG, CW (II) 388–9, 398
92 *Zohar* III.107a, in Scholem *Zohar*, 118. The Kabbalistic interpretation of this passage is discussed in Blumenthal, *Understanding Jewish Mysticism*, 121ff. See also Talmage, 'Apples of Gold: the Inner Meaning of Sacred Texts in Medieval Judaism'.
93 CLG, CW (II) 387–9
94 CLG, CW (II) 384

Chapter 4

1 L (C) 153–4; IC 29
2 Kottman, *Law and Apocalypse: the Moral Thought of Luis de León*. See also Woodward, 'Hebrew Tradition and Luis de León'.
3 Swietlicki, *Spanish Christian Cabala*, 88.
4 Gómez-Menor Fuentes, *El Linaje Familiar de Santa Teresa y San Juan de la Cruz*.

5 Swietlicki, *Spanish Christian Cabala*, 157ff.
6 Larkin, 'St Teresa of Avila and Centering Prayer', 194.
7 Williams, 'St Teresa, Doctor of the Church (Orthodoxy and Public Opinion)', 92–3.
8 Llamas Martínez, *Santa Teresa de Jesús y la Inquisición Española*, 26: '. . . visiones, revelaciones, éxtasis, hablas interiores eran en este tiempo sinónimo de influencia diabólica.'
9 Egido, 'The Historical Setting of St Teresa's Life', 130.
10 In his *Aviso de Gente recogida y especialmente dedicada al servicio de Dios* (1585). See Christian, *Local Religion in Sixteenth-Century Spain*, from which the foregoing information regarding *beatas* is also taken.
11 F, CW (III), 44
12 L (C) 186
13 Domínguez Ortiz, *The Golden Age of Spain: 1516–1659*, 216–17
14 Báñez's report may be read in CW (III) 333ff.
15 Alonso de la Fuente's report, in Rivers, 'The Vernacular Mind of St Teresa', 114.
16 Williams, 'St Teresa, Doctor of the Church', 102. I am indebted to Williams' article in drawing up my account of Teresa's dealings with the Inquisition, and to Llamas Martínez, *Santa Teresa de Jesús y la Inquisición Española*.
17 WP, CW (II) xxvi (this declaration was added by Teresa to the Toledan Codex of WP for the edition of 1583, and is therefore much later than the original ms.); IC viii; IC 151
18 Egan, 'Teresa of Jesus: Daughter of the Church and Woman of the Reformation', 75
19 Ibid., 76
20 Llamas Martínez, *Santa Teresa de Jesús y la Inquisición Española*, 99
21 Morón-Arroyo, ' "I Will Give You a Living Book": Spiritual Currents at Work at the Time of St Teresa of Jesus', 109
22 Romano, 'A Psycho-Spiritual History of Teresa of Avila', 284
23 Hamilton, *The Great Teresa*, 133
24 Rawlinson, 'Attempting to Understand Everything', 88
25 IC, 131
26 IC, 60
27 IC, 2–3
28 Zohar, 3.97a, in Swietlicki, *Spanish Christian Cabala*, 171
29 IC, 2, 134–5
30 Cf. Ortiz, *The Golden Age of Spain*, 221.
31 Egido, 'The Historical Setting of St Teresa's Life', 131
32 Chorpenning, 'St Teresa's Presentation of her Religious Experience', 157
33 O'Donoghue, 'The Human Form Divine: St Teresa and the Humanity of Christ', 88, n. 5

34 Some examples of such approaches to mysticism are discussed in my *A Study of Mysticism and its Forms of Expression*.
35 Ruether, *New Woman, New Earth*, 89ff.

Chapter 5

1 Felipe Sega, in Hamilton, *The Great Teresa*, 158
2 King, 'Goddesses, Witches, Androgyny and Beyond?', 215
3 Cf. McLaughlin, 'Women, Power and the Pursuit of Holiness in Medieval Christianity'.
4 Romano, 'A Psycho-Spiritual History of Teresa of Avila: A Woman's Perspective', 272
5 F, CW (III), 203: *librarlas de estar sujetas a un hombre que muchas veces les acaba la vida, y plega a Dios no sea también el alma* (OC 514)
6 L (C), 30
7 WP, CW (II), 107. 'Slavery': *sujeción*, 'subjection' (OC, 700)
8 McLaughlin, 'Equality of Souls, Inequality of Sexes: Women in Medieval Theology', 234
9 Cf. Ruether & McLaughlin, Introduction to their *Women of Spirit*, 22–3
10 McLaughlin, 'Women, Power and the Pursuit of Holiness . . .'
11 Ramanujan, 'On Women Saints'
12 Fox, commentary to Hildegard of Bingen, *Illuminations*, 13
13 Scholz, 'Hildegard von Bingen on the Nature of Woman', 361
14 Fox, commentary to Hildegard of Bingen, *Illuminations*, 7
15 For example, certain witchcraft groups which see themselves as feminist emphasise that the 'Old Religion' of witchcraft is based on earth-centred, nature-orientated worship of the Goddess and her consort. A similar acceptance of the identification of the feminine with earth, nature etc. can be seen in some feminist Christian writings.
16 McLaughlin, 'Equality of Souls, Inequality of Sexes', 256–7
17 Ruether, *New Woman, New Earth*, 74, 195. Such gender-based polarities are not confined to medieval thought. For example, according to Jungian thought, 'feminine' modes of knowledge are emotional, in tune with the unconscious and the realm of archetypes; 'masculine' modes are technical and analytical. Some have claimed that the two modes are each found within all human beings of either sex, that it is not intended to identify the 'feminine' with women and the 'masculine' with men, and that the ideal is for each individual, whether male or female, to attain a balance between these polarities. While I am in agreement with the ideal of balance for all human beings between these different types of knowledge, I am not convinced that it is wholly possible to speak of 'the feminine' simply as a symbolic archetype without implying that female human beings partake of 'the feminine' in a way that male

human beings do not; and similarly with regard to the notion of 'the masculine'.

18 Gross, 'Women's Studies in Religion', 581
19 'Statement of P. Pedro Ibáñez on the Spirit of Saint Teresa', Appendix to CW (III), 315–16
20 SR, CW (I), 313
21 WP, CW (II), 89
22 King, 'Current Perspectives in the Study of Women and Religion', 5
23 L (C) 153–4; IC 29
24 I Tim. 2:11–12; I Cor. 14:34–5
25 IC, 98
26 Thomas Baker (ed.), *The Letters of St Teresa* (n.i., 1919), cited in Thomas & Gabriel, *Saint Teresa of Avila*, 21
27 Llamas Martínez, *Santa Teresa de Jesús y la Inquisición Española*, 271: Llamas Martínez's words are *más objetivo y menos pasional*.
28 Giles, 'The Feminist Mystic', 28–9
29 Neville Braybrook, cited in Romano, 'A Psycho-Spiritual History of Teresa of Avila', 264
30 Borrowdale, 'The Church as an Equal Opportunities Employer', 65
31 King, *Women and Spirituality*, 100. I am grateful to Dr King for sending me a copy of the manuscript of one chapter of her book before publication. For the reference to Teresa, see WP, CW (II) 35.
32 Auclair, *Saint Teresa of Avila*, 232
33 Quitslund, 'Elements of a Feminist Spirituality in St Teresa', 31.
34 Cf. King, 'Goddesses, Witches, Androgyny and Beyond?', 211–12.
35 King, *Women and Spirituality*, 34
36 See IC 7; L (C) 64; WP, CW (II) 35; CLG, CW (II) 360; SR, CW (I) 317. Other female mystics, for example Catherine of Siena, similarly accept the traditional identification of weakness with femininity, without seeming to perceive themselves as suffering from this weakness! Cf. McLaughlin, 'Women, Power and the Pursuit of Holiness . . .', 121.
37 L (C) 75
38 Hellwig, 'St Teresa's Inspiration for Our Times', 218–19
39 Bichovsky, in *New Statesman*. A similar example of criticism of Teresa which ignores her cultural context is found in Sackville-West, *The Eagle and the Dove*, 66f.
40 Cf. Quitslund, 'Elements of a Feminist Spirituality in St Teresa', 24
41 L (C) 81. 'They should exercise control over themselves and go right ahead': *anden señores de sí mismos* (OC, 67). Allison Peers gives a more literal translation: 'They should be masters of themselves and go on their way.' (L, CW (I) 69)
42 L (C) 167
43 WP, CW (II) 35; cf. Quitslund, 'Elements of a Feminist Spirituality in St Teresa', 35

44 *Way of Perfection*, in Egan, 'Teresa of Jesus: Daughter of the Church and Woman of the Reformation', 71
45 An interesting example within Judaism is Hannah Rahel, the 'Maid of Ludmir', a nineteenth-century ecstatic who insisted on following the full ritual observance prescribed only for males in orthodox Judaism, and on devoting herself to constant prayer and religious study. She attracted a large popular following, but the response of the male religious leaders (*zaddikim*) of her milieu was that an evil spirit was speaking through her. Pressure was put on Hannah to give up her self-appointed role of religious leader and teacher, and to resume her rightful female role in marriage, which she had previously rejected, adopting a celibate way of life. See Rapoport-Albert, 'The Maid of Ludmir'.
46 L (C) 145. 'What power': *señorío*, 'dominion, mastery'. 'Men of prayer': *gente de oración*, 'people of prayer'; the masculine is not actually implied here, though the references to persecution of women in particular, later in the passage, are forceful, and suggest that Teresa had men in mind. 'A storm of persecutions': *mil persecuciones*, 'a thousand persecutions' (OC, 130).
47 Lt., I, 4
48 L (C) 193, 213, 309
49 IC, 62
50 Quitslund, 'Elements of a Feminist Spirituality in St Teresa', 30
51 L (C) 309
52 Hamilton, *The Great Teresa*, 71
53 Giles, 'The Feminist Mystic', 23–4
54 Quitslund, 'Elements of a Feminist Spirituality . . .', 33
55 CLG, CW (II) 393
56 'Statement of P. Pedro Ibáñez on the Spirit of Saint Teresa', Appendix to CW (III), 331
57 As suggested by Lincoln, *Teresa: A Woman*, 170
58 Chorpenning, 'St Teresa's Presentation of her Religious Experience', 181–2. Today, we are beginning to realise that the very distinction between 'subjective' and 'objective' is something of a false dichotomy, and that no one system of thought is entirely 'objective'. Nevertheless, this issue of 'subjectivity' and 'objectivity' was a very real one for the theologians of Teresa's day.
59 L (C) 78ff. See Jennings, 'Teresa of Avila'. Thanks to Barbara Dennis for drawing this poem to my attention.
60 WP, CW (II), 117
61 IC viii
62 IC 36
63 WP, CW (II) 78–85; see also ESG, CW (II) 410
64 IC 36–7

65 IC 5–6; cf. Psalm 1:3. 'Tree of life': *árbol de vida* (OC, 842)
66 See for example WP, CW (II) 115. Cf. the expression 'the other shore' to denote the attainment of *nirvāṇa*, the crossing of the 'stream of life', in Buddhism; the symbolism of journeys to the Otherworld in Celtic and other mythologies.
67 Game of chess: WP, CW (II) 63. Sun: IC 5–6 and elsewhere. Temple: IC 40. Phoenix: L, CW (I) 289. Silkworm: IC, 53ff. Gold in the crucible: L, CW (I) 200, 125.
68 Lewis, *Ecstatic Religion*. The cults referred to here are what Lewis terms 'peripheral possession cults'. As examples of the phenomenon other than those already cited, he includes the Kamba of East Africa, the Luo of Kenya, the Mapuche of Chile, Hindu women in Uttar Pradesh, and others.
69 Bregman, 'Women and Ecstatic Religious Experience'.
70 King, 'Mysticism and Feminism, or Why Look at Women Mystics?', 7
71 King, 'Voices of Protest – Voices of Promise: Exploring Spirituality for a New Age', 3–4
72 Cf. Giles, 'Meditations on Teresa', 4
73 SR, CW (I), 351
74 Letter from Luis de León to Ana de Jesús, one of the Discalced Carmelite Prioresses. This letter appears in the first edition of Teresa's works, edited by Luis de León. CW (III), Appendix, 369.

Bibliography

Alexander, Philip S. *Textual Sources for the Study of Judaism* (Manchester: University Press, 1984)

Allison Peers, E. *Studies of the Spanish Mystics*, I (London: SPCK, 1951)

—— *Mother of Carmel: A Portrait of St Teresa of Jesus* (London: SCM, 1945)

——*A Handbook to the Life and Times of St Teresa and St John of the Cross* (London: Burns Oates, 1954)

Alston, A. J. (trans.). *The Devotional Poems of Mīrābāī* (Delhi: Motilal Banarsidass, 1980)

Asín Palacios, Miguel, 'El símil de los castillos y moradas del alma en la mística islámica y en Santa Teresa', *Al-Andalus*, 9, 1946

Auclair, Marcelle. *Saint Teresa of Avila* (London: Burns Oates, 1953)

Baer, Yitzhak. *A History of the Jews in Christian Spain*, II (Philadelphia: Jewish Publication Society of America, 1961)

Beinart, Haim. 'The *Converso* Community in Sixteenth and Seventeenth Century Spain', in R. D. Barnett (ed.) *The Sephardi Heritage*, I (New York: C. Vallentine, 1971)

Bension, Ariel. *The Zohar in Moslem and Christian Spain* (London: George Routledge & Sons, 1932)

Bichovsky, Hilary. Review of *The Life Story of St Theresa [sic] of Avila by Herself*, *New Statesman*, 20 November 1987

Blau, J. L. *The Christian Interpretation of the Kabbalah in the Renaissance* (Columbia: University Press, 1944)

Blumenthal, David. *Understanding Jewish Mysticism* (New York: Ktav, 1978)

Borrowdale, Anne. 'The Church as Equal Opportunities Employer', *Crucible*, April–June 1988

Bregman, Lucy. 'Women and Ecstatic Religious Experience', *Encounter*, 38, 1977

Carroll, Eamon R. 'The Saving Role of the Human Christ for St Teresa', *Carmelite Studies*, 3, 1984

Chorpenning, Joseph F. 'The Image of Darkness and Spiritual Development in the *Castillo Interior*', *Studia Mystica*, VIII, 2, Summer 1985

——'The Literary and Theological Method of the *Castillo Interior*', *Journal of Hispanic Philology*, III, 2, Winter 1979

——'The Monastery, Paradise, and the Castle: Literary Images and Spiritual Development in St Teresa of Avila', *Bulletin of Hispanic Studies*, LXII, 1985

——'St Teresa's Presentation of her Religious Experience', *Carmelite Studies*, 3, 1984

Christian, W. A. *Local Religion in Sixteenth-Century Spain* (New Jersey: Princeton University Press, 1981)

Clissold, Stephen. *St Teresa of Avila* (London: Sheldon Press, 1979)

Cuevas García, Cristóbal. 'El significante alegórico en el "Castillo" teresiano', *Letras de Deusto*, 12, 24 (1982)

Dan, Joseph. 'The Religious Experience of the Merkavah', in Arthur Green (ed.) *Jewish Spirituality*, I (London: Routledge & Kegan Paul, 1986)

Daniel-Rops, H. *The Catholic Reformation* (London: Dent, 1962)

Davies, Gareth Alban. 'St Teresa and the Jewish Question', in Margaret A. Rees (ed.) *Teresa de Jesús and her World* (Leeds: Trinity and All Saints' College, 1981)

De Manhar, N. (trans.). *Zohar* (San Diego: Wizards Bookshelf, 1978)

Domínguez Ortiz, Antonio. *The Golden Age of Spain, 1516–1659* (London: Weidenfeld & Nicolson, 1971)

Edwards, J. H. 'Religious Belief and Social Conformity: the "Converso" Problem in late-Medieval Córdoba', *Transactions of the Royal Historical Society*, 31, 1981

Egan, Keith J. 'Teresa of Jesus: Daughter of the Church and Woman of the Reformation', *Carmelite Studies*, 3, 1984

Egido, Teófanes. 'The Historical Setting of St Teresa's Life' (trans. M. Dodd & S. Payne), *Carmelite Studies*, I, 1980

Ermanno, Fr. 'The Degrees of Teresian Prayer', in Frs. Thomas and Gabriel (eds.) *St Teresa of Avila: Studies in her Life, Doctrine and Times* (Dublin: Clonmore & Reynolds, 1963)

Giles, Mary E. 'The Feminist Mystic' in her *The Feminist Mystic and other essays on Women and Spirituality* (New York: Crossroad, 1982)

——'Meditations on Teresa', *Studia Mystica*, 5, 1, Spring 1982

Ginsburg, Christian D. *The Kabbalah: its Doctrines, Development and Literature* (London: Routledge & Kegan Paul, 1955)

Gómez-Menor Fuentes, José. *El Linaje Familiar de Santa Teresa y San Juan* de la Cruz (Toledo: Gráficas Cervantes, 1970)

Green, Arthur. 'The Song of Songs in Early Jewish Mysticism', *Orim: A Jewish Journal at Yale*, II, 2, Spring 1987

Green, Deirdre. 'St Teresa of Avila and Hekhalot Mysticism', *Studies in Religion/Sciences Religieuses*, 13, 3, Summer 1984; also published as 'Santa Teresa de Avila y la Mística Hekhalot', in *Homenaje a Luis Morales Oliver* (Madrid: Fundacion Universitaria Española, 1986)

——'St John of the Cross and Mystical "Unknowing"' *Religious Studies*, 22, 1986

——'Mysticism and the Sevenfold Castle', *Shadow*, II, 2, December 1985

——'Unity in Diversity', *Scottish Journal of Religious Studies*, III, 1, Spring 1982

——*A Study of Mysticism and its Forms of Expression* Unpublished Ph. D. thesis, University of Stirling, 1983

——'Living Between the Worlds: Bhakti Poetry and the Carmelite Mystics', in Karel Werner (ed.) *The Yogi and the Mystic: Studies in Indian and Comparative Mysticism* (Durham: University of Durham Indological Series, 1989)

——'Kuṇḍalinī Yoga and Kabbalistic Meditation', *Avaloka*, forthcoming.

——'The Seven Palaces in early Jewish Mysticism', *Hermetic Journal*, 31, Spring 1986

Gross, Rita M. 'Women's Studies in Religion: the State of the Art, 1980', in P. Slater & D. Wiebe (eds.) *Traditions and Change: Selected Proceedings of the XIVth Congress of the International Association for the History of Religions* (Ontario: Wilfred Laurier Press, 1983)

Gruenwald, Ithamar. *Apocalyptic and Merkavah Mysticism* (Leiden: E. J. Brill, 1980)

Hamilton, Elizabeth. *The Great Teresa* (London: Chatto & Windus, 1960)

Hatzfeld, Helmut A. *Santa Teresa de Avila* (New York: Twayne, 1969)

Hellwig, Monika. 'St Teresa's Inspiration for our Times', *Carmelite Studies*, 3, 1984

Hildegard of Bingen. *Illuminations of Hildegard of Bingen*, with commentary by Matthew Fox (New Mexico: Bear & Co., 1985)

Jennings, Elizabeth. 'Teresa of Avila', in Peter Levi (ed.) *The Penguin Book of English Christian Verse* (Harmondsworth: Penguin, 1987)

Kaplan, Aryeh. *Meditation and Kabbalah* (Maine: Weiser, 1982)

King, Ursula. 'Mysticism and Feminism or Why Look at Women Mystics?', in Margaret A. Rees (ed.) *Teresa de Jesús and her World* (Leeds: Trinity & All Saints' College, 1981)

——'Goddesses, Witches, Androgyny and Beyond?' in her *Women in the World's Religions, Past and Present* (New York: Paragon House, 1987)

——'Current Perspectives in the Study of Women and Religion', *Women Speaking*, October–December 1982

——'Voices of Protest – Voices of Promise: Exploring Spirituality for a New

Age' (The Hibbert Lecture 1984) (London: Hibbert Trust, 1984)
——*Women and Spirituality* (London: Macmillan, 1989)
Kottman, Karl A. *Law and Apocalypse: the Moral Thought of Luis de León* (The Hague: Nijhoff, 1972)
Larkin, Ernest. 'St Teresa of Avila and Centering Prayer', *Carmelite Studies*, 3, 1984
Laski, Marghanita. *Ecstasy: A Study of some Secular and Religious Experiences* (London: Cresset Press, 1961)
Leuba, James H. *The Psychology of Religious Mysticism* (London: 1925)
Lewis, I. M. *Ecstatic Religion* (Harmondsworth: Penguin, 1971)
Lincoln, Victoria. *Teresa: A Woman: A Biography of Teresa of Avila* (Albany: State University of New York Press, 1984)
Llamas Martínez, Enrique. *Santa Teresa de Jesús y la Inquisición Española* (Madrid: Consejo Superior de Investigaciones Cientificas, 1972)
López-Baralt, Luce. 'Santa Teresa y el Islam', *Teresianum*, 33, 1982
——'Simbología mística musulmana en San Juan de la Cruz y en Santa Teresa de Jesús', *Nueva Revista de Filología Hispánica*, 30, 1, 1981
McLaughlin, Eleanor. 'Equality of Souls, Inequality of Sexes: Women in Medieval Theology', in Rosemary Radford Ruether (ed.) *Religion and Sexism: Images of Women in the Jewish and Christian Traditions* (New York: Simon & Schuster, 1974)
——'Women, Power and the Pursuit of Holiness in Medieval Christianity', in Rosemary Radford Ruether and Eleanor McLaughlin (eds.) *Women of Spirit: Female Leadership in the Jewish and Christian Traditions* (New York: Simon & Schuster, 1979)
Morón-Arroyo, Ciriaco. ' "I Will Give you a Living Book": Spiritual Currents at Work in the Time of St Teresa of Jesus', *Carmelite Studies*, 3, 1984
O'Donoghue, N. D. 'The Human Form Divine: St Teresa and the Humanity of Christ', in Margaret A. Rees (ed.) *Teresa de Jesús and her World* (Leeds: Trinity & All Saints' College, 1981)
Quitslund, Sonya A. 'Elements of a Feminist Spirituality in St Teresa', *Carmelite Studies*, 3, 1984
Ramanujan, A. K. 'On Women Saints', in John Stratton Hawley & Donna Marie Wulff (eds.) *The Divine Consort: Rādhā and the Goddesses of India* (Boston: Beacon Press, 1986)
Rapoport-Albert, Ada. 'The Maid of Ludmir', *Kabbalah*, II, 2, 1987
Rawlinson, Andrew. 'Attempting to Understand Everything', *Religion*, 13, 1983.
Rivers, Elias R. 'The Vernacular Mind of St Teresa', *Carmelite Studies*, 3, 1984
Romano, Catherine. 'A Psycho-Spiritual History of Teresa of Avila: A Woman's Perspective', in Matthew Fox (ed.) *Western Spirituality: Historical Roots, Ecumenical Routes* (New Mexico: Bear & Co., 1981)

Ruether, Rosemary Radford. *New Woman, New Earth: Sexist Ideologies and Human Liberation* (New York: Seabury, 1975)

Sackville-West, V. *The Eagle and the Dove* (London: Quartet, 1973)

Scholem, Gershom G. *Major Trends in Jewish Mysticism* (New York: Schocken, 1961)

——*On the Kabbalah and its Symbolism* (New York: Schocken, 1969)

——*Kabbalah* (New York: Quadrangle/New York Times Book Co., 1974)

——*Jewish Gnosticism, Merkabah Mysticism, and Talmudic Tradition* (New York: Jewish Theological Seminary of America, 1965)

——(ed.) *Zohar* (London: Rider, 1977)

——'Zohar', *Encyclopedia Judaica*, vol. XVI.

——*Origins of the Kabbalah* (New Jersey: Princeton University Press, 1987)

Scholz, Bernard W. 'Hildegard von Bingen on the Nature of Woman', *American Benedictine Review*, December 1980

Silverio de Santa Teresa, Padre. *Vida de Teresa de Jesús* (Burgos: 1935–37)

Smith, Morton. 'Observations on Hekhalot Rabbati', in Alexander Altmann (ed.) *Biblical and Other Studies* (Massachusetts: Harvard University Press, 1963)

Swietlicki, Catherine. *Spanish Christian Cabala: the Works of Luis de León. Santa Teresa de Jesús, and San Juan de la Cruz* (Columbia: University of Missouri Press, 1986)

Talmage, Frank. 'Apples of Gold: the Inner Meaning of Sacred Texts in Medieval Judaism', in Arthur Green (ed.) *Jewish Spirituality*, I (London: Routledge & Kegan Paul, 1986)

Teresa of Jesus, St. *Complete Works of Saint Teresa of Jesus*, 3 vols. trans. & ed. E. Allison Peers (London: Sheed & Ward, 1946)

——*Santa Teresa de Jesús: Obras Completas*, eds. Enrique Llamas, Teófanes Egido et. al. (Madrid: Editorial de Espiritualidad, 1984)

——*The Letters of Saint Teresa of Jesus*, 2 vols. Trans. & ed. E. Allison Peers (London: Burns Oates & Washbourne Ltd., 1951)

——*The Life of Saint Teresa*, trans. J. M. Cohen (Harmondsworth: Penguin, 1957)

Trueman Dicken, E. W. *The Crucible of Love: A Study of the Mysticism of St Teresa of Jesus and St John of the Cross* (New York: Sheed & Ward, 1963)

——'The Imagery of the Interior Castle and its Implications', *Ephemerides Carmeliticae*, 21, 1970

Underhill, Evelyn. *Mysticism* (London: Methuen & Co., 1930)

——*The House of the Soul* (London: Methuen, 1933)

Williams, M. E. 'St Teresa, Doctor of the Church (Orthodoxy and Public Opinion)', in Margaret A. Rees (ed.) *Teresa de Jesús and her World* (Leeds: Trinity and All Saints' College, 1981)

Woodward, L. J. 'Hebrew Tradition and Luis de León', *Bulletin of Hispanic Studies*, 61, July 1984

Index